IMAGES
of America

IRISH CINCINNATI

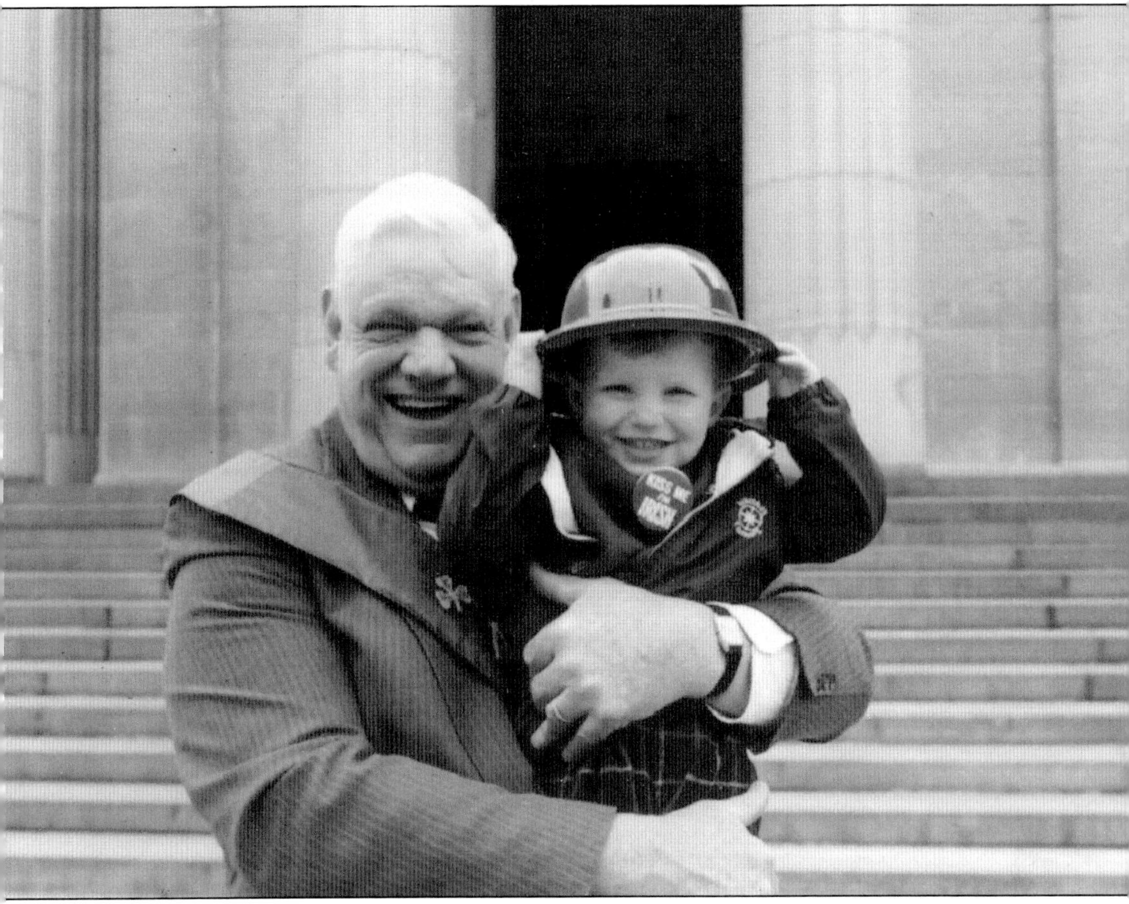

Pictured in the 1980s holding his grandson Joe Coz on the steps of St. Peter in Chains Cathedral during a St. Patrick's Day celebration, "Big Jim" Murphy had every reason to smile. Just one of the several local Hibernians responsible for reviving Cincinnati's annual Irish parade in 1967, Murphy was a great bear of a man who grew up in Price Hill and received his education at Elder High School and Xavier University. It was a matter of fierce pride to him that the Irish heritage of the city received due appreciation. (Courtesy of Joe Coz and Colleen Klosterman.)

On the Cover: Shown here around 1900, the Tyler Davidson Fountain is the iconic symbol of Cincinnati. It was designed and cast in Germany and presented to the city by Henry Probasco in 1871, but every March, the "Genius of Waters" becomes an Irish landmark for the beginning of the St. Patrick's Day festivities and the parade that passes today's Fountain Square. (Courtesy of the author's collection.)

IMAGES
of America

IRISH CINCINNATI

Kevin Grace

ARCADIA
PUBLISHING

ISBN 978-0-7385-9435-4

Published by Arcadia Publishing
Charleston, South Carolina

Printed in the United States of America

Library of Congress Control Number: 2012937512

For all general information, please contact Arcadia Publishing:
Telephone 843-853-2070
Fax 843-853-0044
E-mail sales@arcadiapublishing.com
For customer service and orders:
Toll-Free 1-888-313-2665

Visit us on the Internet at www.arcadiapublishing.com

For the Graces and the Deneens of Emmetsburg, Síochán.

Contents

ACKNOWLEDGMENTS

This book is about the community of Irish in Cincinnati, and it certainly would not have been possible to write it without a community of encouragement and assistance. Thank you very much to everyone who helped in contributing their expertise and information to *Irish Cincinnati*: Andy Butler, Meghan Cappel, Kent Covey, Joe Coz, Sabrina Darnowsky, Lauren Fink, Bob Flischel, The Gilligan Funeral Home, Susie Kauck, Maureen Kennedy, Patti Kinsinger, Colleen Klosterman, Kate Kreuger, Tim McCabe, Mary McGing, Sue Maggard, Michael O'Bryant, John O'Connor, Ed Rider, Nancy Riesenbeck, Michael Ruddy, Janice Schulz, Todd and Kellie Siler, Brother Tim Sucher, Gail Sweeney, Mark Sweeney, Andrew Sweeny Jr., Danny Thomas, and Chris von Volborth. As with everything else, I am fortunate enough to accomplish this project with the support of my family: Joan, Josh, Sean, Courtney, Bonnie, Lily, Zo, and Honora. Special gratitude is due to Stacey Walsh for her kindness and hard work on my behalf, and especially to Pat Mallory, who so generously and graciously shared his wide knowledge of Irish Cincinnati.

Unless otherwise noted, all images are from the collection of the author.

INTRODUCTION

More than 36 million people in the United States today identify themselves as having Irish ancestry. What started as a trickle in the 18th century, primarily with immigrants from the northern counties of Ireland who came to America to seek new lives as farmers and merchants, became a veritable flood of people by the mid-19th century as a result of the devastating potato crop failures in the 1840s that led to famine, displacement, and migration across the oceans to North America, Australia, and New Zealand. The reason was not just that they were seeking new lives and opportunities, but that they were just striving to survive. Smaller waves continued in the following decades and well into the 20th century. And, of no small account either, are the Irish who came here to escape the yoke that England had on them in their native land until full independence, though partitioned from Northern Ireland, in 1949.

When the Irish came to America, they landed variously in New York, Boston, Philadelphia, New Orleans, Montreal, and other eastern cities available by waterway. They lived in urban enclaves and neighborhoods with their fellow countrymen who preceded them. The Irish brought their faith with them, of whatever denomination or religion they followed, though in truth, they were primarily Catholic. In fact, the Irish dominated the American Catholic hierarchy of cardinals, bishops, and priests for well more than a century. And, the Irish scrabbled for a living, often facing tremendous resistance and discrimination from nativists and Know-Nothings. They also persevered and eventually took a fair and rightful place in American society.

But that place in our nation's culture goes much beyond the "wearing of the green" on St. Patrick's Day by everyone who likes a good time, or the sentimental songs and comic routines of vaudeville, or the politicians and celebrities who hold their heritage aloft like a banner. It is really all the everyday people, the teachers, the writers, the artists, the civic leaders and boosters, the businessmen, and those in fraternal organizations who have stitched the banner together. In Cincinnati, there were more than 13,000 Irish in the city's population by the 1850s, and 20 years later, the number climbed to nearly 19,000. It is a reasonable bet to make that there are more Irish community and cultural organizations in Cincinnati than there are for any other group. That sounds a bit like boasting, and certainly the "firstests" and "mostests" ultimately are of wee importance, but it does illustrate the notion that Cincinnati's Irish community is a vibrant and diverse one. There are the traditional Hibernians and Friendly Sons of St. Patrick, but also the Belles of Ireland, and the Irish American Theater Company, the Irish Salon and the Irish Table, the Northern Kentucky Fenians, the EuroCeltic Institute, and the Ulster Project Cincinnati. And of course, there is Hap's, Crowley's, Molly Malone's, and O'Bryon's, where the conversation flows right along with the Guinness.

Dividing a book like this into chapters is always a hedged endeavor. Years and ages tend to fly toward each other, swarm, and divide. So, instead of specific dates, each chapter begins with a line from an Irish American song that is contemporary with the relevant era of images. These tunes indicate the culture of the times—political, social, and emotional. At their best, songs are evocative instruments for marking history, and in this book, they serve to set the stage for understanding the Cincinnati Irish heritage. Chapter One begins with a line from "The Emigrant's Farewell," written in 1852, that speaks of the Irish leaving their native land behind in an often necessary search for a better life across the sea. Chapter Two, concerning the Civil War years and the subsequent failed Fenian effort in America, is headed by a line from "The Irish Volunteer," a popular war tune in 1862 about the courage of the Irish soldier fighting for the Yankees while still holding on to his desire for full freedom back home in Ireland. For Chapter Three, the song line is from a comic song about suffrage, "The Rights of Ladies," written by A.G. Weeks under the pseudonym of Dennis McFlinn. The indication here is to mark the increased involvement of the Irish in important civic affairs, from service as policemen, firemen, and politicians to community leaders, casting aside years of "No Irish Need Apply." In Chapter Four, the images are about a new century and an increased sentimentality about the Irish heritage at the beginning of the 1900s, fostered in no small part by the tunesmiths of Tin Pan Alley. The line for this chapter is from "Killarney Moon," a song published by Olympic Music Publishers in Cincinnati in 1915, complete with quaint shamrocks on the cover. Chapter Five represents a signature Bing Crosby tune, "McNamara's Band," which he recorded in 1945. It has the particular connotation of the intense desire on the part of second, third, and fourth generation Irish to overly-romanticize the land of their ancestors, but more importantly, to assert and demonstrate their ethnic pride in America. And finally, Chapter Six begins with a line from "Thousands Are Sailing" by the seminal Irish punk rock group, The Pogues. Written by Philip Chevron and forever identified with Pogues front man Shane MacGowan, the song is a deeply poignant account of the men and women who left Ireland over the past 175 years to come to America. Some succeeded and embraced their new country, while others found heartbreak, poverty, and disappointment. Taken all together, the song speaks to the hope that brought all of them, and perhaps this song says more than most what it is like to be an Irish American.

As with most American cities in the 21st century, there are those individuals who have Irish ancestors in Cincinnati that extend well back into the 19th century, and those who have toted the steamer trunks of heritage into the city when they moved here. I am among the latter, the Graces and their affinity families traveling from Cork and Mayo to New Brunswick, Maine, Massachusetts, Wisconsin, and Iowa over two centuries time, and finally, to Cincinnati. Others, like Pat Mallory, Stacey Walsh, and Andy Sweeny, for example, are among the former. Listening to Mallory, in his energetic, hop-skip manner of telling the tales of his relatives, Cincinnati's Irish history comes to vivid life. Walsh earnestly builds links between people and organizations to establish a connection between past and present, and Sweeny, with his extensive knowledge of local Irish political and social connections over the decades, is an invaluable source of information. These "long-timers" are among the many Irish Cincinnatians who make a community's ethnicity a rich part of life. It is said that time is a great storyteller. Talking about a lot of different things over beers one evening, Mallory said of one Cincinnati tale, "Well it's not exactly true, but partly," a sentiment that is a fine old tradition in itself. But what follows in these pages are the true stories, at least as much truth as can be made of them. *Sláinte*!

One

"Old Home of Our Childhood, Forever From Thee"

In 1788, John Cleves Symmes, who had purchased two million acres of land in the Ohio Valley from the Confederation Congress the year before, sold 800 acres to Israel Ludlow, Robert Patterson, and Matthias Denman. The three men platted a town on the Ohio River opposite the mouth of the Licking River to the south and called it Losantiville. In 1790, Arthur St. Clair, governor of the Northwest Territory, renamed the settlement Cincinnati in honor of the Revolutionary War soldiers who formed the Society of Cincinnati. That is the standard beginning of the city's history, factual and often told. What may not be generally known is that of the 700 people in Cincinnati in 1790, the Irish were among them.

Cincinnati is most often identified as a German city because of the vast numbers of those immigrants who came here throughout the 19th century. And, of course, their contributions were numerous, continuing to this day, but there were other ethnic groups in early Cincinnati. One of them, an Irishman by the name of Joseph Lloyd, is accorded the place of the first schoolteacher when he established a log cabin school in 1791 on a plot of land just west of what is today Sycamore Street. And John Dunlap, from Coleraine, Ireland, would name the farthest northern reaches of the settlement Colerain Township in honor of his nativity, now with the "e" dropped. Dunlap's Station would become a fort in defense against Indian attacks.

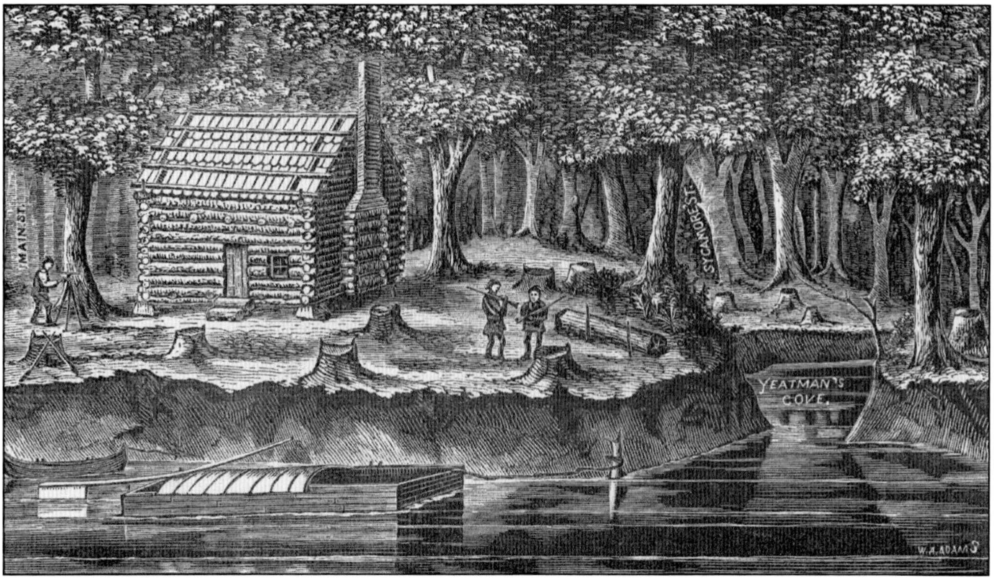

In chronicling the settlement of Cincinnati, accepted wisdom is that the first Irishman to arrive was Francis Kennedy, who journeyed with his wife and seven children down the Ohio River during the winter of 1788. Arriving in February, the family spent the remainder of the season on their boat before venturing ashore and building a house among the few cabins that were then standing. The village was soon surveyed into lots within the natural basin formed along the Ohio River. Kennedy established the first ferry service in Cincinnati, carrying people back and forth from the north riverbank to the Licking River on the Kentucky side of the Ohio. His descendants eventually moved north of the river, and over the surrounding hilltops to farm in Pleasant Ridge. The Kennedy Heights neighborhood is named for one of those early farmers.

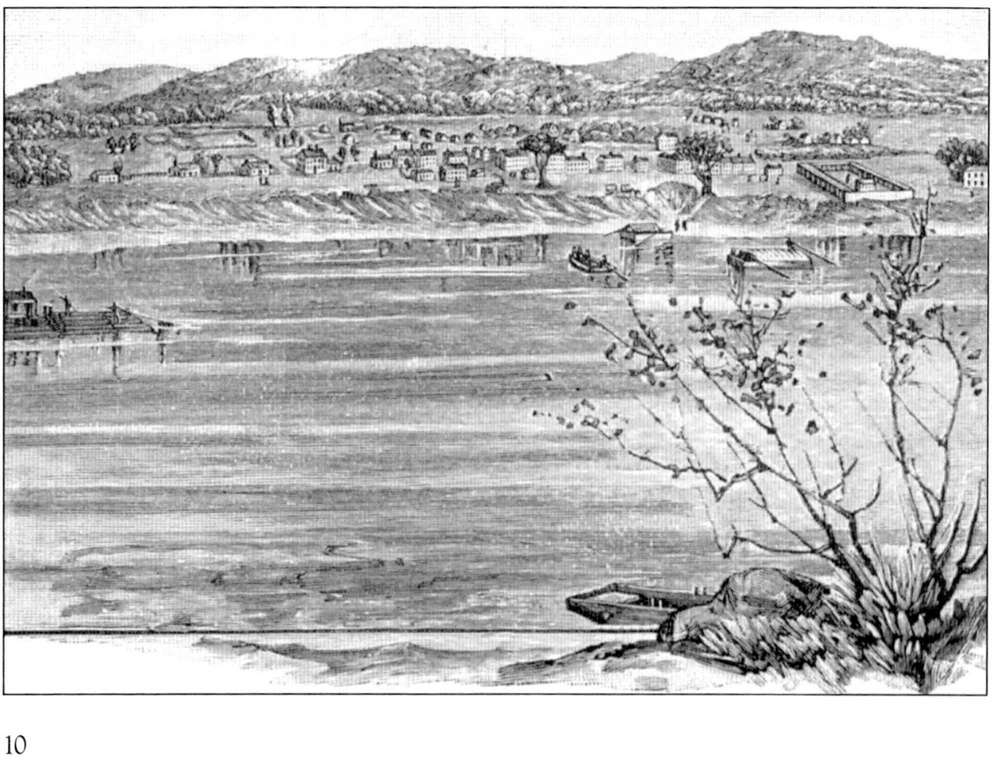

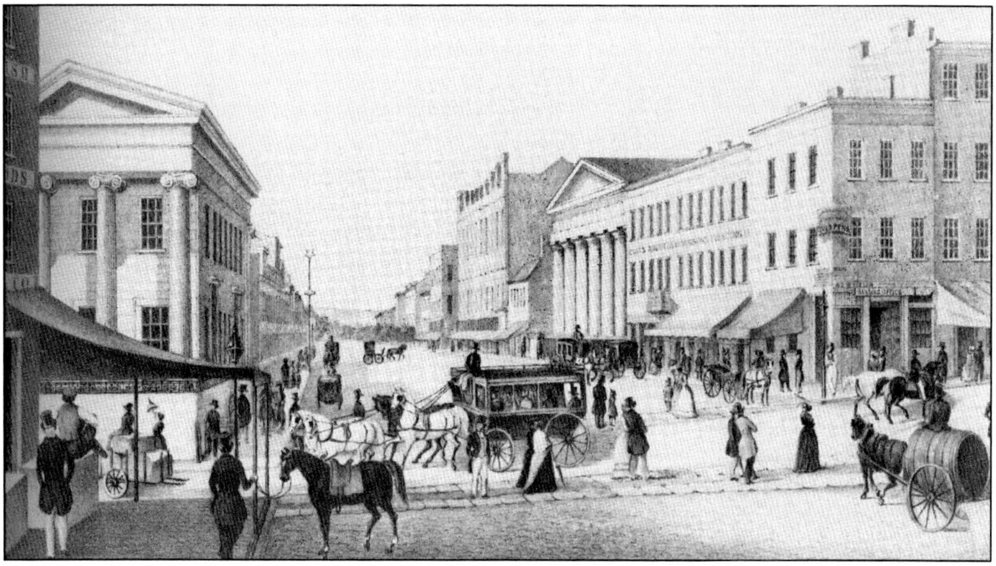

By 1820, the basin area of the settlement was taking shape as a real city. Cincinnati College and a medical college were established in 1819, banks were flourishing as well as factories, and Cincinnati was on its way to becoming the major trading point in the Northwest Territory. However, religious tolerance was somewhat lacking. The first Catholic church, called Christ Church, was forced to build in the "Liberties" because of city ordinances forbidding its construction within the city limits. The first Catholic congregation was formed by Fr. Edward Fenwick in 1819, followed by the 1821 building on the northwest corner of Liberty and Vine Streets, just north of the corporation line. Surrounding the church was the Catholic cemetery, final resting place for the earliest Irish congregants.

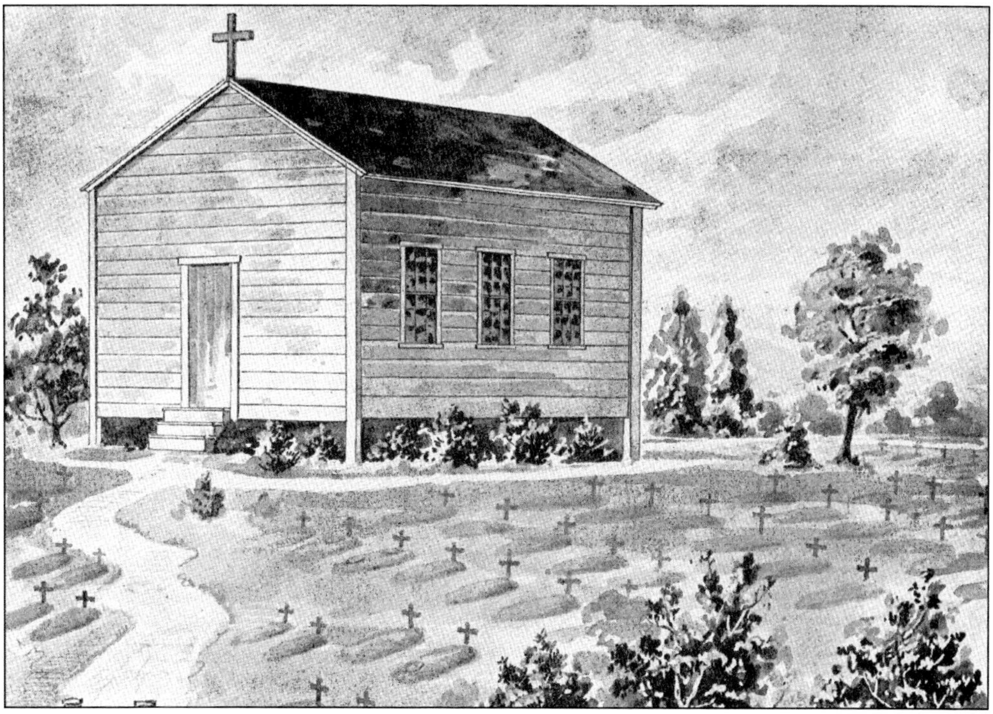

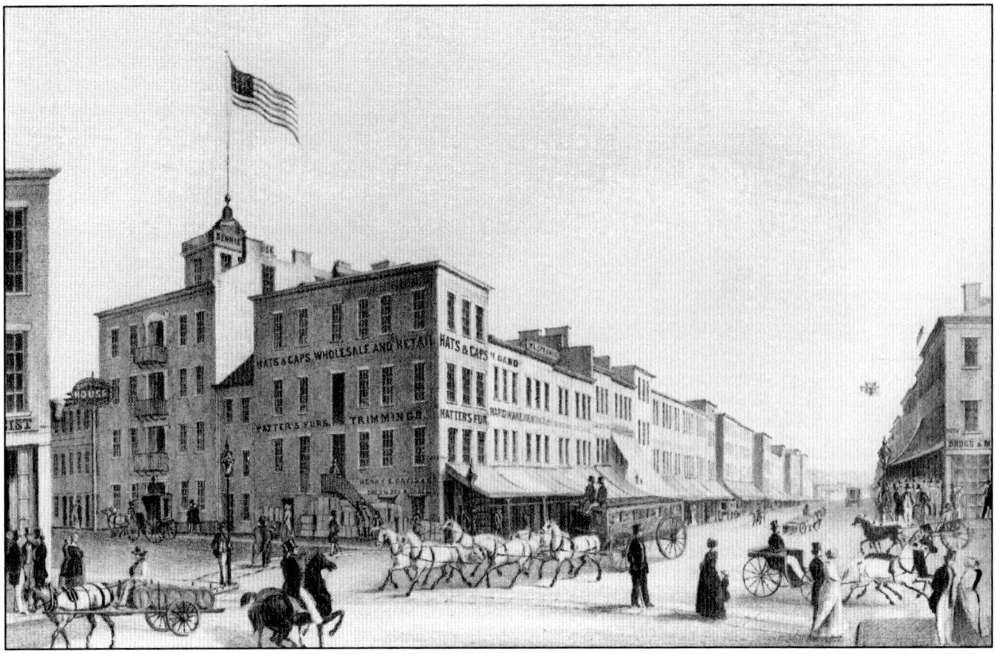

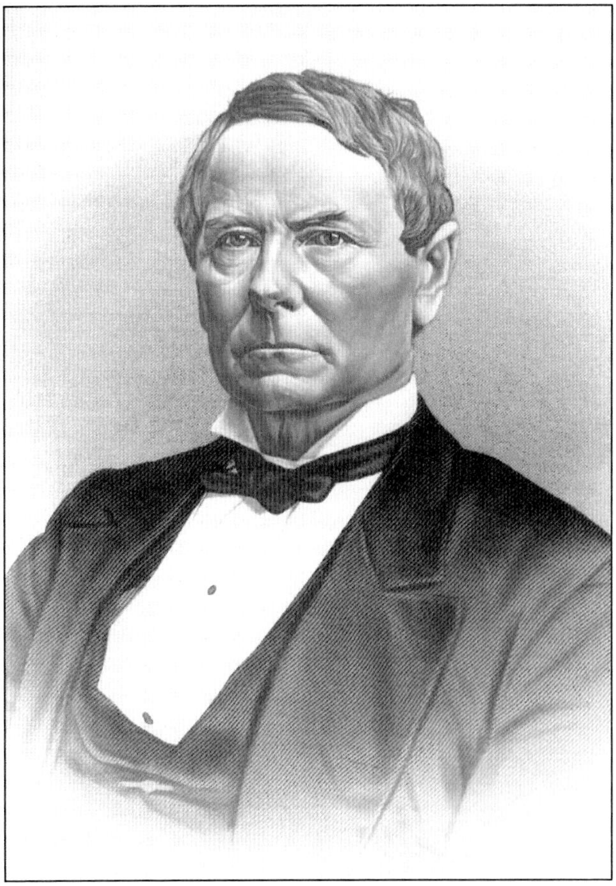

As the city's business, cultural, and economic opportunities continued to expand, social class differences within ethnic groups naturally developed. For example, David Sinton, a Quaker born in County Armagh in 1808, came to America with his family when he was three years old. After moving to Cincinnati in adulthood, he became one of the richest men in America through his business in pig iron during the Civil War. He used his immense wealth for several philanthropic endeavors in Cincinnati and died in 1900 at the age of 93. On the other end of the scale from Sinton's standing were the Irish of "Dublin," a spread of shanties just north and east of downtown. One commentator on the denizens there said of them, "The inhabitants are chiefly Paddies and of a very rough character . . . the neighborhood has been annoyed by Irish rows and chicken-stealing."

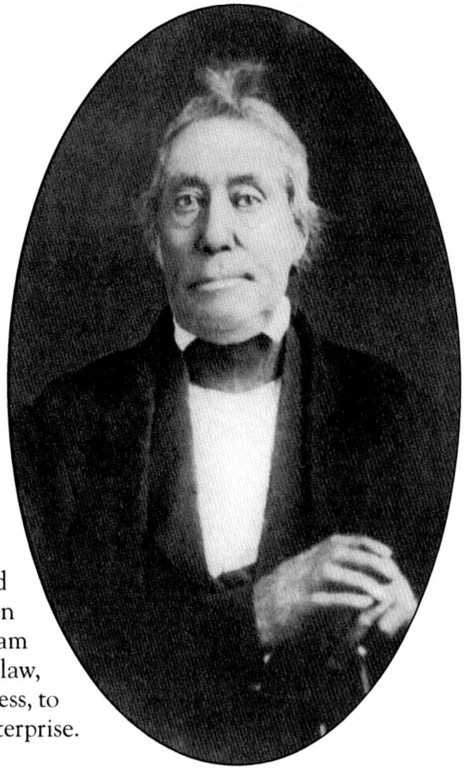

An early Irish immigrant to Cincinnati, Alexander Norris was born in Caledon, County Tyrone, Ireland, in 1771. The date of his arrival in Cincinnati is uncertain, but it was before 1819 when he appears in the city directory as a chandler. Norris (right) came with his family, which included his daughter Elizabeth Ann (below), born in Ireland in 1811. After establishing a successful tallow business, he moved in the local social circles of candle makers, where Elizabeth met and married another Irish immigrant, James Gamble, in 1833. The couple had 10 children and further joined business interests when Elizabeth's sister Olivia married the widowed William Procter. Alexander Norris persuaded his sons-in-law, both of whom were involved in the animal fat business, to join together and form a mutual manufacturing enterprise. (Courtesy of Procter and Gamble Archives.)

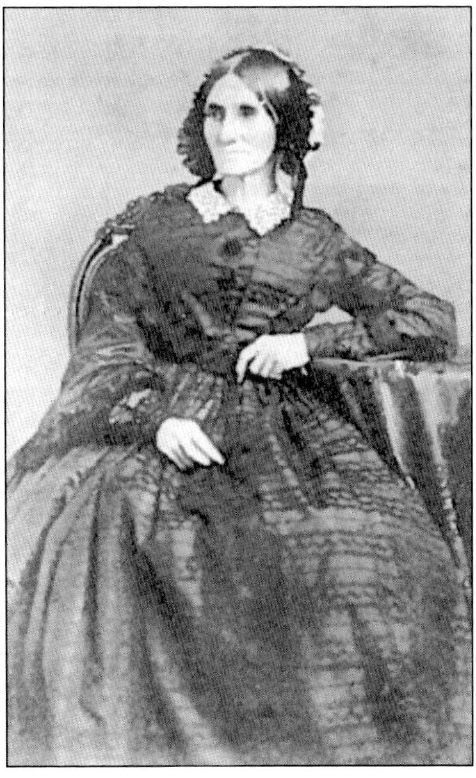

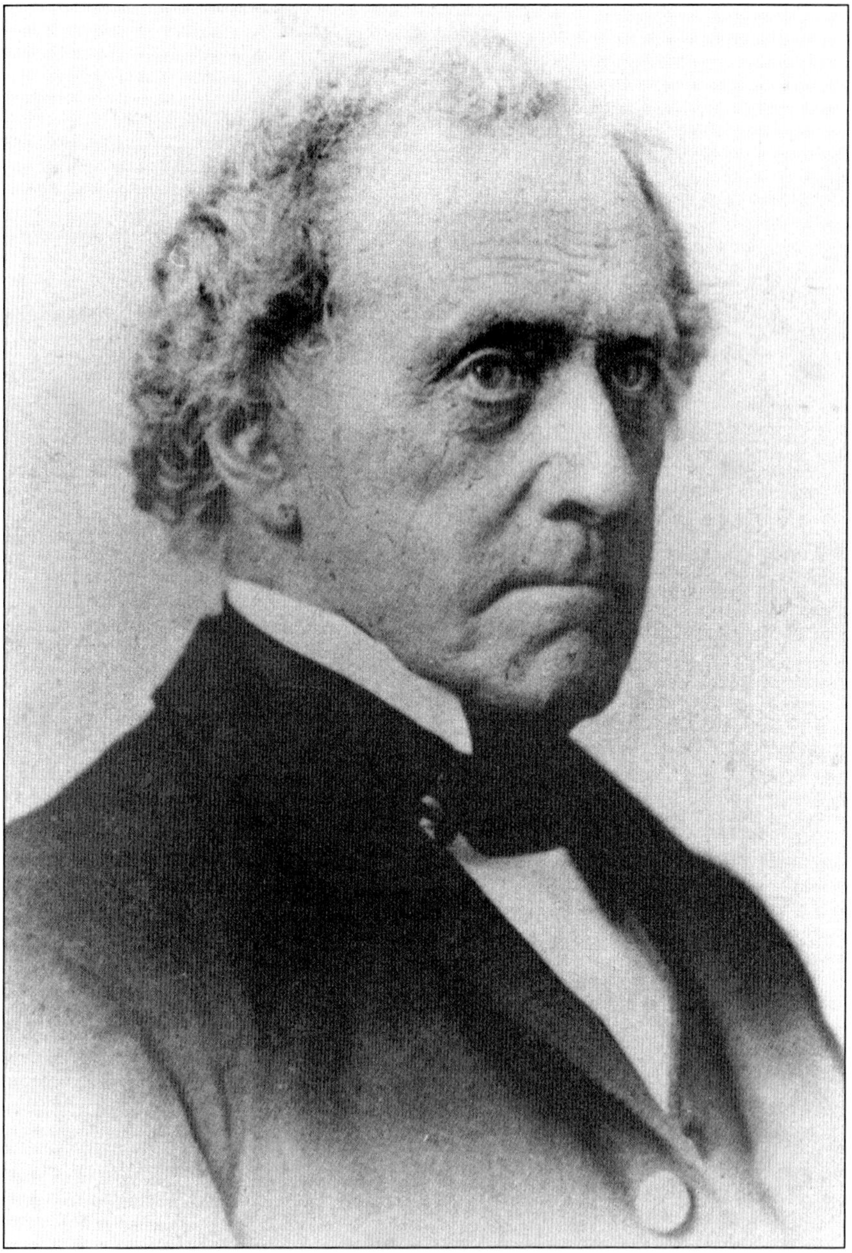

James Gamble was born in Enniskillen, in the Northern Ireland county of Fermanagh, in 1803. His father, George, was a farmer who went bankrupt, so he packed up his young family and left for America. The elder Gamble's intent was to move to Illinois, but as their flatboat made its way down the Ohio River, 16-year old James became seriously ill so a stop was made in Cincinnati. The family decided to settle here, and George opened a nursery and worked as a grocer. James Gamble was apprenticed to a small soap factory and in 1828, at the age of 25, decided to start his own business. Opening his own soap factory on Walnut Street, the success of his business soon made it necessary to move to a larger space at Water Street and Central Avenue. In less than a decade, his firm would grow to the point that he would take on a partner. The resulting concern was called Procter & Gamble.

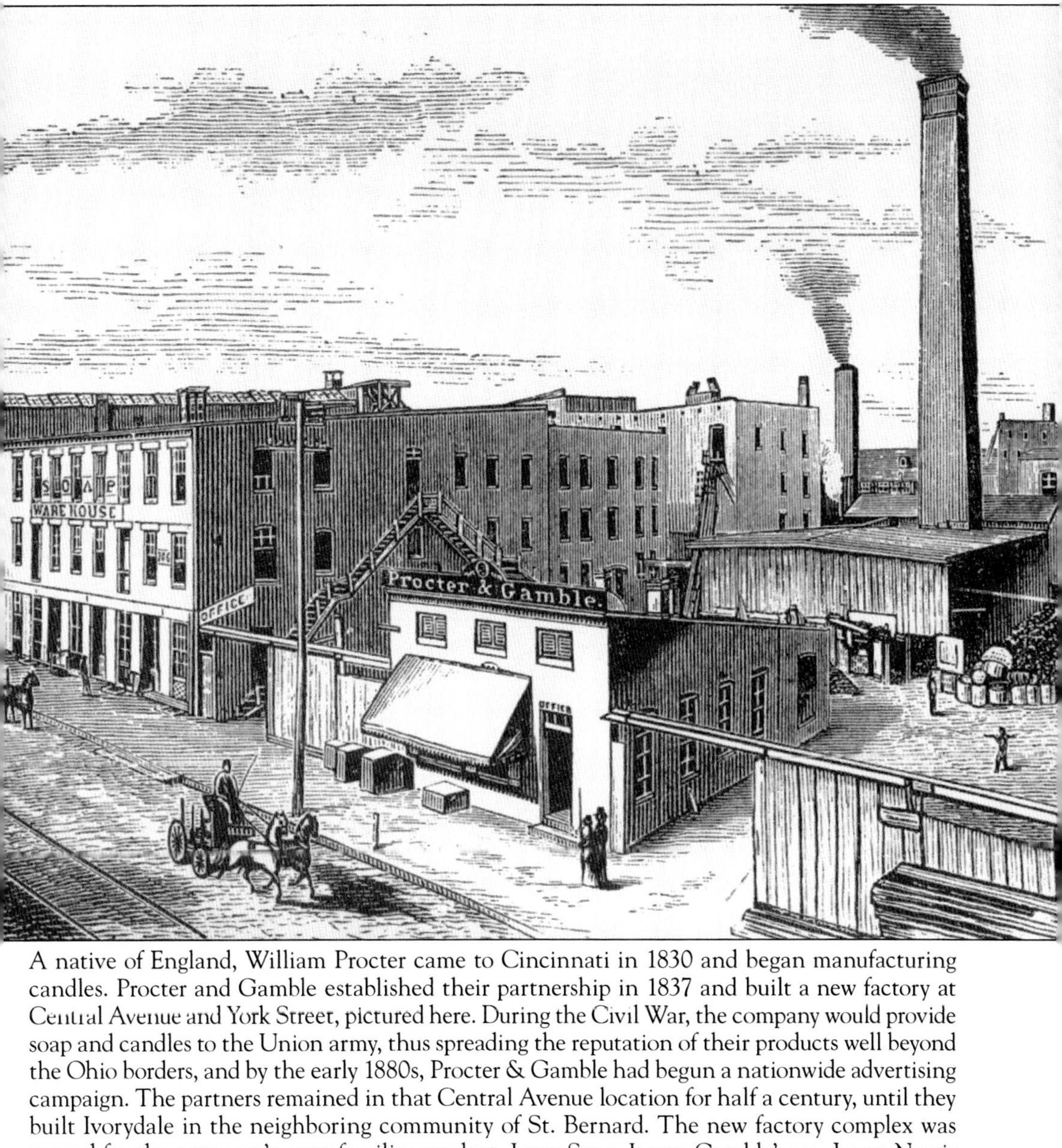

A native of England, William Procter came to Cincinnati in 1830 and began manufacturing candles. Procter and Gamble established their partnership in 1837 and built a new factory at Central Avenue and York Street, pictured here. During the Civil War, the company would provide soap and candles to the Union army, thus spreading the reputation of their products well beyond the Ohio borders, and by the early 1880s, Procter & Gamble had begun a nationwide advertising campaign. The partners remained in that Central Avenue location for half a century, until they built Ivorydale in the neighboring community of St. Bernard. The new factory complex was named for the company's most familiar product, Ivory Soap. It was Gamble's son James Norris Gamble who was trained as a chemist at Kenyon College and developed the process for the floating soap in 1879.

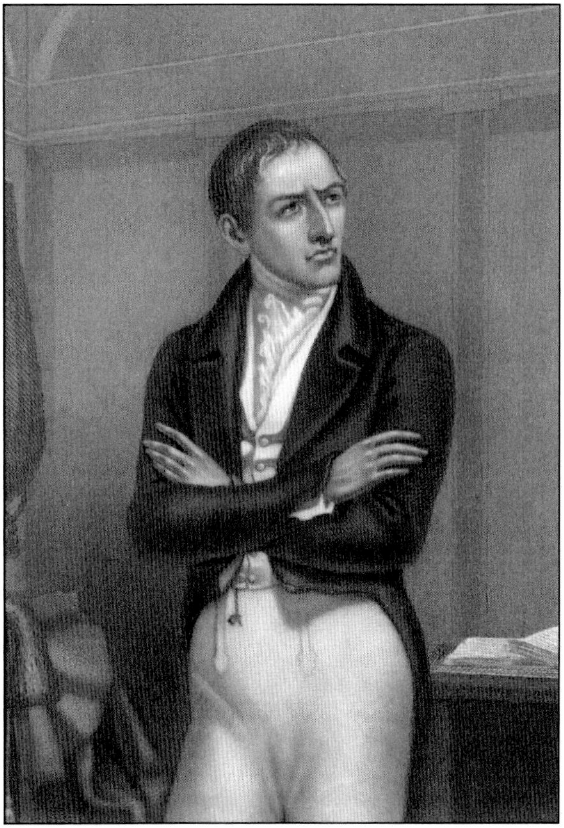

The Irish newcomers to Cincinnati often maintained their political points of view regarding the rights and freedom denied them back in Ireland and fostered them in the sons and daughters who were born here. One organization that strived to keep Irish Americans involved in the struggle against the British was the Robert Emmet Emigrant Aid Society. In 1856, several members were called into district court and questioned about their intent to support rebellion against England. Their president, Dan Conahan, addressed the court about their society formed in tribute to Emmet (shown here, along with a scene of his death), the Irish nationalist executed by the British in 1803 following a failed rebellion. Emmet's final words after his sentencing were "When my country takes its place among the nations of the earth, then and not till then, let my epitaph be written." He was hanged and then beheaded. Local Irishmen did not want his words forgotten.

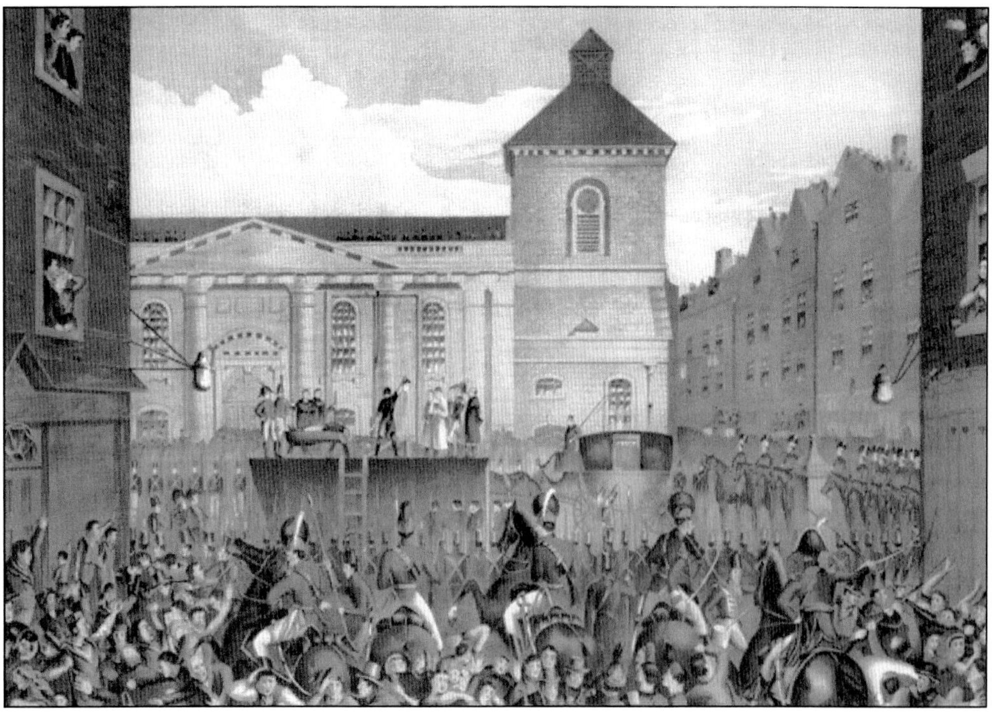

In 1842, Charles Dickens journeyed to America and visited Boston, New York, Washington, Pittsburgh, and Cincinnati. In the Queen City, the author and his wife, Catherine, stayed at the Burnet House, a popular hotel for visiting dignitaries. One noted guest, landscape designer Frederick Law Olmstead, stayed at the same hotel several years later as part of the US Sanitary Commission during the Civil War and biliously complained about the Irish hotel staff's uncouth habits. Dickens, however, found Cincinnati's Irish charming. In noting a parade celebrating the Irish temperance leader Fr. Theobald Mathew, Dickens said, "I was particularly pleased to see the Irishmen, who formed a distinct society among themselves, and mustered very strong with their green scarfs carrying their national harp and their Portrait of Father Mathew high about the people's heads . . . and doing any kind of sturdy labor that came in their way, were the most independent fellows there, I thought."

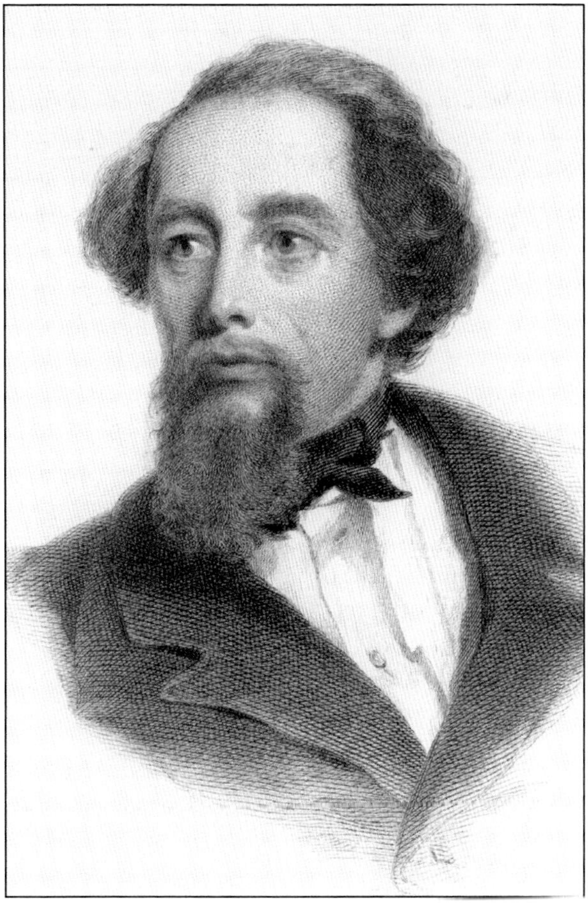

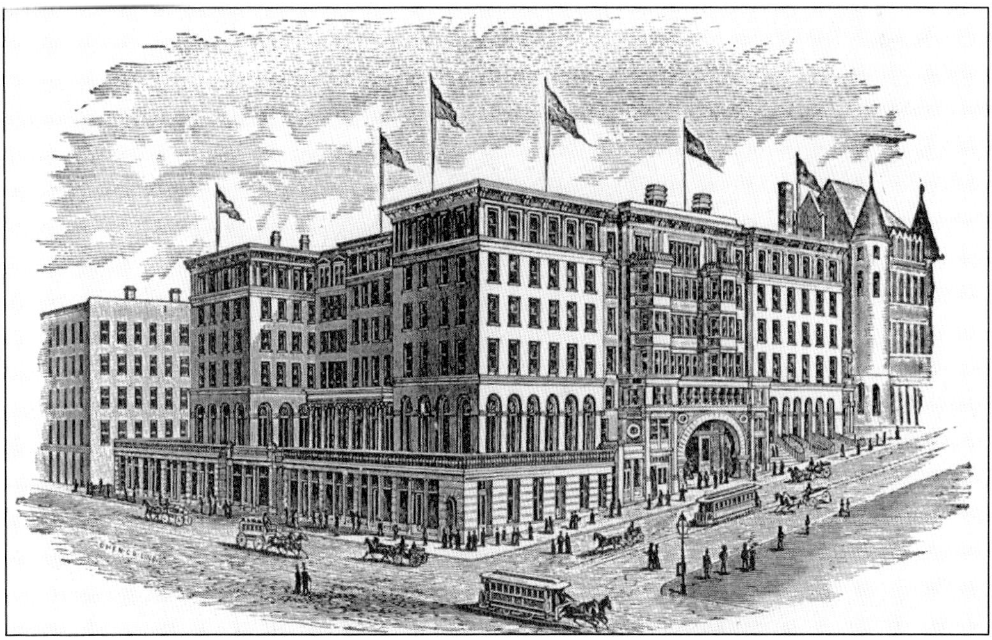

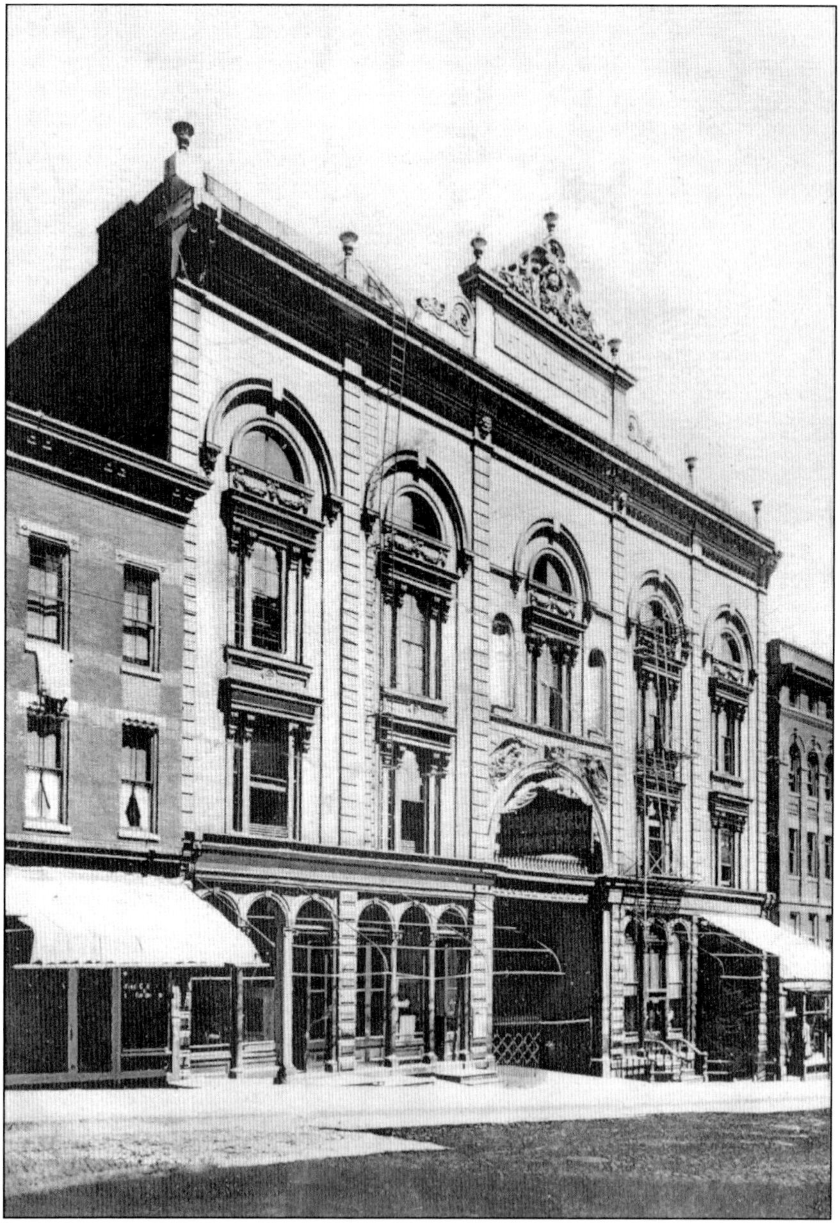

Opening its doors in 1837, the National Theater was one of the main venues for drama and musical performance during the 19th century. The theater's reputation was such that it was sometimes referred to as Old Drury, after London's redoubtable Drury Lane Theatre. In a city that was quickly embracing its cultural inclinations, the National presented numerous Irish and English plays over the next several decades but often was lumped with the disreputable doings of other theaters. In 1846, for example, the People's Theatre was the site of a love match gone wrong between performers. One night backstage, Irish comedian John Reeve had taken up with a certain Mrs. Cook, a "danseuse." Enraged by the situation, her husband and the theater's treasurer, Mr. Cook, killed the Irishman with a knife thrust to the heart. There were no encores that evening, Cook lit out of town, and the next day the National Theater joined the People's in offering a reward for the arrest of the murderer.

Known for his melodramas on both sides of the Atlantic, Irish playwright and actor Dionysus Lardner Boucicault toured America from 1854 to 1860 to launch new productions and to write and direct the occasional play. His years in the United States were prompted by his elopement with actress Agnes Robertson after the mysterious death of his first wife in Switzerland. He married Robertson upon their arrival in New York, and when they reached Cincinnati, the couple found favorable audiences already familiar with *Andy Blake: Or, The Irish Diamond*, which he wrote and produced in Boston. He produced and acted in several plays here, most starring Agnes, and then debuted *Grimaldi: Or, Scenes in the Life of an Actress* at the National Theater on September 24, 1855.

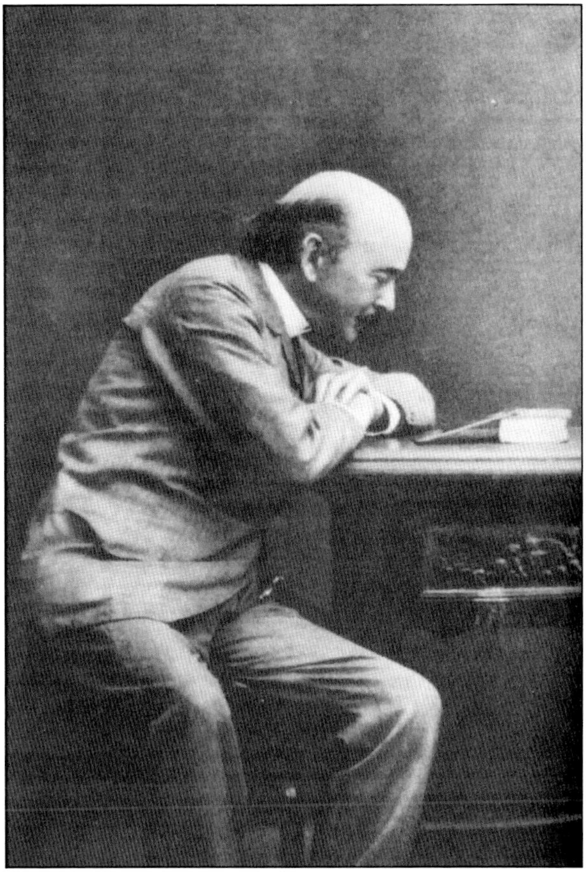

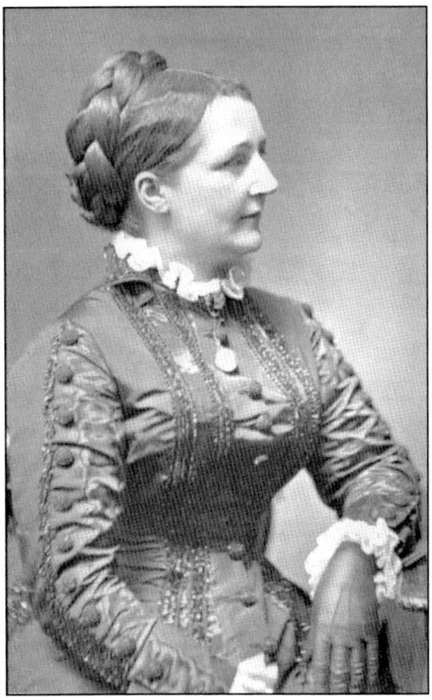

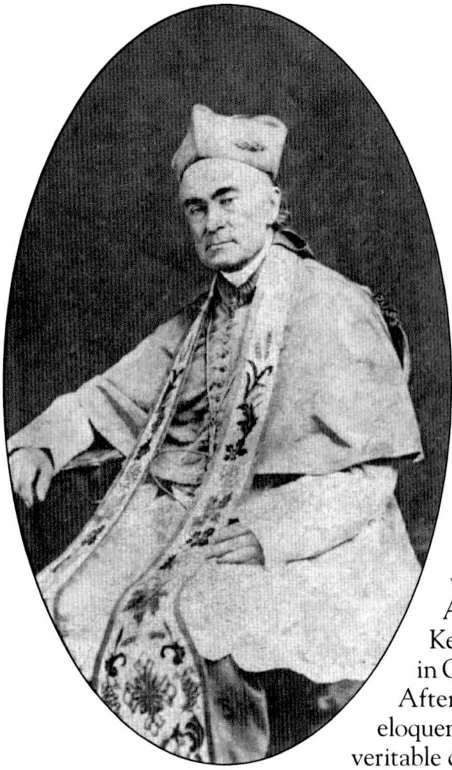

Cincinnati was a hotbed of debates in the 1800s, most of which were centered around religion, public education, temperance, or abolitionism. One of the great debates of the century was the one between two Irishmen who were powerful religious figures in their own right. John Baptist Purcell (pictured left) was born in Mallow, Ireland, in 1800, and as bishop of the archdiocese, ruled Catholic Cincinnati with an iron hand. He also had the civic stature to fight for the rights of the local Irish. Alexander Campbell, born near Ballymena in Northern Ireland in 1788, was raised as a Presbyterian but after his arrival in America in 1809, began the Restoration Movement in Kentucky and Virginia. In 1837, these two ministers met in Cincinnati to debate Protestantism versus Catholicism. After seven days of debate, two sessions each day, the eloquence of both men left them in what was considered a veritable draw.

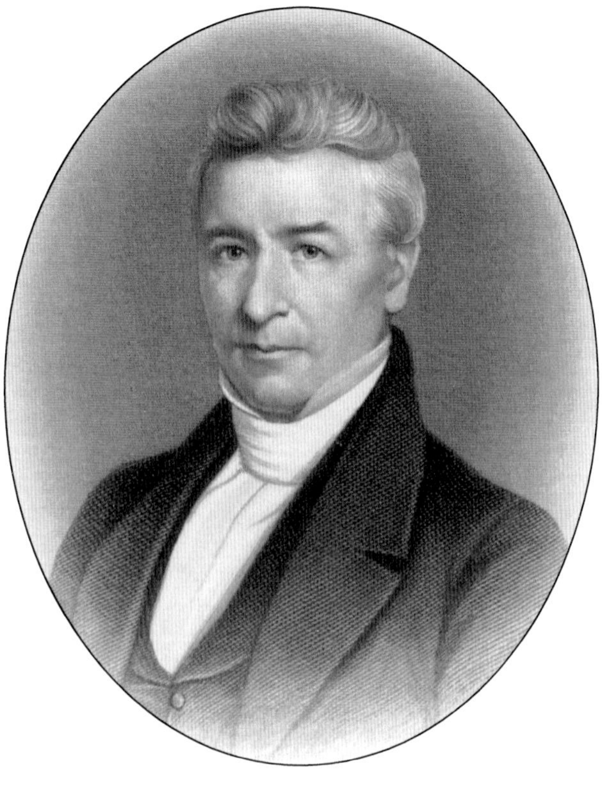

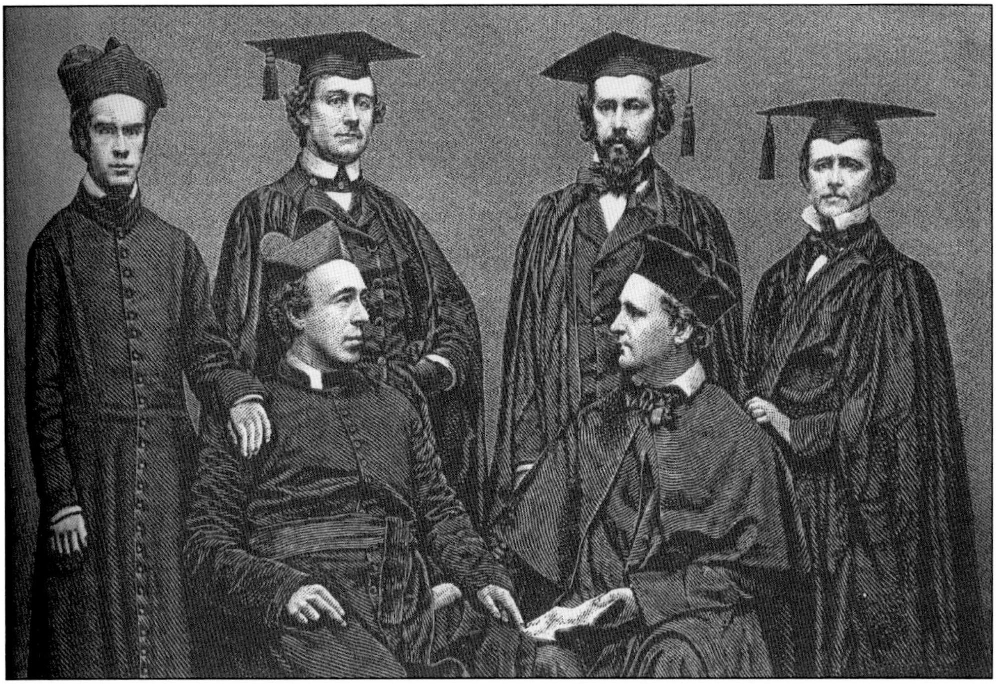

In developing the Catholic presence in Cincinnati and in order to provide pastoral care for his congregants, Purcell needed to build a permanent seminary in Cincinnati. Two Irish brothers, John and James Slevin, pledged to build the seminary, and two other Irish brothers, Michael and Patrick Considine, donated five acres on Price's Hill. Rebuffed by his efforts to build a faculty with priests from the Sulpician and Vincentian orders, Purcell opened Mount St. Mary's Seminary in 1851, and the faculty was soon decidedly Celtic: Barry, Mcleod, O'Leary, Scammon, Quinlan, and Rosecrans.

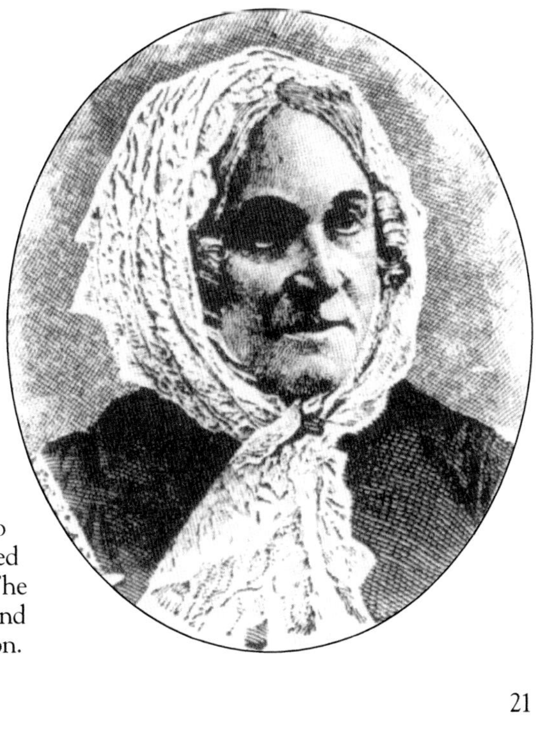

Sarah Worthington King Peter, a wealthy Cincinnatian who was an important arts patron, converted to Catholicism in 1855 and maintained a close association with Purcell. With the bishop's blessing, Peter journeyed to Kinsale, Ireland, in 1857 to recruit nuns in the Order of the Sisters of Mercy to come to Cincinnati. When they arrived, Peter opened her home to them until they were settled. The Irish nuns began what has been a century and a half of service in health care and education.

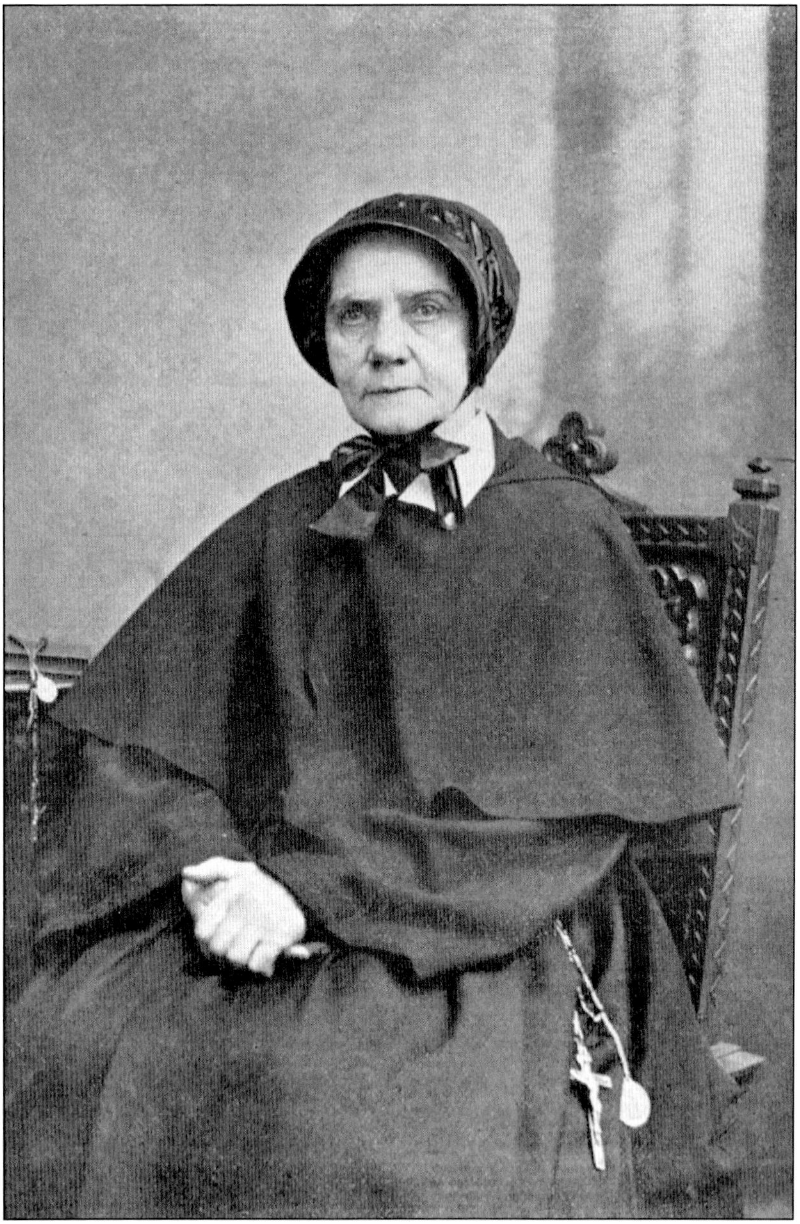

Sr. Anthony O'Connell was a young novitiate when she emigrated from Ireland to the United States in 1837. Born as Mary Ellen O'Connell in Limerick in 1814, she took her vows shortly after her arrival in America and entered the Sisters of Charity in Maryland. As Sr. Anthony O'Connell, she came to Cincinnati in 1837 to work in St. Peter's Orphanage and later, in an invalid hospital. Working with other sisters at Camp Dennison at the outbreak of the Civil War, she would soon be in the middle of battlefields in Tennessee and Virginia. Sister Anthony became known as the "Angel of the Battlefield" during the war, as she and the other nuns provided medical care to the soldiers both in the field and on the hospital ships that plied the rivers during the conflict. And, it was her work in developing battlefield triage that won her praise from both Abraham Lincoln and Jefferson Davis. After the war, she was honored with membership in the Grand Army of the Republic.

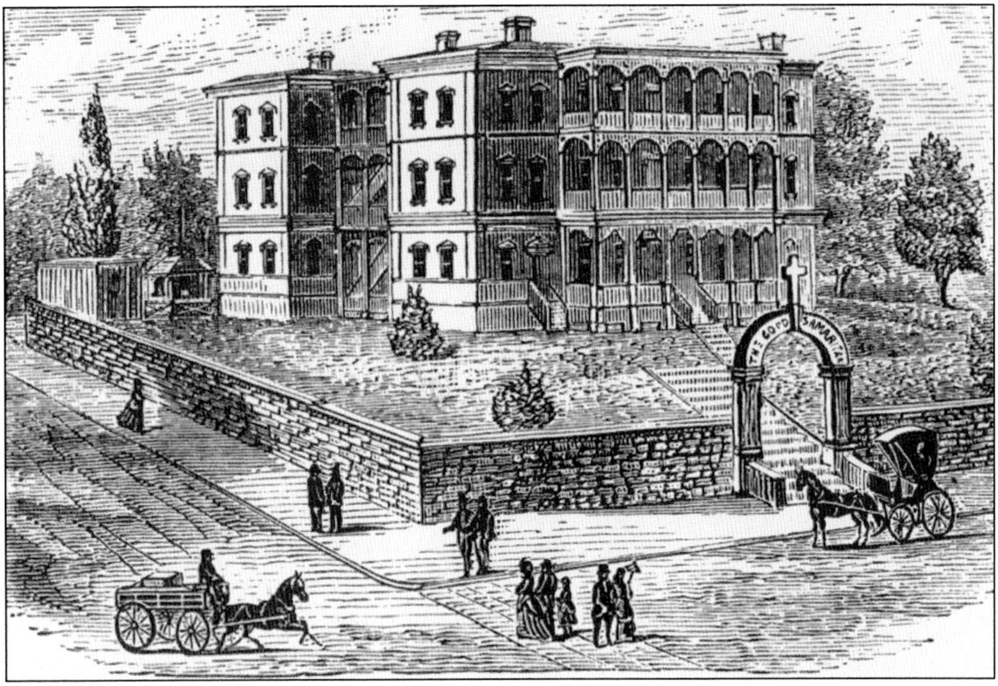

These two views of Good Samaritan Hospital, one from the 19th century and one from the early 20th century, show the establishment that flourished because of the work of Sr. Anthony O'Connell and the Sisters of Charity. In the late 1860s, Sister O'Connell resumed her work with orphans and unwed mothers, as well as providing medical care. In 1866, two local businessmen, Joseph Butler and Lewis Worthington, bought the federal government's Marine Hospital in Cincinnati and donated the building to Sister Anthony. Though non-Catholics, both men were deeply impressed by her devotion to the sick, and it was Butler who suggested the hospital be renamed "Good Samaritan." The Sisters of Charity took on the operation of the hospital, and Sr. Anthony O'Connell continued her medical ministry until her death in 1897.

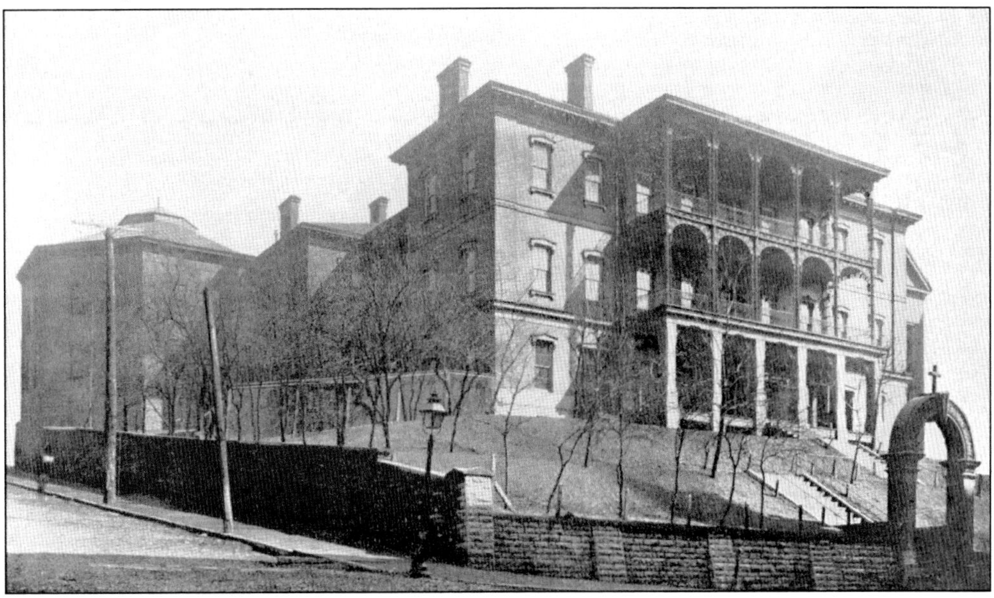

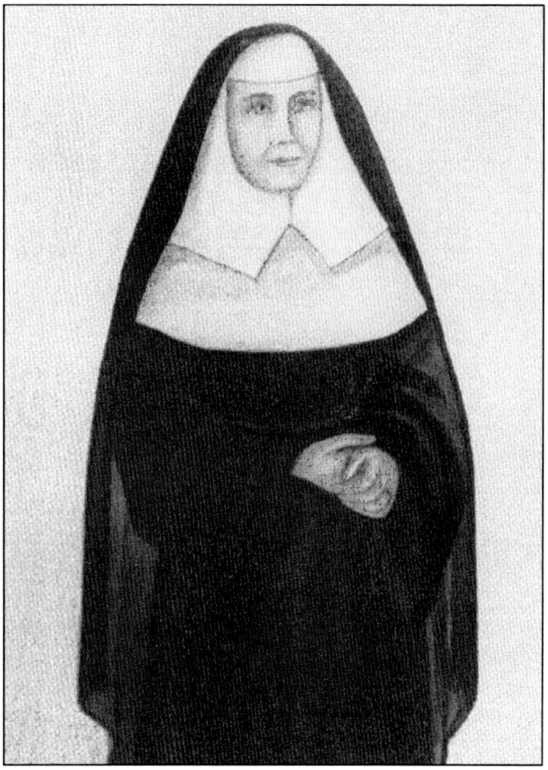

In 1858, Mother Mary Teresa Maher led a group of 10 Sisters of Mercy from Kinsale, Ireland, to Cincinnati in order to minister to the poor and establish schools to educate women and children. After arriving in Cincinnati that August, Mother Maher and the nuns first stayed in the sumptuous home of Sarah Peter but soon established a convent in a poor area of Sycamore Street between the Bottoms and Over-the-Rhine. From there, they purchased an old German orphanage, and in 1869 they formed their first school at St. Patrick's School on Third and Mill Streets.

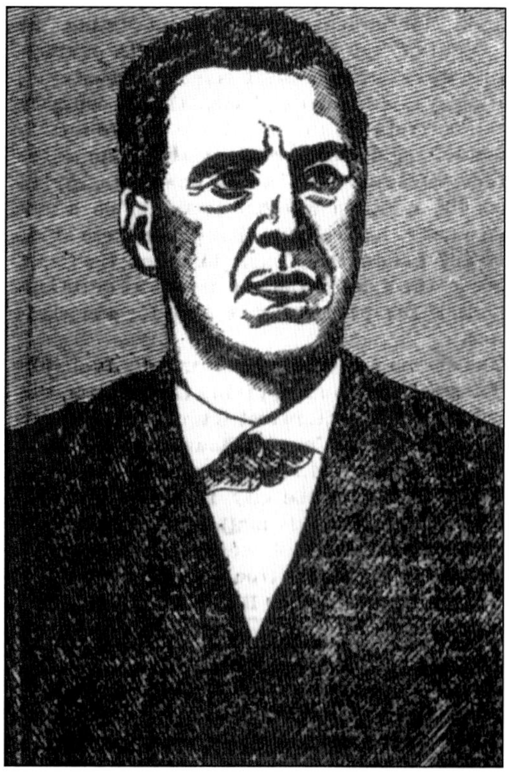

A burly bargeman on the Ohio River, Mike McCoole emigrated from Ireland to Cincinnati around 1850. A character known for his overall belligerence, McCoole turned his massive muscles earned on the river to bare-knuckle prizefighting. He won and lost a number of bouts from Pittsburgh to Louisville, and in 1867, he took on Aaron Jones in Cincinnati's first championship match. In order to escape possible arrest in Hamilton County, the pugilists met at a railroad crossing in Butler County, attracting more than 3,000 people from Cincinnati and neighboring towns. After 34 bruising rounds, Jones had to quit because of his injuries, and McCoole was declared the heavyweight champion.

Born in 1826 in a family strongly aware of its northern Irish ancestry, composer Stephen Collins Foster came to Cincinnati in 1846 to work as a bookkeeper in his brother's steamboat business. Foster's grandfather, Alexander, emigrated from Londonderry in Ulster, Ireland, around 1728, and his brother maintained a membership in the Scotch-Irish Society of America. In Cincinnati, though he only stayed for a few years, Foster found his musical inspiration in the river culture, a life that was largely Irish or African American. Before leaving to return to his native Pennsylvania, Foster composed "Oh Susannah" during his waterfront days. Though his compositions are an integral part of the American songbook, Foster's life ended in poverty and despair. After his untimely death in 1864 in New York City, a sole scrap of paper taken from his billfold had only the words, "Dear friends and gentle hearts."

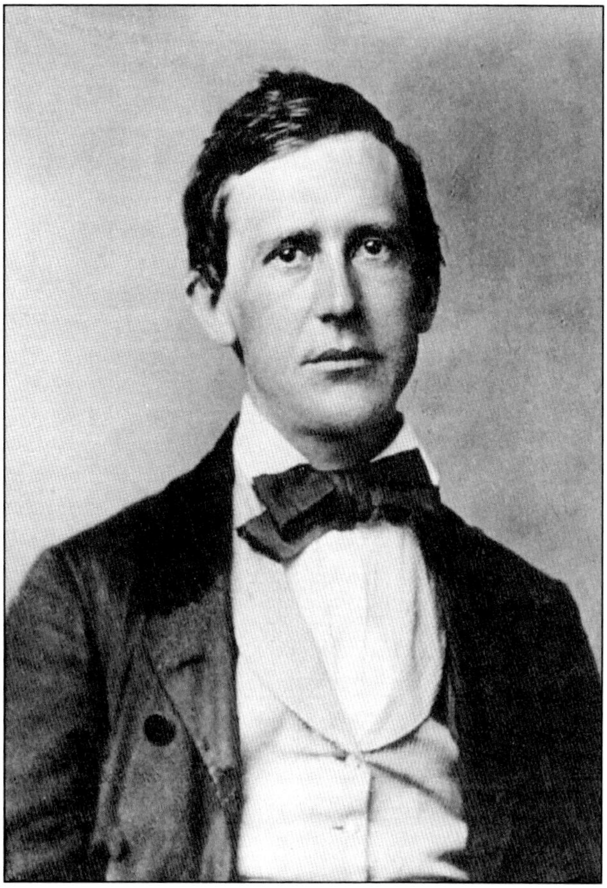

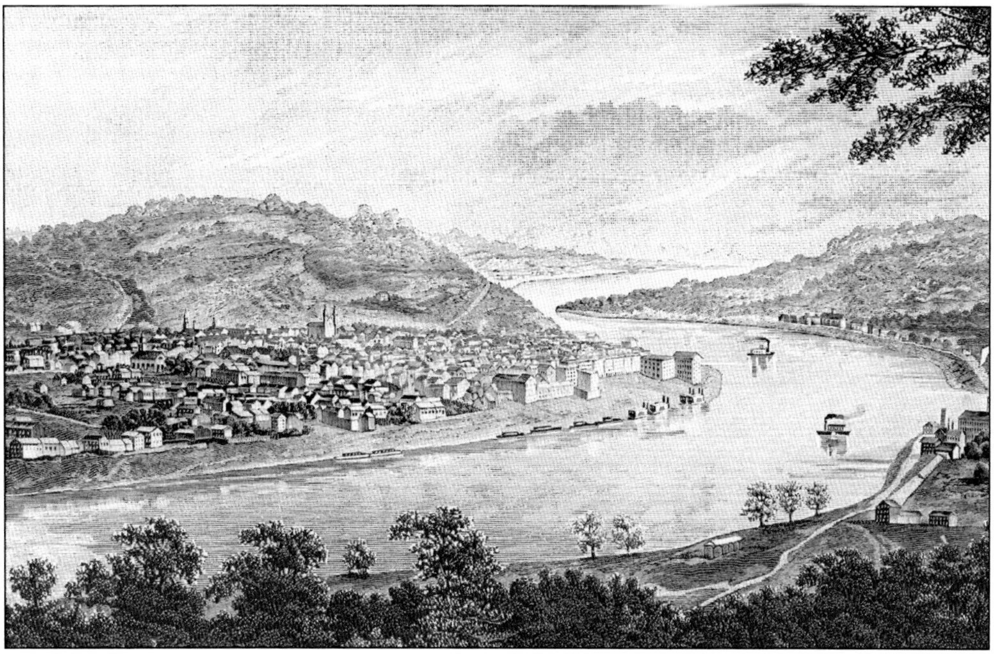

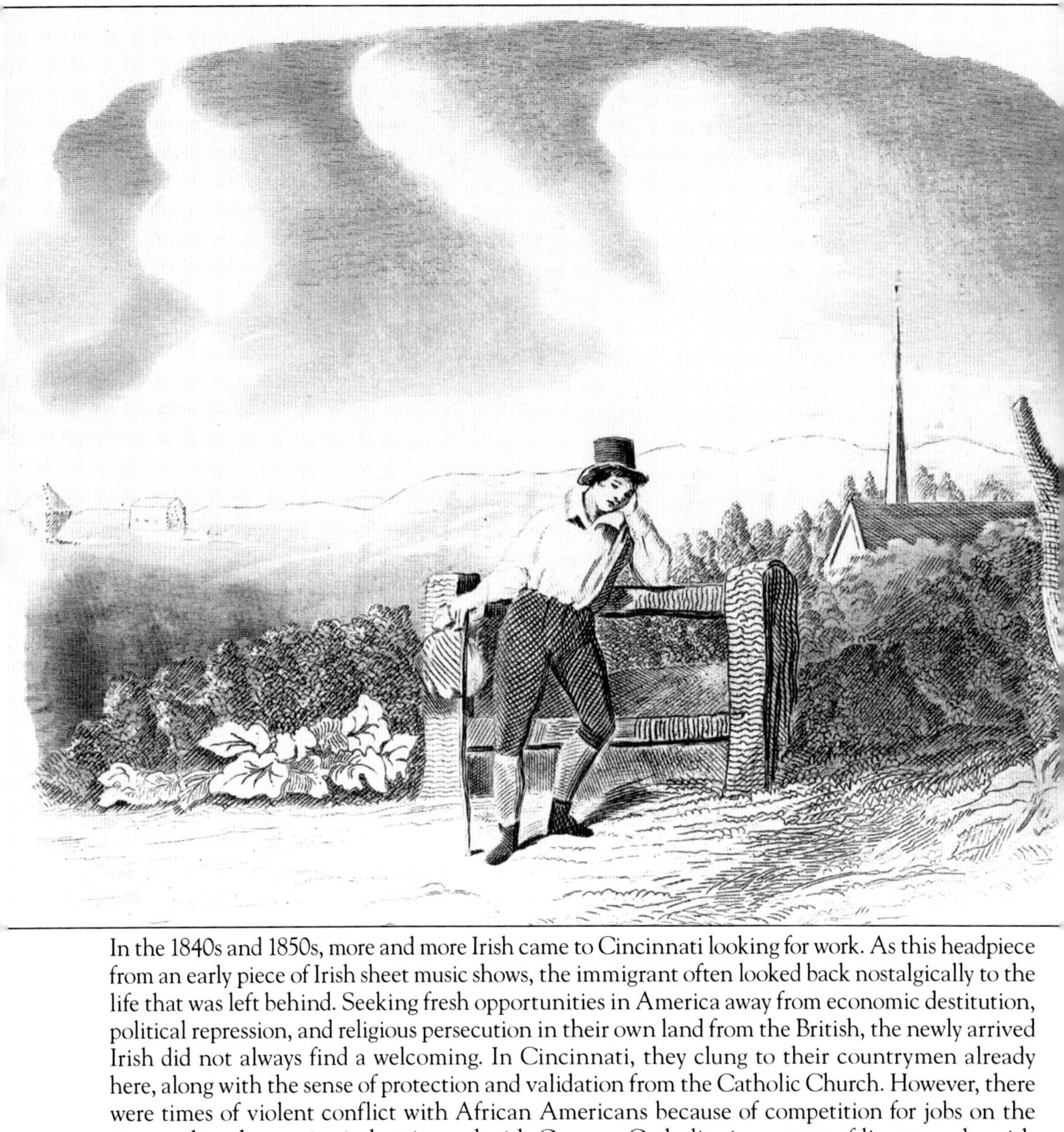

In the 1840s and 1850s, more and more Irish came to Cincinnati looking for work. As this headpiece from an early piece of Irish sheet music shows, the immigrant often looked back nostalgically to the life that was left behind. Seeking fresh opportunities in America away from economic destitution, political repression, and religious persecution in their own land from the British, the newly arrived Irish did not always find a welcoming. In Cincinnati, they clung to their countrymen already here, along with the sense of protection and validation from the Catholic Church. However, there were times of violent conflict with African Americans because of competition for jobs on the river and in the service industries and with German Catholics in matters of liturgy and parish control. On the other hand, the Irish joined with Germans and African Americans in fighting against nativists and anti-abolitionists.

The arguments both for and against slavery raged in Cincinnati for many years. And the Irish found themselves on both sides of the issue, sometimes divided not only by social and economic class, but also by their memory of the ongoing struggles in Ireland. Irish nationalist Daniel O'Connell, pictured here, fought for the repeal of slavery in the British Empire and in the United States. As a Catholic leader in Ireland, O'Connell used that influence in carrying his message to America. But the Irish leaders in Cincinnati, he felt, were not doing enough. In 1843, O'Connell sent a response to an address made by the Irish Repeal Association of Cincinnati: "How can the generous, the charitable, the humane, the noble emotions of the Irish heart, have become extinct amongst you? . . . Irishmen, I call on you to join in crushing slavery, and in giving Liberty to every man of every caste, creed, and color."

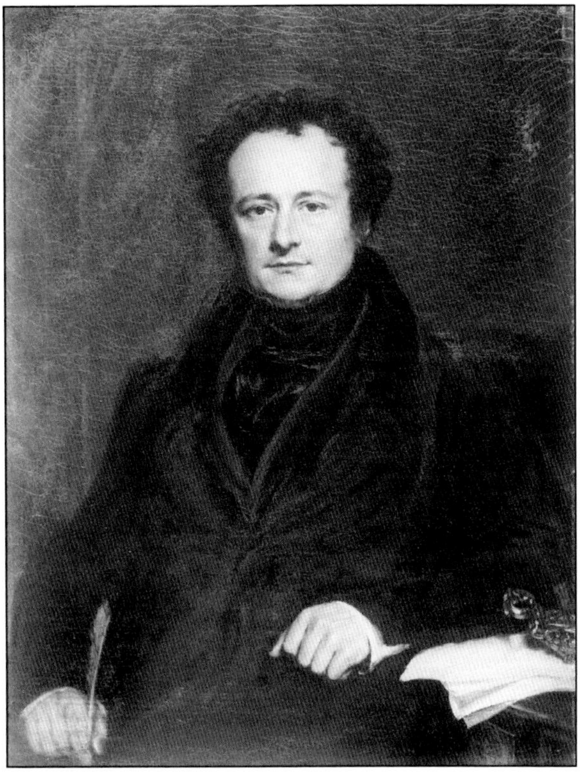

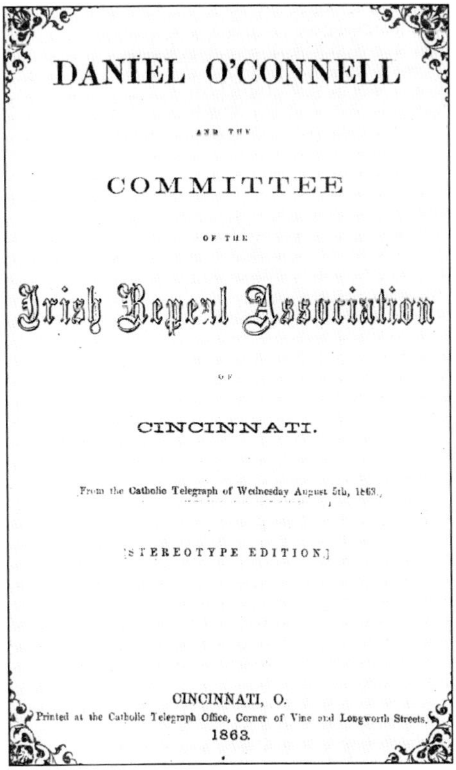

DANIEL O'CONNELL

AND THE

COMMITTEE

OF THE

Irish Repeal Association

OF

CINCINNATI.

From the Catholic Telegraph of Wednesday August 5th, 1863.

[STEREOTYPE EDITION.]

CINCINNATI, O.
Printed at the Catholic Telegraph Office, Corner of Vine and Longworth Streets.
1863.

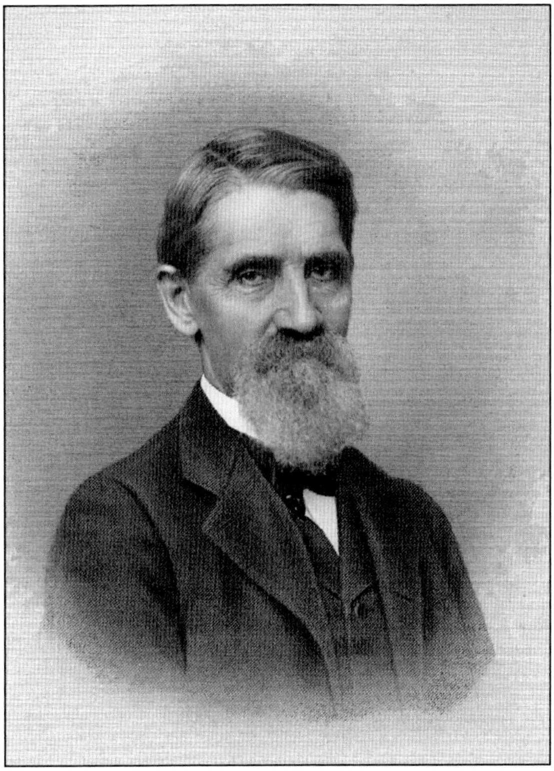

The Pogue brothers, Henry (left) and Samuel (below) were from County Cravan, Ireland. Working in the dry goods business in Cravan, Henry came to Cincinnati in 1851, the year after the rest of his family immigrated to America. First working as a clerk in a local store, by 1865 Henry had the financial means to set up his own business with his brother, the H. & S. Pogue Company. Later, the two brought their other brothers Thomas, Joseph, and William into the business as well, and by 1878, their store was located in the center of the Cincinnati business district on Fourth Street between Race and Vine Streets. The five built Pogue's into one of the largest department stores in the Midwest, an enterprise that survived for over a century.

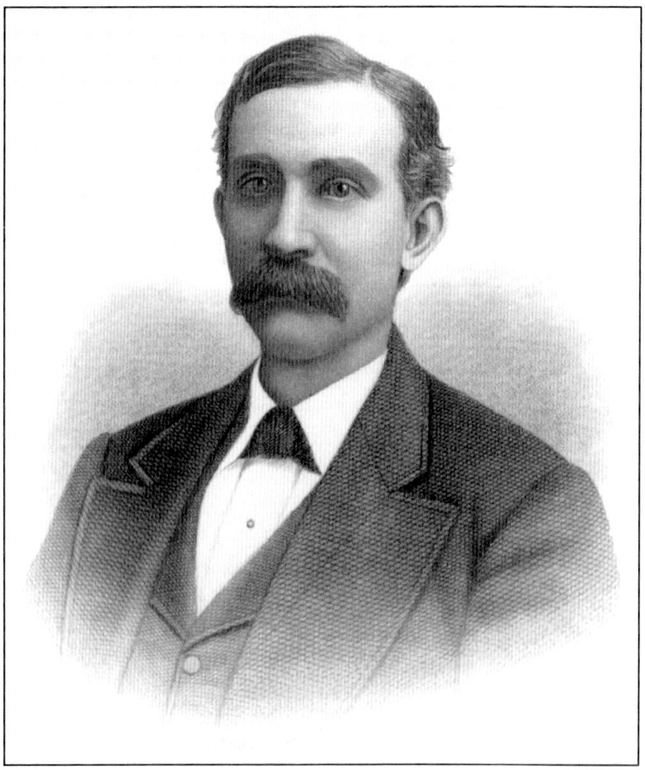

Two

"We'll Drive Them All to Blazes, Says the Irish Volunteer"

By the end of the 1850s, the Irish in Cincinnati were as diverse in their civic roles as any other group. And though there may have been differences in denominational faiths and economic achievement, the Irish heritage most often coalesced around the influence of the Catholic Church. Archbishop Purcell used the *Catholic Telegraph* to solidify the Church's influence on daily life. One reason this worked was because of the relative illiteracy of fresh immigrants and those of the lower classes. One of Purcell's trusted friends, bookseller and printer Daniel Conahan, would read the *Telegraph* to the local Irish. The paper would have the diocesan views on politics and faith, but it also contained the news from the cities, towns, and counties of Ireland, helping Cincinnati Irish Americans maintain a connection to the land they left behind.

There were several Irish nationalist groups in the city, as well as church sodalities and fraternal groups. And these organizations would find themselves on both sides of the slavery issue, some vehemently opposing slavery but many opposing abolitionism as well. These topics were especially important in antebellum Cincinnati and southern Ohio. Some of these differences could be traced to the competition for jobs. In 1829, again in 1836, and once more in 1841, Irish workers and African American workers rioted, clashing over employment opportunities and the issue of abolitionism. And sometimes the Irish were fighting alongside German immigrants as both groups staved off attacks by nativists and Know-Nothings. The Civil War would clarify matters somewhat, but that competition for jobs and influence would persist.

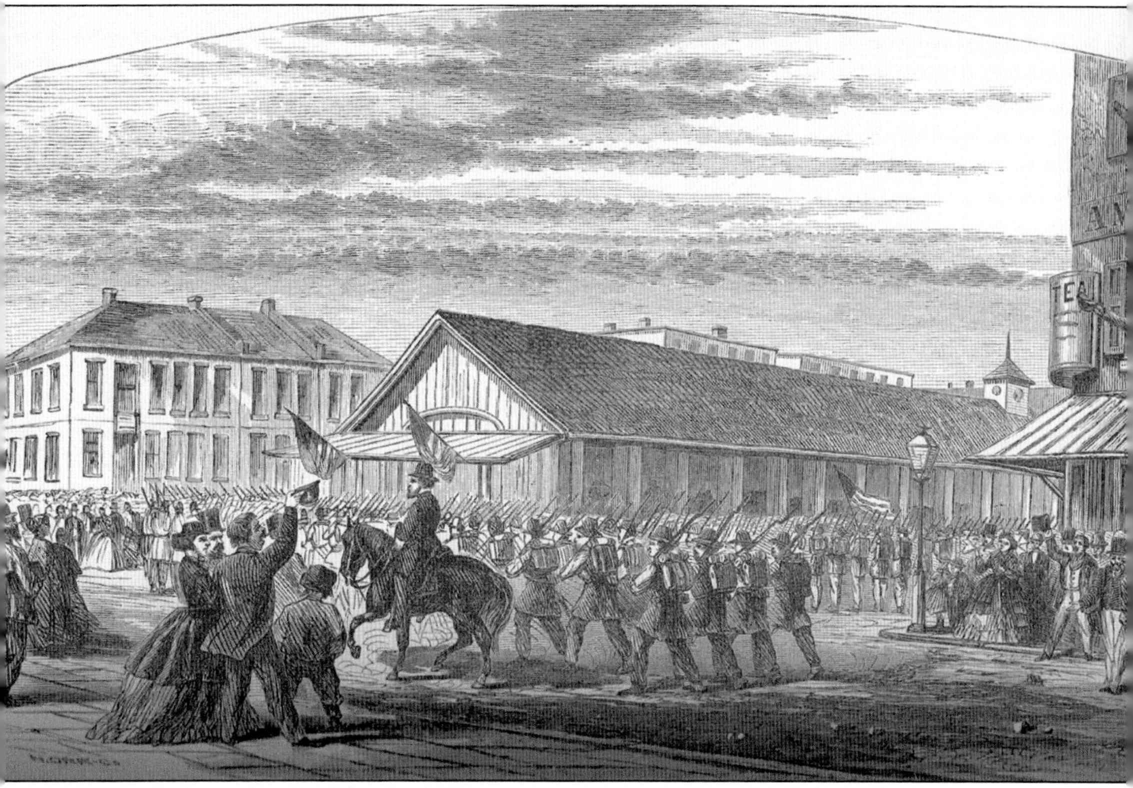

With the outbreak of the Civil War in 1861, Cincinnatians girded themselves for the roles they would play in the unfolding conflict. Many citizens were somewhat at odds as to the Union or Confederate cause, as Cincinnati was essentially a border city with economic and political interests extending on both sides of the Mason-Dixon Line. The passions regarding slavery and abolitionism had built for decades. Nevertheless, as this image of a mustering parade at the Fifth Street Market shows, regiments were raised for the Union, and planning began for the protection of the city in case of attack from the South.

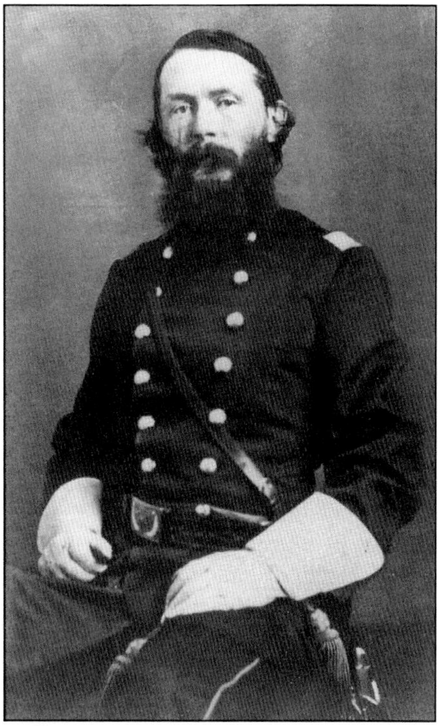

The city's Irish citizens quickly rose to the situation. On May 7, 1861, less than a month after the firing on Fort Sumter that began the war, the 10th Ohio Volunteer Infantry Regiment was formed and mustered at Camp Harrison under poet-soldier William Haines Lytle (right), who was a veteran of the Mexican-American War and had been appointed colonel. The 10th Ohio Volunteer Infantry Regiment (below) was an Irish regiment and would become known as the "Bloody Tinth" for its battlefield service. Initially a three-month service regiment with nine of the ten companies composed of Irishmen under the names of the Montgomery Guards and Sarsfield Guards, the three-year service company formed thereafter held seven companies of Irish American soldiers. (Below, courtesy of Pat Mallory.)

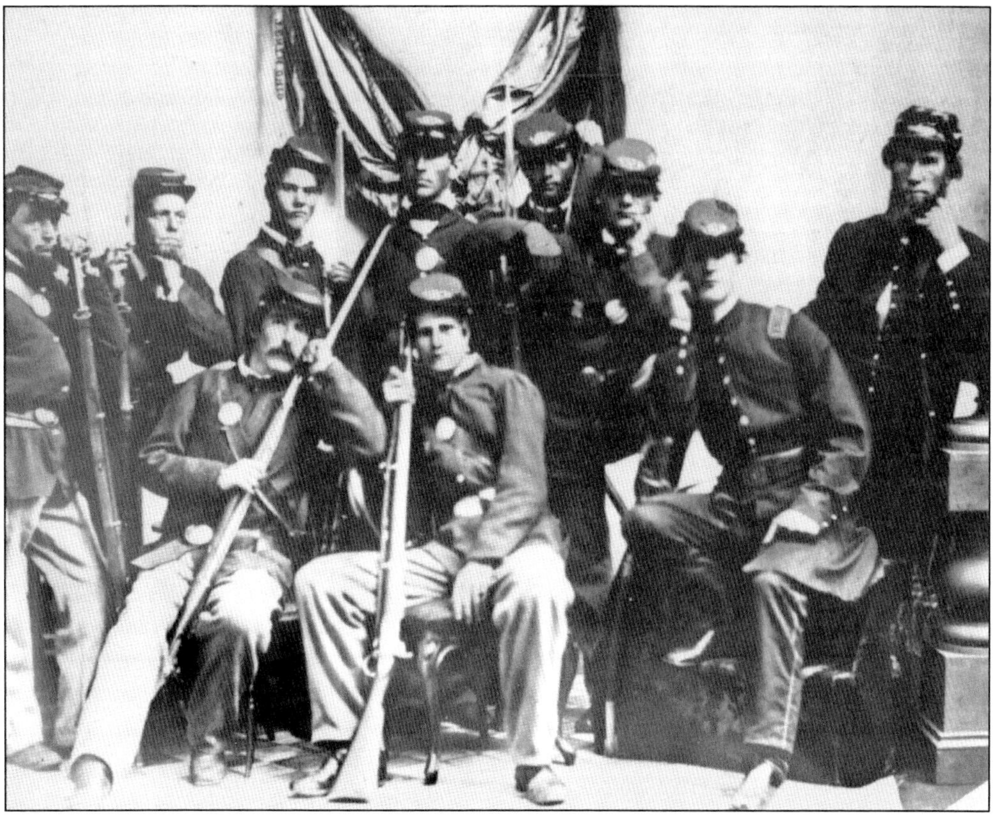

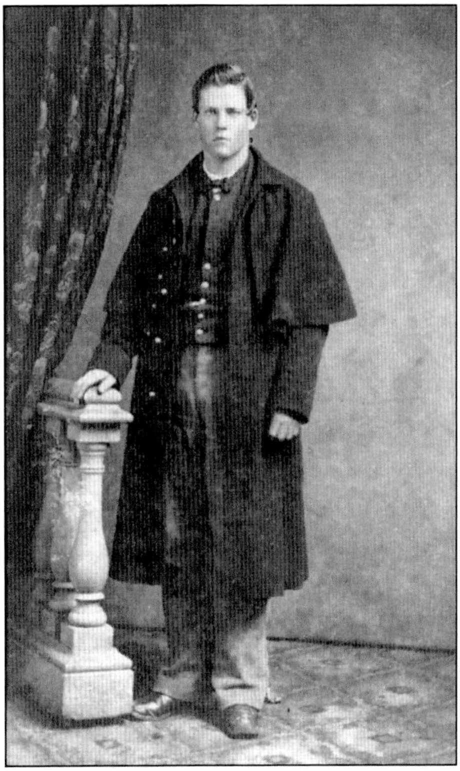

Pictured here is an unknown soldier of the 10th Ohio Volunteer Infantry Regiment (left), posing in a photographer's studio before marching off to battle, providing his family with a memento in case he did not return. It was important to the Irish both in the regiment and to their families in Cincinnati that they have the services of a Catholic priest. Forty-two years old at the time, William T. O'Higgins (below) joined the regiment on June 3 as it was ready to move out of camp and into the war theater. A regimental chaplain, O'Higgins remained in the regiment for three years and was mustered out with the rest of the soldiers on June 17, 1864. (Left, courtesy of Pat Mallory.)

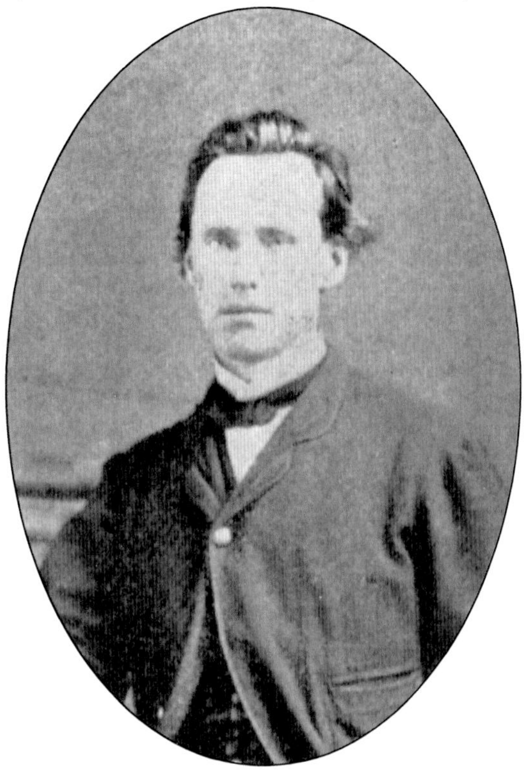

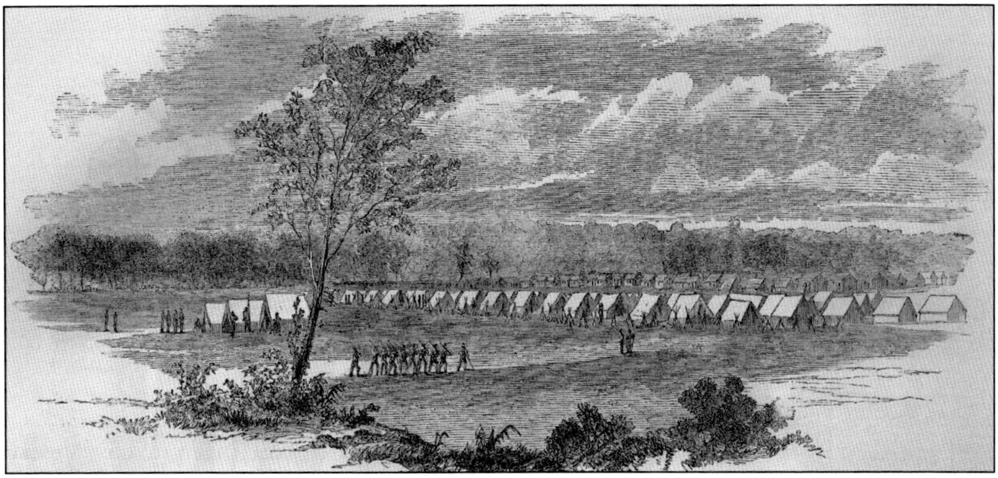

After mustering at Camp Harrison, the 10th Ohio Volunteer Infantry Regiment moved to Camp Dennison, to the northeast of Cincinnati, on May 12 and remained there until June 3. Camp Dennison was used as a training base for more than 50,000 Yankee soldiers over the course of the war and also served as the site for a military hospital. It was a strategic location because from there the regiments would be sent to fight in Virginia and Tennessee. In the image below of the camp, Father O'Higgins celebrates mass for his Irish American countryman before they broke camp and marched to the east, en route to battle.

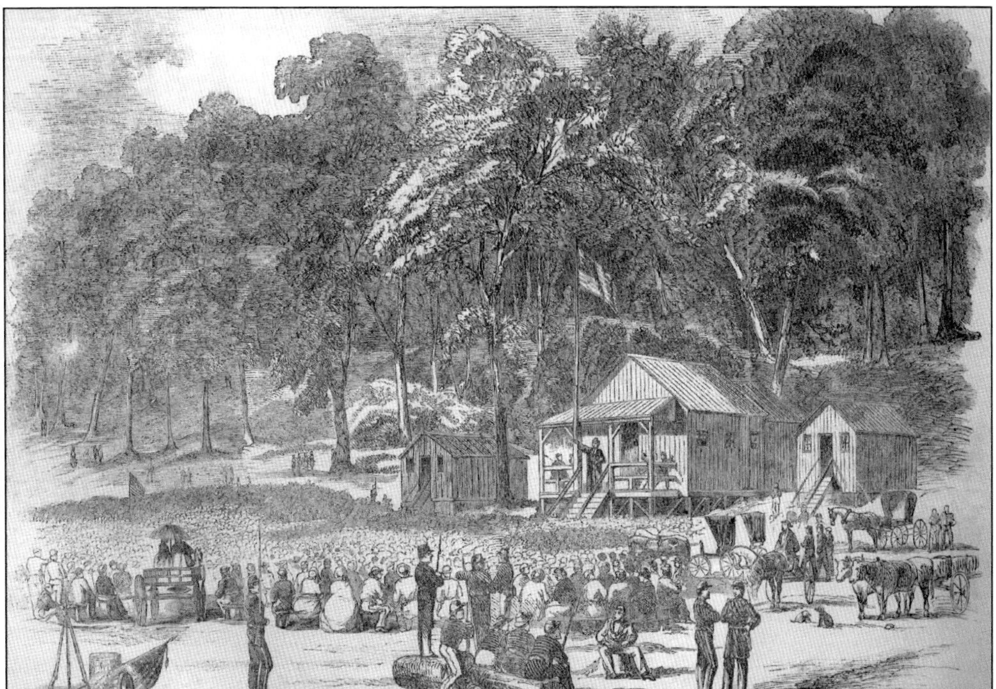

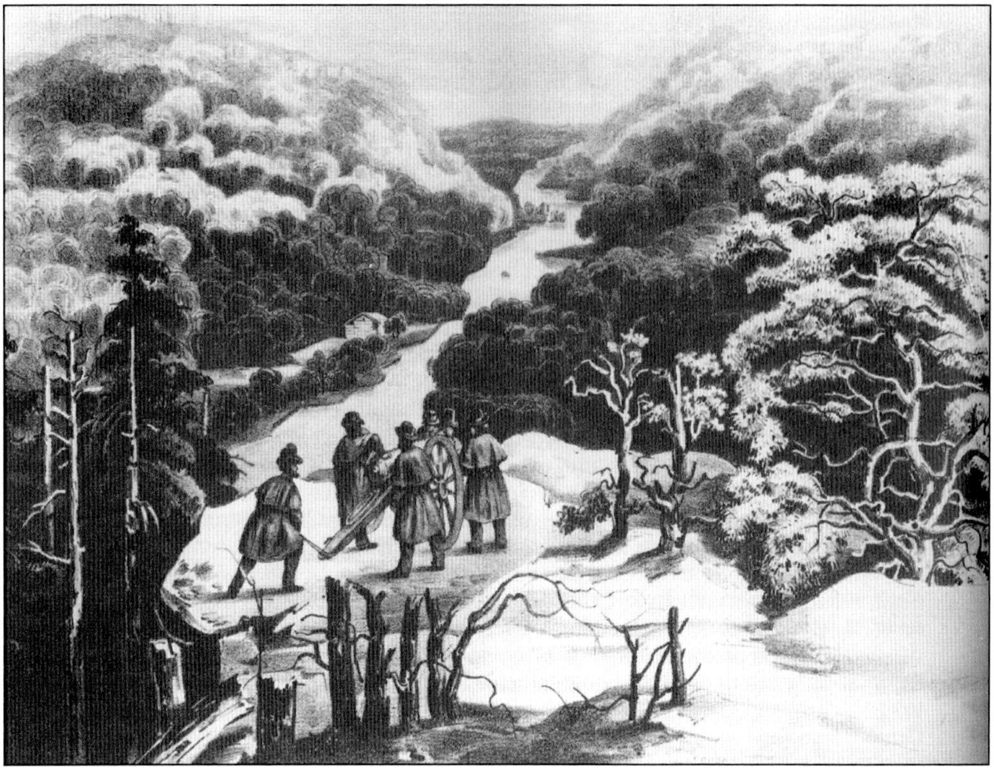

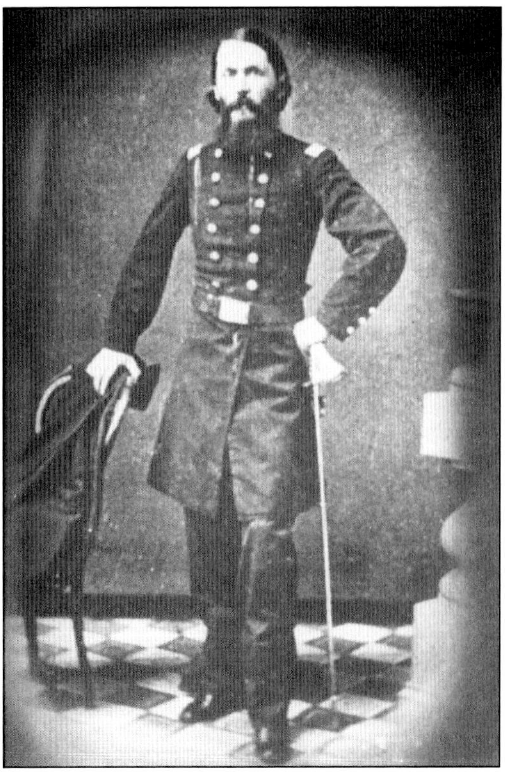

In the West Virginia Campaign, the 10th Ohio Volunteer Infantry Regiment entered the fray at Carnifex Ferry, Virginia. Lytle assigned men to reconnoiter the enemy along the Gauley River. Marching through dense woods, the 10th engaged the Confederate force and began fighting. Of all the regiments involved in the battle, the 10th suffered the most casualties, with 10 soldiers killed and 50 wounded.

Lytle was wounded in the Carnifex Ferry fighting when a bullet hit him and then killed his horse. After recovering back home in Cincinnati, Lytle was assigned to fight in Kentucky. He was again wounded. He was promoted to brigadier general and was later killed in the Battle of Chickamauga on September 20, 1863. Beloved by his men, he was also respected by the Confederates who guarded his body until it could be removed. That night, his soldiers recited his poetry around the campfires: "I gazed, till to the sun the drums, Rolled at the dawn, 'He comes, he comes.'"

An attorney in Cincinnati, Col. Stephen J. McGroarty was originally commissioned as a captain in the 10th Ohio Volunteer Infantry Regiment but quickly rose in rank as he was transferred to other regiments. He was born in County Donegal in 1830 and was three years old when his parents moved the family to Cincinnati. At Carnifex Ferry, he was shot in the lung, and though wounded, he rescued the company flag, wrapped it around his body, and hid under a corncrib until he could be rescued himself. The blood-soaked flag was sent home to Cincinnati. After his recovery, he had his arm shattered by a bullet in another battle. Throughout the war, he was wounded 23 times, finally dying in 1870 from the lasting damage of his first wound.

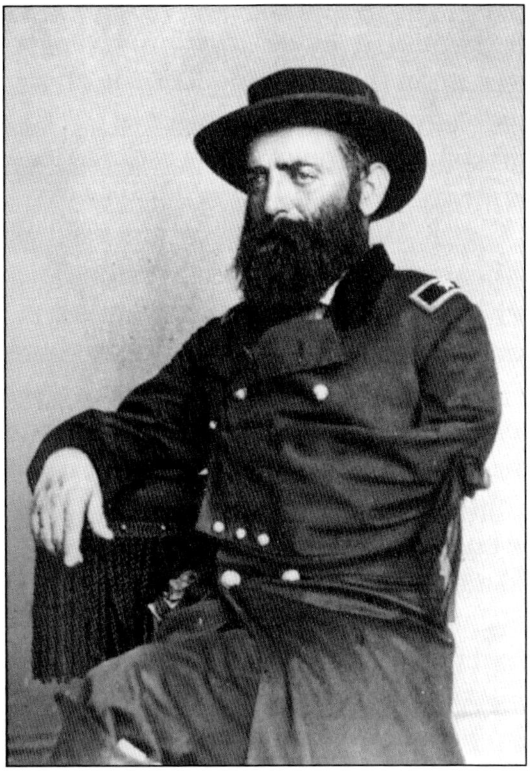

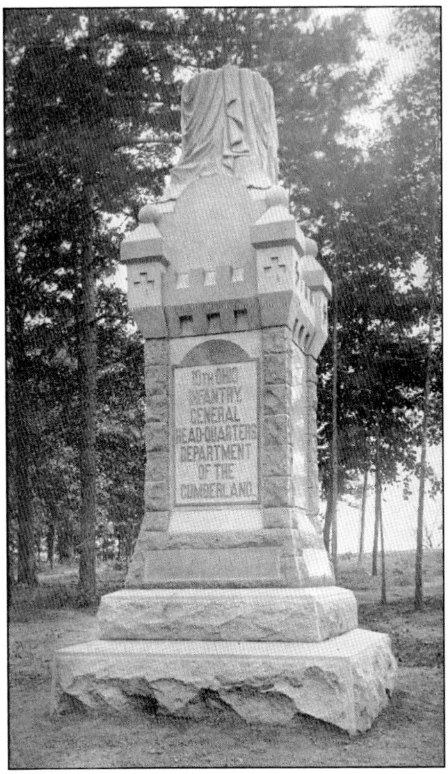

Erected in 1896, this monument at the Chickamauga Battlefield honors the brave Irishmen of the "Bloody Tinth." The regiment fought in 10 major battles, as well as numerous skirmishes during its service to the Union cause. During the 1862 fighting at Perryville, the 10th Ohio Volunteer Infantry Regiment lost half of its soldiers as dead, wounded, or missing. The monument was provided by an act of the Ohio General Assembly in 1891.

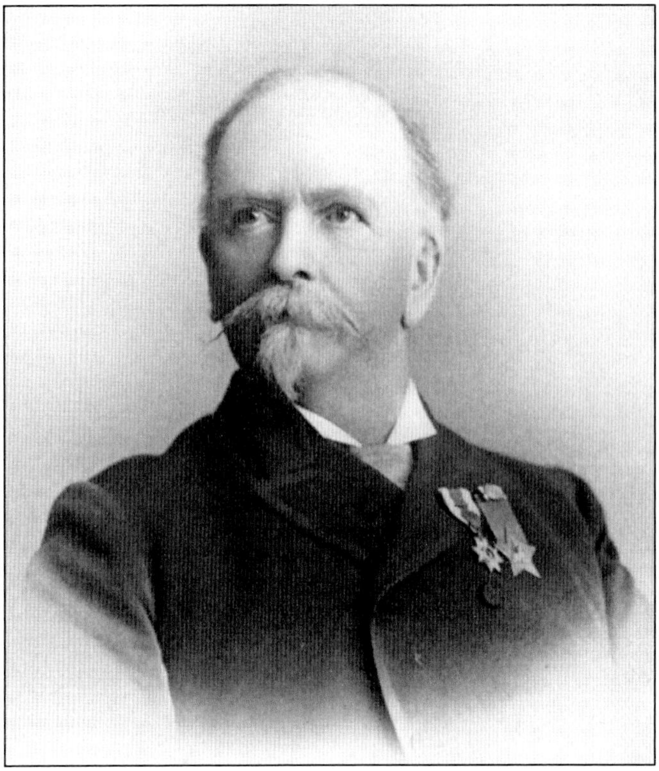

Joseph Burke was another Cincinnati Irishman who served in the Civil War. Born in Ireland in 1835, he worked as a lawyer in Cincinnati until he was commissioned as a major with the 10th Ohio Volunteer Infantry Regiment. He rose to the rank of colonel and was an important aide to both Lytle and to Gen. William Rosecrans. Highly respected by his men, it was Burke who often was able to control their rowdiness in camp. After the war, Burke moved to the South, becoming the collector at the Port of Mobile. He died in Jacksonville, Alabama, in 1900, donating his estate for the establishment of what is now Jacksonville State University.

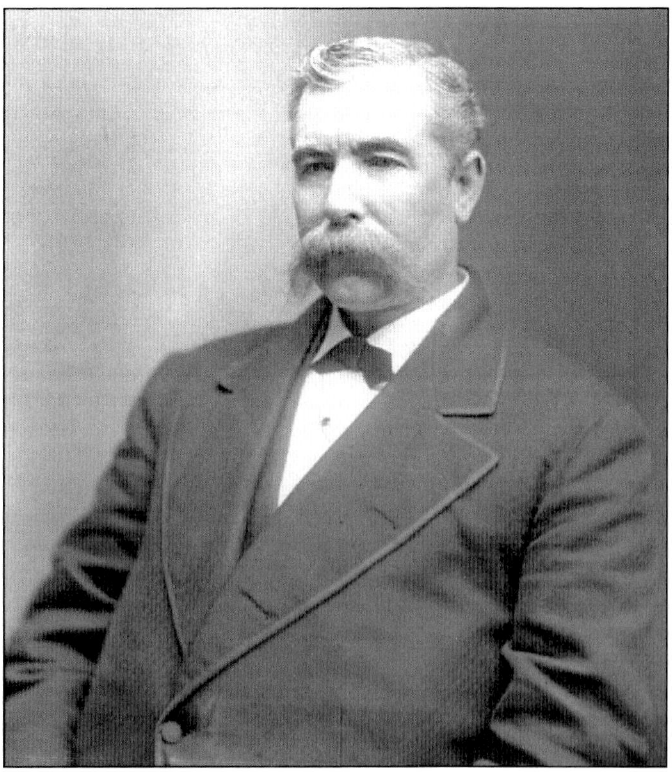

Thomas Lowry Young was born in County Down, Ireland, in 1832. He grew up in New York City, and after serving as a military musician in the last days of the Mexican-American War, he came to Cincinnati to teach in the Ohio State Reform School. During the Civil War, Young served with a regiment of Missouri volunteers and then with the 118th Ohio Infantry. Following his discharge in 1864 due to illness, he attended the Cincinnati Law School and embarked on a political career, elected to the Ohio State Legislature, serving as lieutenant governor under Rutherford B. Hayes and winning election to the US Congress. Young died in Cincinnati in 1888.

The strong ties that Cincinnati Irish maintained with their homeland made the city a fertile ground for recruiting support for Irish independence. The Fenian Movement, with its pledge of fighting for "the establishment of a Free and Independent Government on the Irish Soil," had several Cincinnatians in its ranks as it planned a military action in Canada that, they hoped, would help force the English out of Ireland. In January 1865, the Fenian Brotherhood held a congress here to prepare its strategy. Led by James Stephens (pictured here), who came to America to help organize Fenian efforts, the brotherhood's officers met in Cincinnati's Metropolitan Hall. Stephens was very popular, and his arrival in the United States occasioned the writing of poetry, and in Cincinnati, the welcoming of him at the train station by hundreds of local Irish. The Congress ended with a resolution for its members to "Be of good cheer! All is well!" The battle would soon be joined.

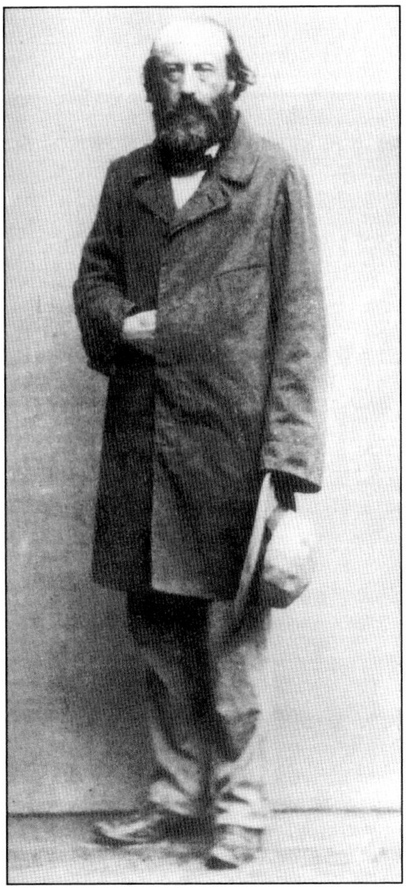

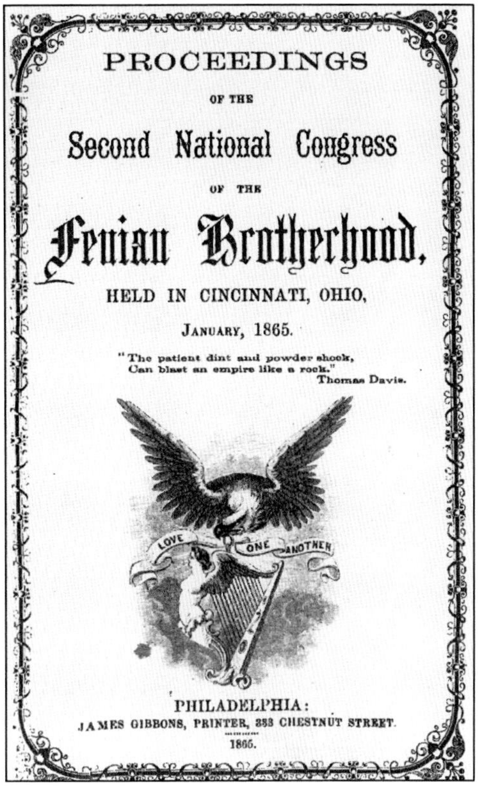

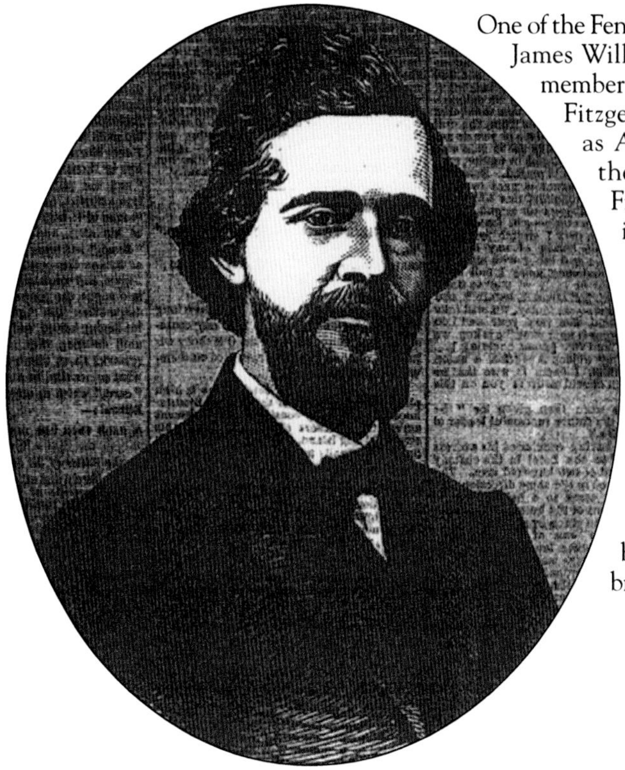

One of the Fenian representatives was Cincinnatian James William Fitzgerald. A lawyer and loyal member of the Friendly Sons of St. Patrick, Fitzgerald had to keep Fenian secrets as Archbishop Purcell railed against the organization as a secret society. Fitzgerald would find himself drawn into the coming conflict in Canada, a battle he considered as folly. Later in his life, Fitzgerald became a police judge in Cincinnati, making the newspaper accounts one time in 1887 when he bravely fought off an intruder in his home who attempted to kill him because of Fitzgerald's harsh sentence he imposed on a ring of cockfighters. He did all this with an injured shoulder; the week before someone else had thrown a brick at him.

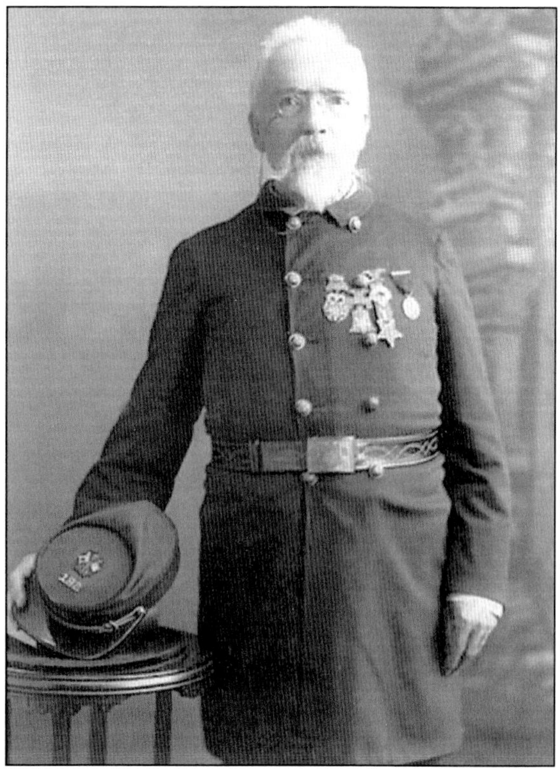

Thomas J. Kelly was another local Irish nationalist loyal to the Fenian cause. Born in County Galway in 1833, Kelly worked as a printer in New York and as a newspaper publisher in Nashville. Forced to leave that city in 1861 because he supported the Union, Kelly came to Cincinnati and joined the 10th Ohio Volunteer Infantry Regiment. Despite being shot in the jaw at Carnifex Ferry, Kelly finished his service in 1864, and following the war, joined the Fenian Movement and the Irish Republican Brotherhood. He became a deputy to Stephens, planned Fenian raids in Ireland, was arrested, escaped capture during a rescue attempt at a prison in Manchester, England, and made his way back to America, where he died in 1908.

Present at the Cincinnati Fenian convention was John Francis O'Mahony, who, like Stephens, was welcomed by a throng of Irish supporters when he arrived in town. O'Mahony was born in County Limerick, entered Trinity College and became a Gaelic scholar of some note, and after immigrating to New York, helped found the Fenian Brotherhood in America. During the Civil War, he served as a colonel in the famous 69th New York Regiment of Irish soldiers under Thomas Meagher. He was prominently in control during the 1865 Fenian meeting in Cincinnati and helped plan the subsequent raids in Canada.

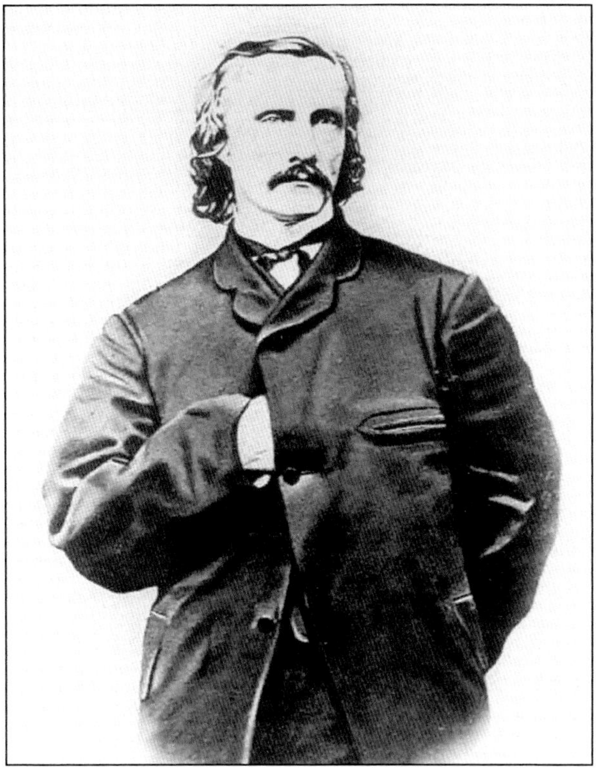

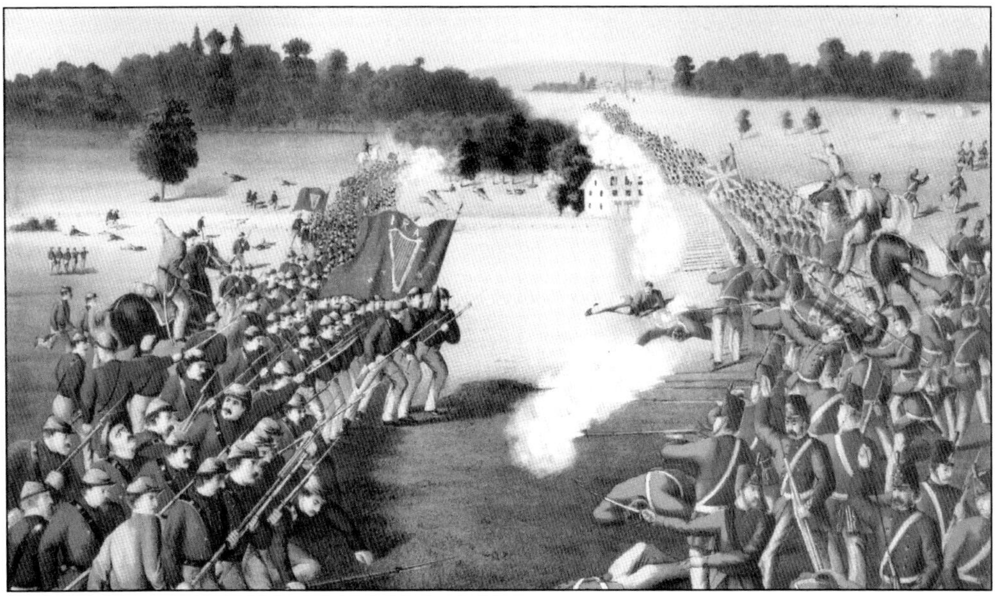

Fenian forces, including many Cincinnatians, gathered near Buffalo, New York, at the beginning of June 1866 to launch their raid into Canada. While the US government kept a close eye on the situation, the Fenians were not interfered with as they set up along the Niagara River. The intent of the invasion of Canada was to confront England and force the negotiation of an independent Irish nation. On June 2, the Battle of Ridgeway began, as this lithograph shows the Fenian troops under an Irish flag confronting the Canadian forces.

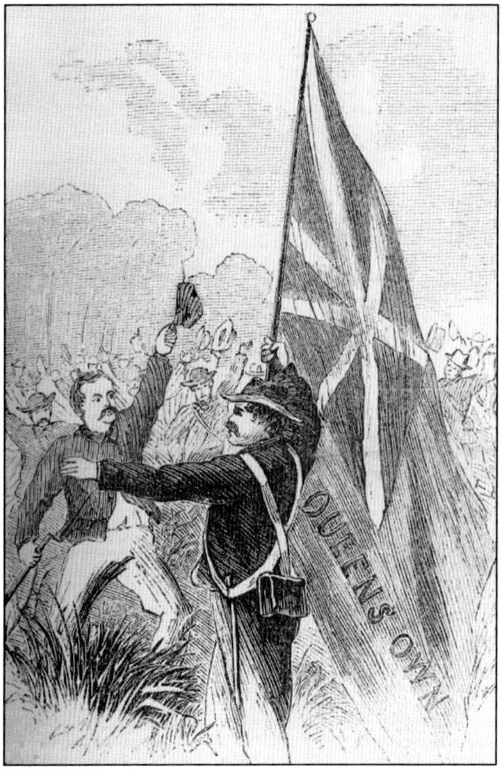

Because the American Civil War had just ended, there was an availability of arms and munitions, along with mustered-out soldiers who not only had military training, but an allegiance to a free Ireland. Earlier in April, there had been a desultory raid into Canada by the Fenians, but no real battle. For the Battle of Ridgeway, both English soldiers and local militia rallied to the battle for the Canadian side and ultimately prevailed. Fenians were taken prisoner by the score, including 85 Cincinnati-area Irishmen. Most of them were quickly paroled. The Fenian Movement attempted to continue its military actions in Canada with another invasion in 1870, but Fitzgerald withheld Cincinnatians from this fighting and it, too, failed.

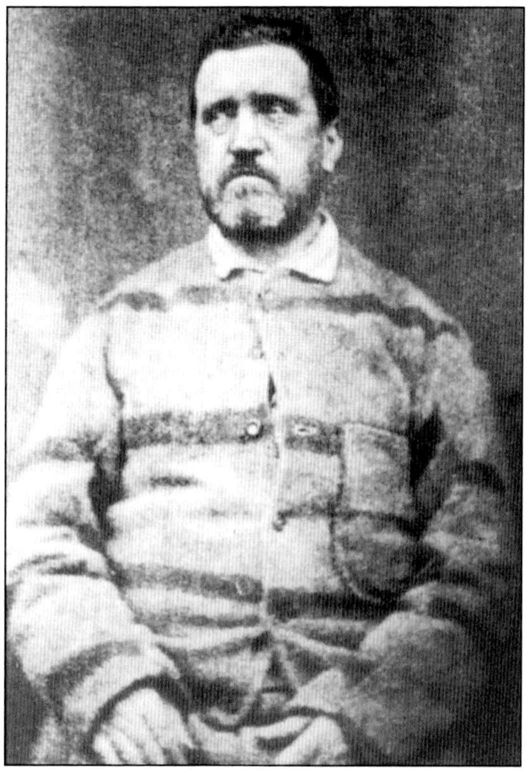

Since his arrival in Cincinnati in 1847, William Halpin was deeply committed to winning freedom for his native Ireland. He was a member of the local Robert Emmett Irish Immigrant Aid Society and the Exiled Sons of Ireland, both organizations working to oust England. After fighting in the Civil War, Halpin joined the Fenian movement and took part in an uprising back in Dublin, where he was arrested in 1867. He was sentenced to 15 years in penal servitude.

Three

"Ye Can Find Them Now in Public Life, in Private Life as Well"

As the years passed after the Civil War, the local Irish became more and more involved in supporting their parochial schools and their parish communities. More of them moved into the middle class and the professional ranks in the business community. Establishing some influence at the election polls, the Irish would find new opportunities in civil service and city politics. By 1870, the Irish constituted 21 percent of Cincinnati's population. As Sir James Macaulay, an English writer, noted as he passed through Cincinnati on his travels in the United States: the Irish had been here long enough to acquire social and political features of American life, "The foreign or immigrant element, both Irish and continental, is larger and influences the affairs of the city in the same ways, and much in the same proportion as they do the whole Union. . . . They [Irish] are distinguished by qualities that tend to make men interesting rather than prosperous."

It was a bit of travelogue hyperbole, somewhat true but rather disingenuous on the whole. The Irish in Cincinnati were, in fact, becoming more and more prosperous, and in that regard, they compared well to the Germans, the Italians, and the old-line Anglo-Saxons. In terms of being "interesting," as Macaulay noted, that became more and more the case as local Irish worked hard to preserve and celebrate their heritage during America's Gilded Age, as it moved into the progressivism of the late 19th and early 20th centuries.

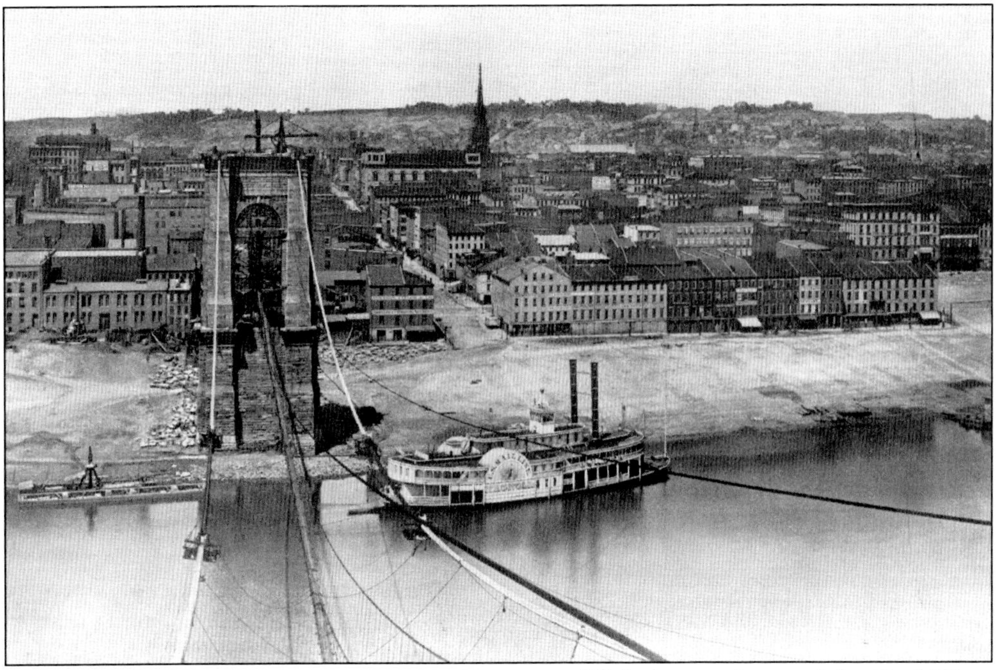

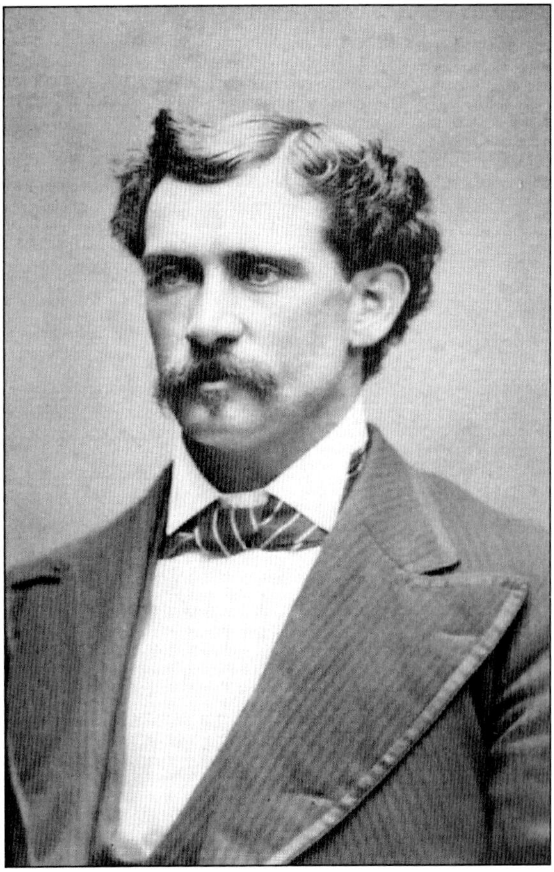

With the conclusion of the Civil War, the John A. Roebling Suspension Bridge would be completed in 1866, connecting Cincinnati with northern Kentucky. For Cincinnatians, it would symbolize a rebirth of local commerce and would indicate a forward-looking city of diverse neighborhoods and ethnicities.

County Cavan native Andrew Jackson Leonard was born in 1846 and raised in Newark, New Jersey. He began his ball-playing career when he was 18, playing for various clubs in New York and New Jersey and coming to Cincinnati in 1868 to join the amateur Buckeyes. The next year, when he signed with the Cincinnati Red Stockings to play left field for a salary of $800, he became the first Irish-born professional baseball player.

Known variously as a "sack 'em up man" and a "resurrectionist," William Cunningham was a supplier of dead bodies. At a time when numerous medical schools were operating in Cincinnati and the procurement of cadavers for anatomy classes was forbidden by law, Cunningham stole fresh bodies from the city infirmary or local cemeteries to sell to the colleges. He was born in Ireland in 1807 and is thought to have lived in Virginia before coming to Cincinnati, where, in snatching a corpse, his methods usually involved a couple of unsavory cohorts, late moonless nights, and a big revolver. Ever watchful for the police, "Old Cunny" escaped one time by putting an old coat around a corpse, sitting it next to him in a buggy, and carrying on a drunken conversation with his "friend." He died in 1871 of heart disease, previously arranging payment from the Cincinnati Medical College of Ohio for his body. His widow wrangled an extra $5 from the anatomists and for several years, continued her husband's business herself.

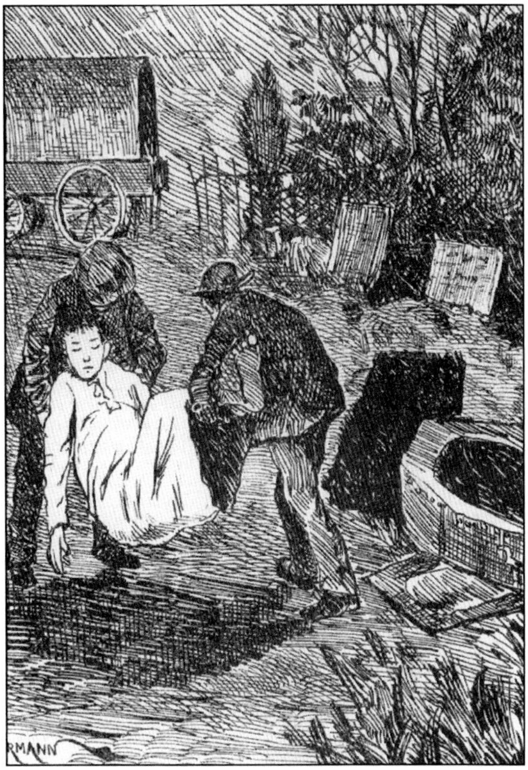

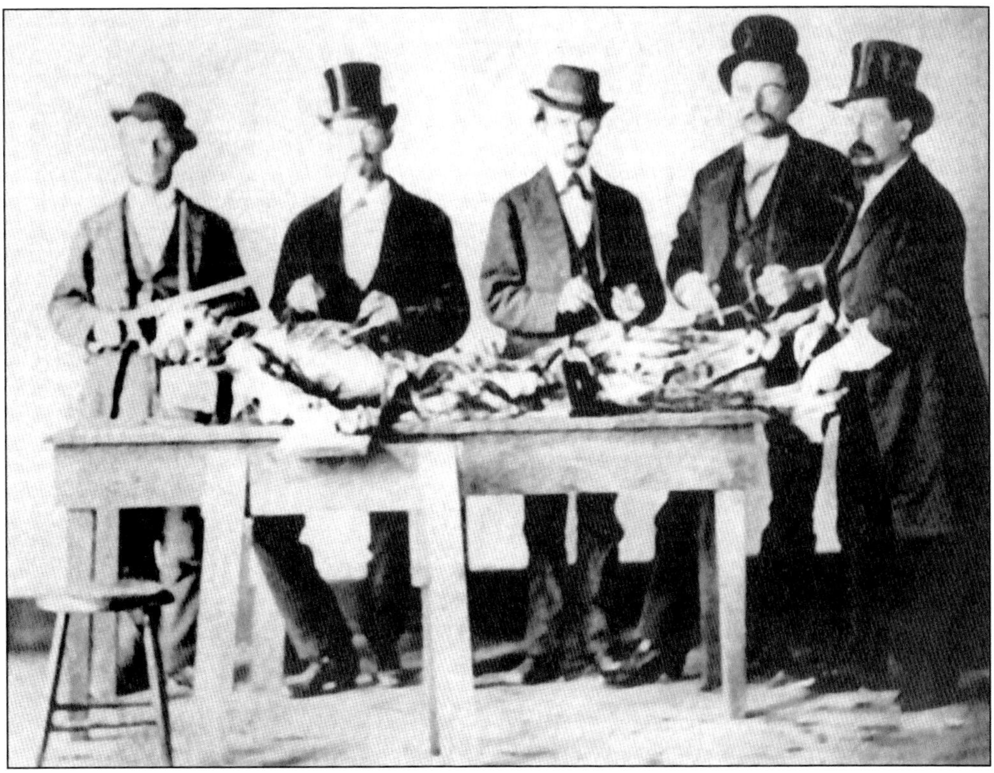

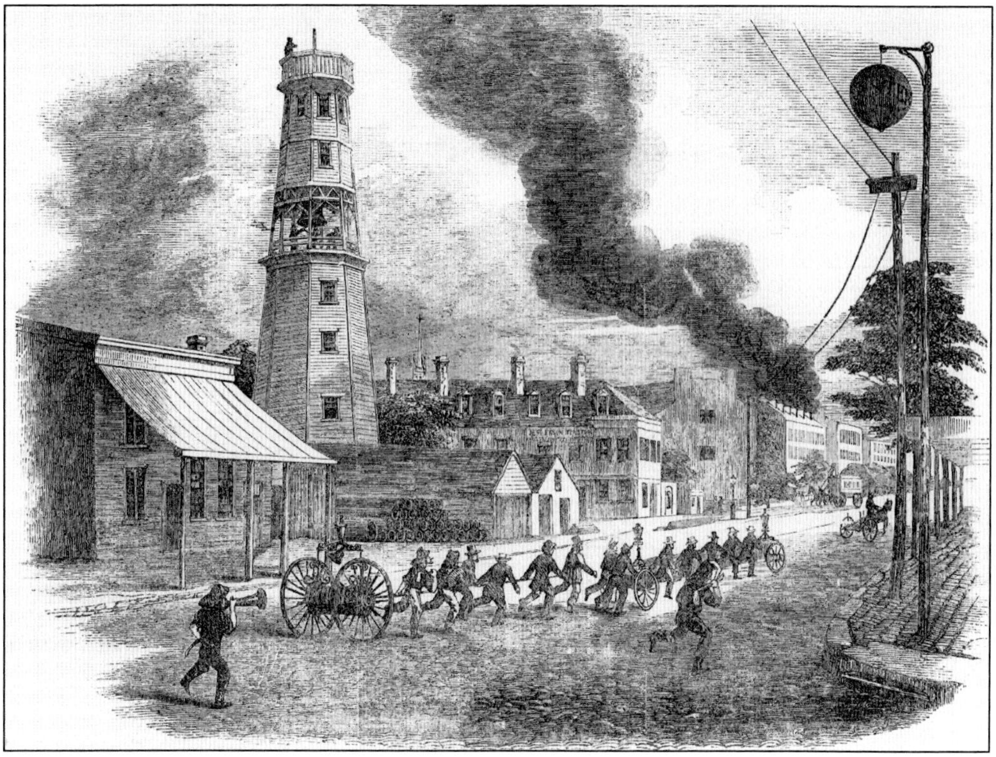

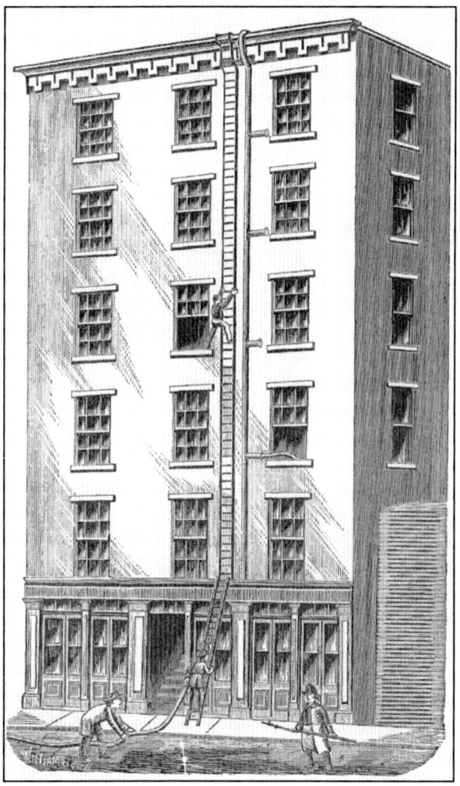

In 1853, Cincinnati established the first fully professional fire department in the United States, and the city boasted the first practical steam fire engine as well. As the department expanded and as more Irish citizens became enfranchised, they would help fill the ranks of firefighters in the city. This was particularly the case as Irish Cincinnatians became more involved in ward politics, thus opening up opportunities for patronage jobs, and as Irish benevolent societies helped members establish the contacts they needed to apply for city positions. The Cincinnati Fire Department became a division of city affairs in which there was a rapid rise of Irish in the 1870s and 1880s.

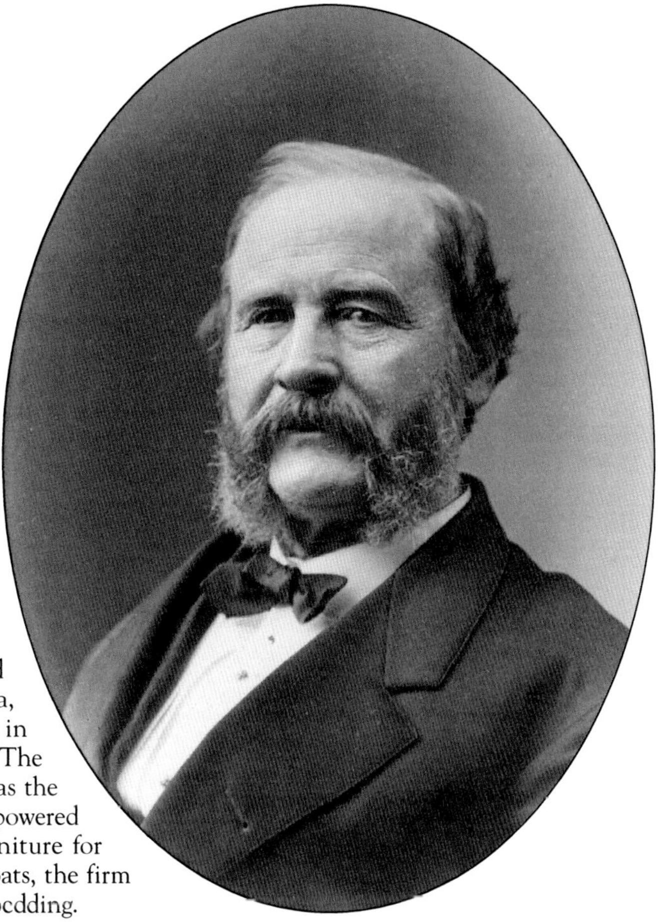

Robert Mitchell was a furniture manufacturer in Cincinnati, first entering as a partner with Frederick Rammelsberg until 1863 when Rammelsberg died and Mitchell and his brother bought that share of the company from the heirs of his late partner. Mitchell was born in 1811 in Ireland and came to America with his family in 1824. The Mitchells first settled as farmers in Franklin, Indiana, but Robert came to Cincinnati in 1829 to work as a cabinetmaker. The Mitchell Furniture Company was the first in Cincinnati to use steam-powered machinery. In addition to furniture for homes, businesses, and steamboats, the firm also imported carpets and fine bedding.

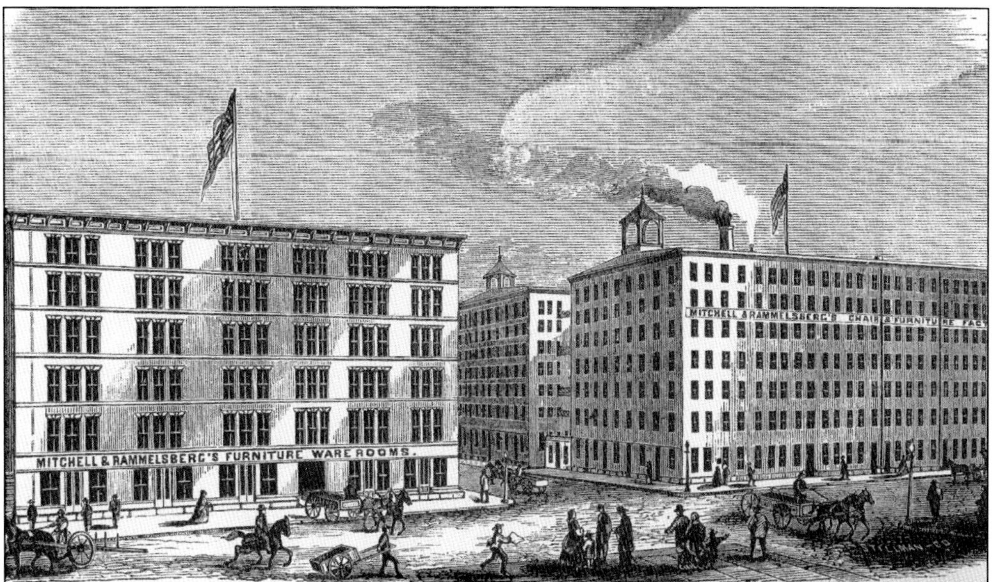

MITCHELL & RAMMELSBERG.

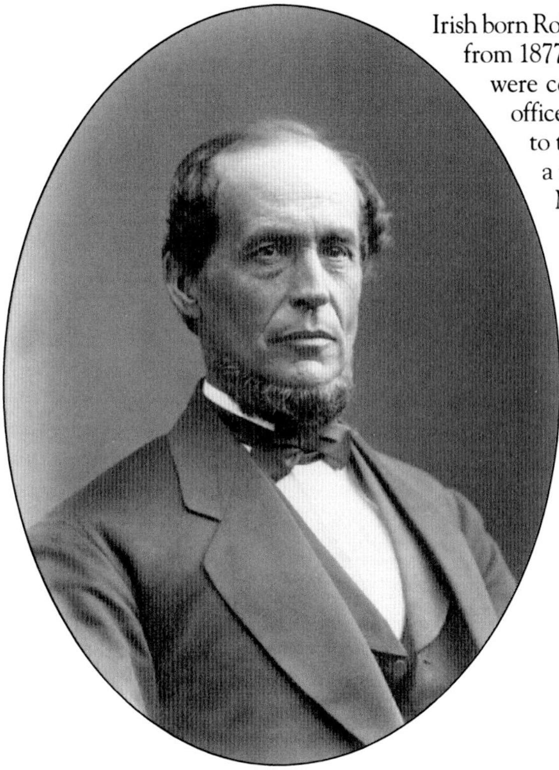

Irish born Robert M. Moore served as mayor of Cincinnati from 1877 to 1879, a time when the Cincinnati Irish were coming into their own in terms of elected office and civic appointments. He was well-suited to the mayor's office and its authority: he had a military background, having fought in the Mexican-American War and then served as an officer in Cincinnati's famed Irish Civil War regiment, the 10th Ohio.

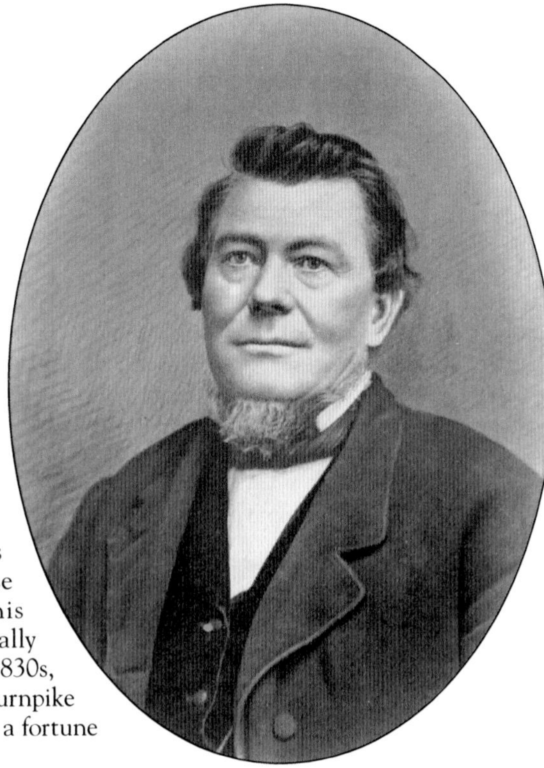

A native of County Tyrone, James Beatty was born in 1814 and came to America when he was 17 years old. His journey was at the behest of his widowed uncle, who intended to name his nephew as his heir. But when the uncle remarried, those plans went astray, so Beatty earned his living as a jockey for a few years. Eventually he made his way westward, and by the 1830s, was constructing the Lebanon Canal and turnpike roads. He spent the next decades making a fortune in banking and livestock.

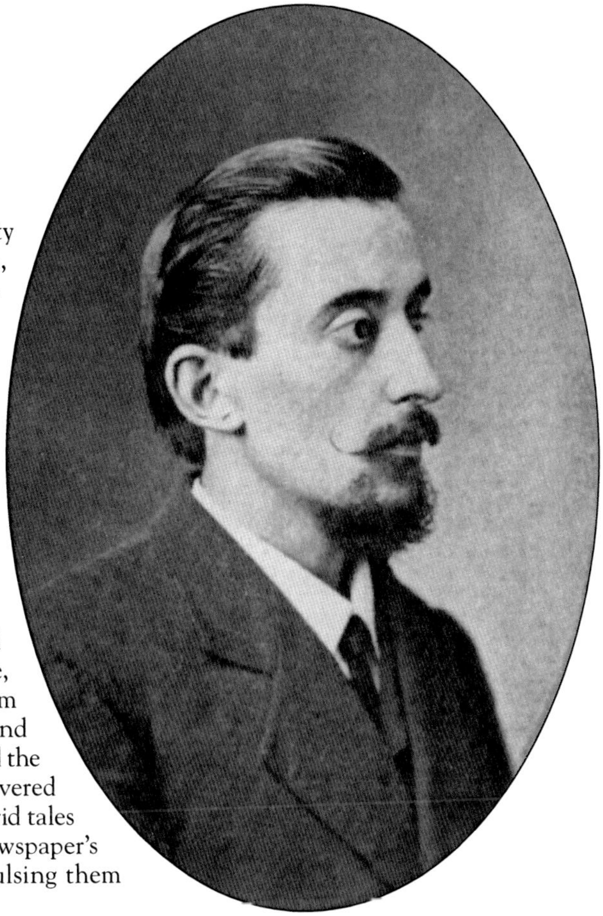

The son of a military man from County Offaly, Ireland, and a Greek woman, Patrick Lafcadio Hearn was born on a Greek island in 1850. Young Lafcadio was sent to live with his Irish Protestant relatives in Ireland when he was two years old and was educated there until he left home at the age of 19, ending up in Cincinnati. Desperately poor, he lived in the city's alleys, but managed to make some contacts in local journalism and wrote for the *Cincinnati Enquirer* and the *Cincinnati Commercial* from 1872 to 1877. Hearn's beat was the morbid oddities and exotica of Cincinnati life, as he creatively constructed tales from the stories he heard in the Irish and African American riverfront slums and the working-class neighborhoods. He covered murders, ghost stories, and various lurid tales of the underworld, thrilling the newspaper's readers while at the same time repulsing them just a little.

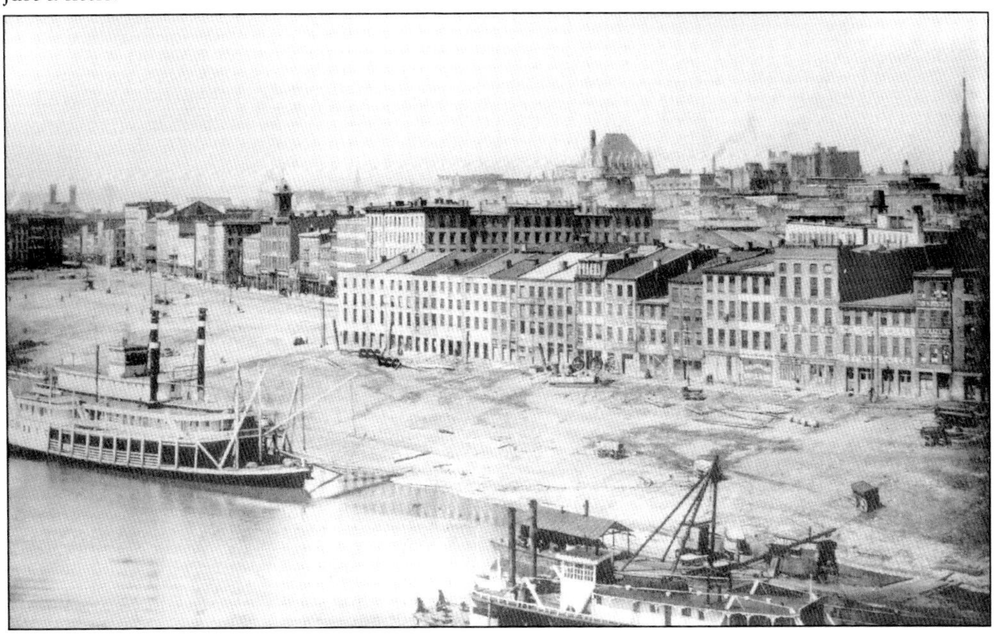

WILLIAM HALLER,

WILL LECTURE IN

ROBINSON'S OPERA HOUSE,

—ON THE—

ROMAN CATHOLIC CHURCH,

—AS—

THE ENEMY OF FREE GOVERNMENT.

On Sunday Afternoon, October 10, 1880.

Admission to all parts of the House, Twenty-Five Cents.

DOORS OPEN AT 2 P. M.

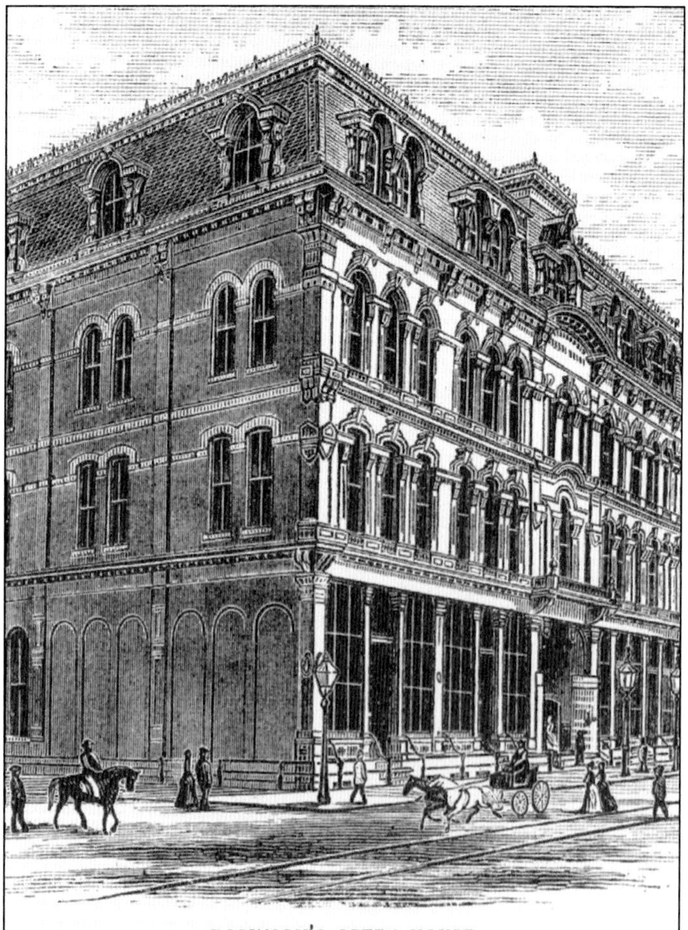

ROBINSON'S OPERA-HOUSE.

Viewing the American Catholic Church as an enemy of the workingman, socialist William Haller worked in a variety of jobs in Cincinnati from the 1860s through the 1880s as he built his reputation as a labor organizer. He was part of the Trades and Labor Assembly formed in Cincinnati in 1864, and drew his supporters from the working class Irish and Germans. A powerful orator, Haller helped organize the Eight Hour League for better working conditions and wages but ran into staunch opposition from the Archdiocese because of his socialist politics. In 1880, Haller went on the attack, renting Robinson's Opera House for a lecture against the Roman Catholic stance regarding organized labor. His intent was to draw local Irish workers away from the influence of the Church.

Thomas Mullen was a successful contractor in Cincinnati following the Civil War. Born in County Monaghan in 1839, he first crossed the ocean to Toronto when he was 15, apprenticing himself as a carpenter. He arrived in Cincinnati in 1858, continued his trade until the outbreak of the war, upon which he enlisted with the 55th Ohio Volunteer Infantry Regiment. After the war, he resumed his trade, constructing numerous schools and other public buildings in Cincinnati, including the city infirmary.

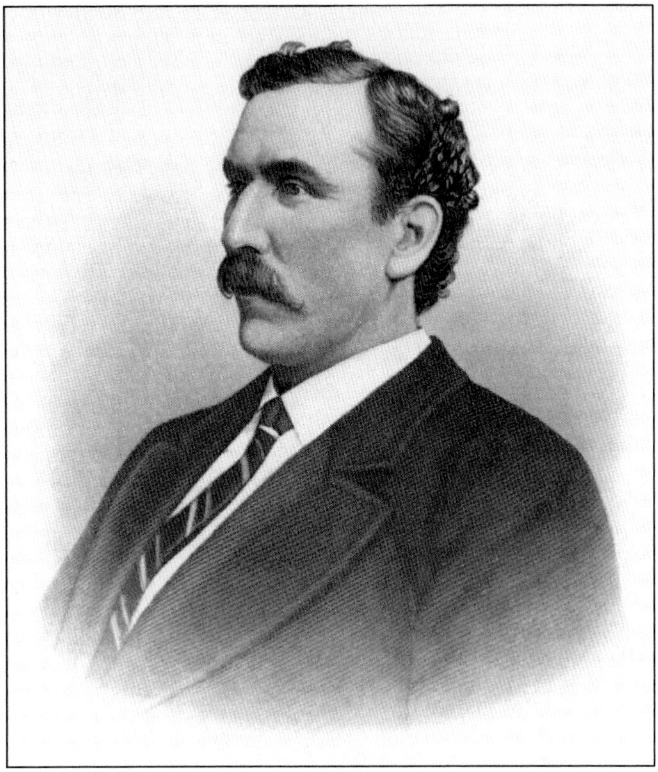

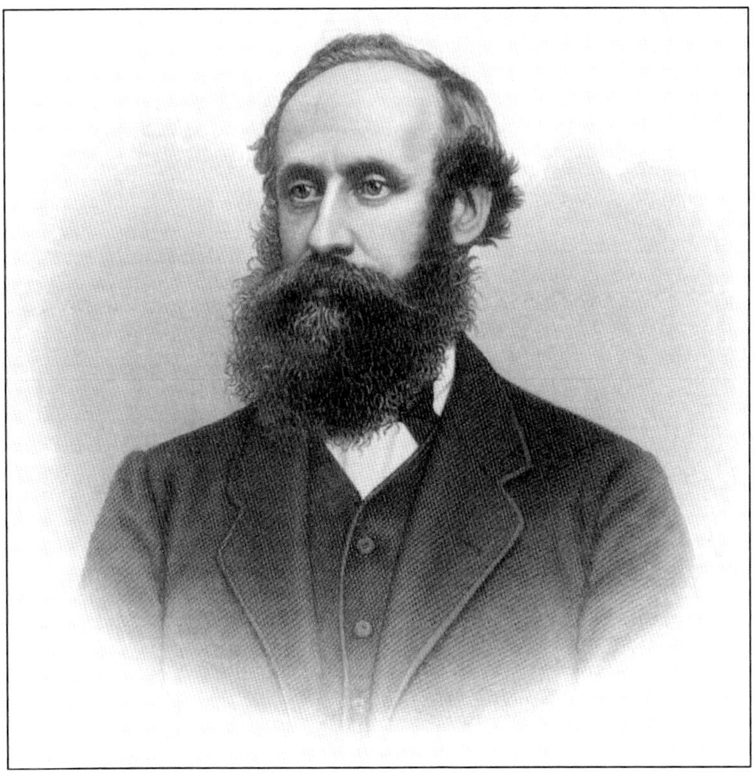

Manufacturer Neil MacNeale was born in County Down in 1826, the son of an Irishman who fought for the British army in the East Indies. Trained as an engineer, MacNeale came to Cincinnati in 1849, and 10 years later, he headed a company that made store and bank safes, at the time one of the three largest in the country. MacNeale also helped found the Board of Trade of Cincinnati in 1868.

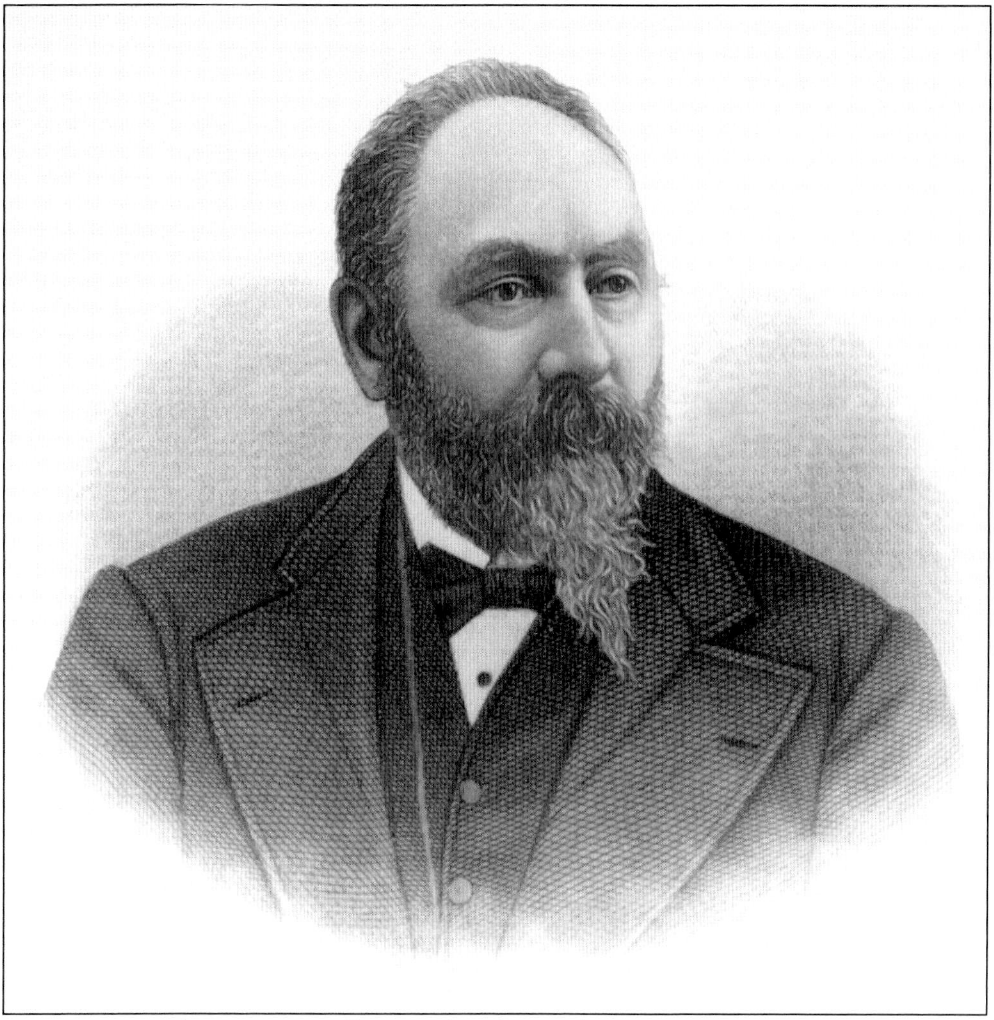

R.D. Norris was from County Kilkenny, where he was born in 1829. He apprenticed with dry goods firms in Wexford and Dublin before immigrating to New York in 1851 where he worked for Lord & Taylor. Shortly thereafter, he journeyed farther west to Cincinnati, establishing his own store and specializing in fine imported fabrics from England and France. In addition to the success of his store, Morris also speculated in real estate. He was a significant member of the Irish fraternity of dry goods and department store owners in Cincinnati in the mid- to late 19th century. As Cincinnati flourished before the Civil War, and still maintained some considerable importance in manufacturing and brewing in the decades after the war, men like Morris were able to garner trade from an increasingly secure middle class.

Irish immigration picked up again in the 1880s, joining what were now second- and third-generation Irish families who had settled in the United States. Many of the newcomers left from the harbor of Queenstown, now called Cobh, in County Cork. When they arrived in Cincinnati, they found established Irish American organizations like the Friendly Sons of St. Patrick and the Ancient Order of Hibernians, as well as a vast number of church-affiliated societies and charities that provided a support base. But although their place in American culture was becoming more status quo, there lingered an element of disdain for the immigrants, as shown in the postcard cartoon ridiculing an Irishwoman for taking on airs above her working-class station. Over the next several decades, while the Irish assumed a greater number of professional positions, many continued to find work in domestic service. One wealthy young Cincinnati girl wrote a Christmas letter to Santa asking, "please, an Irish maid to clean my room."

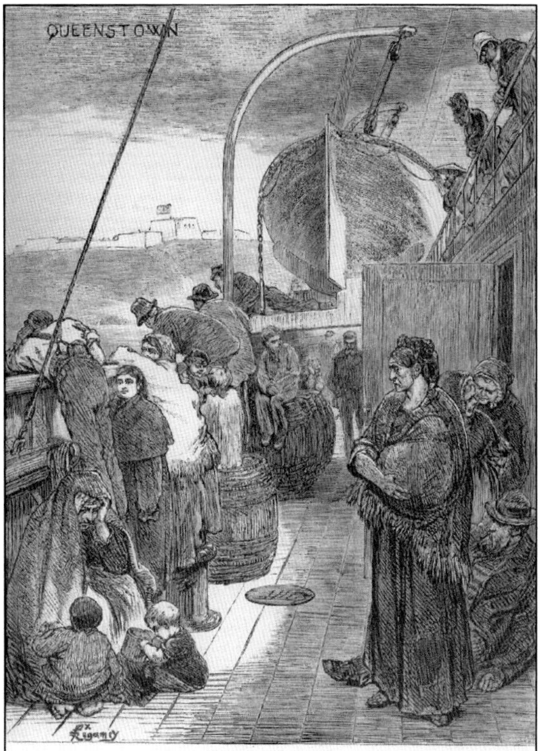

FAREWELL TO THE OLD WORLD.

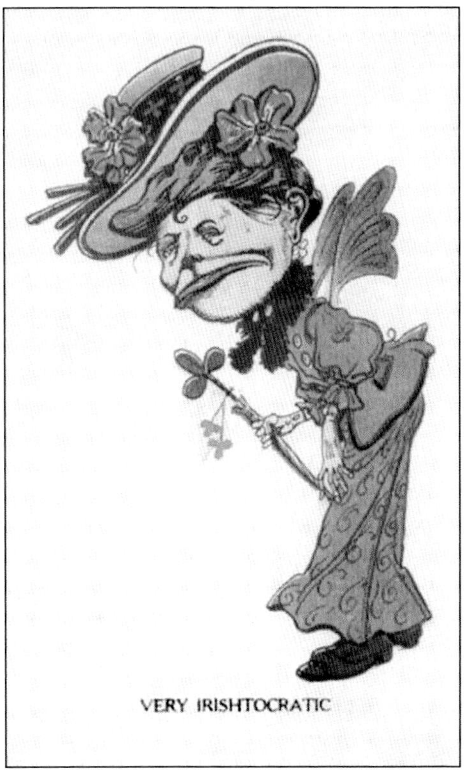

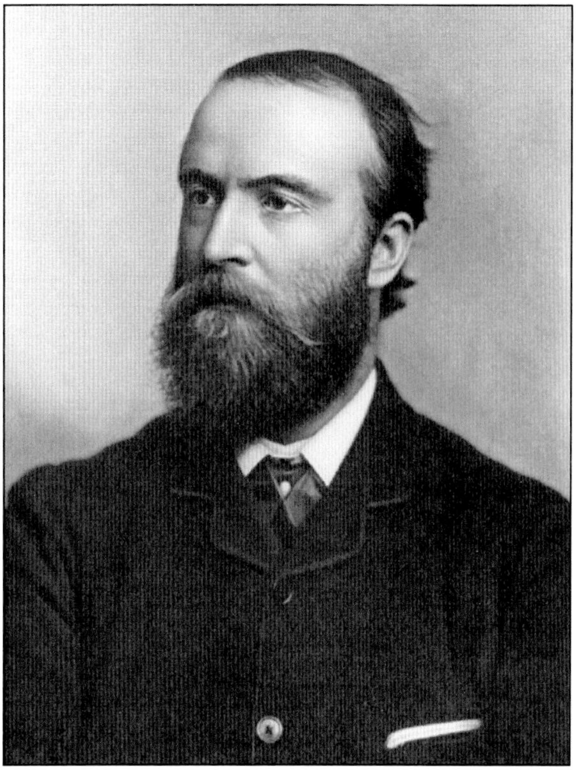

Irish nationalist Charles Stewart Parnell exerted an immense influence on Irish Cincinnatians. As a leader for land reform, he called upon Fenians and American Irish to support his proposals in Britain's House of Commons. Parnell was able to raise considerable funds and awareness of the necessities for reform with the hope that Ireland would eventually achieve self-rule. In 1880, he made a trip to America to further the cause, and on his Cincinnati stop on February 20, he made a speech that would become part of the his legacy: "When we have given Ireland to the people of Ireland we shall have laid the foundation upon which to build up our Irish nation . . . None of us, whether we be in America or in Ireland, or wherever we may be, will be satisfied until we have destroyed the last link which keeps Ireland bound to England."

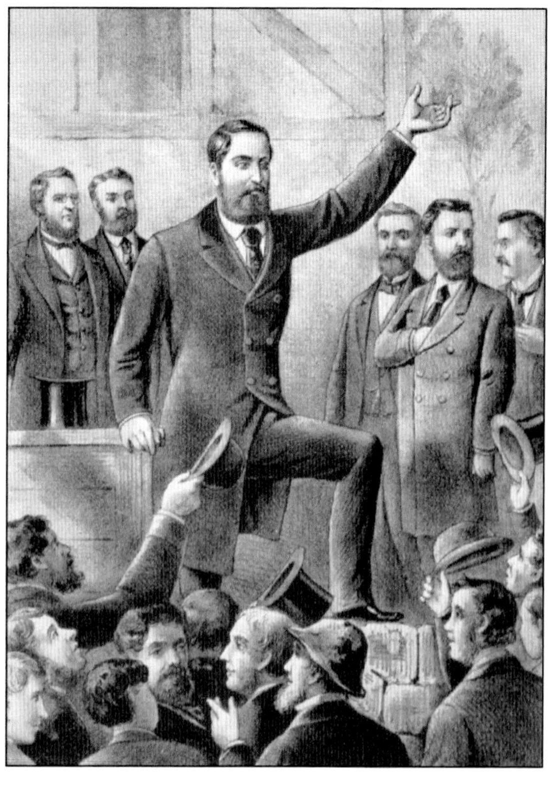

On May 26, 1876, Archbishop John Baptist Purcell celebrated his Golden Jubilee in Cincinnati. Ordained 50 years earlier in Paris, the thoroughly Irish Purcell became one of the most important religious leaders in the country, and an immense power in the American Catholic Church. He governed Catholic Cincinnati with authority, one of his main strengths being the ability to accommodate both Irish and German congregants. By 1876, his diocese had grown to over 150 priests and 150,000 Catholic faithful. Purcell used the *Catholic Telegraph* not just to promote and defend the Church, but also as a community newspaper for the Irish, bringing them news from home and inquiries from relatives trying to find one another. Undeterred by a torrential downpour, thousands of schoolchildren, members of fraternal organizations, and community members marched in a parade before the archbishop's reviewing stand.

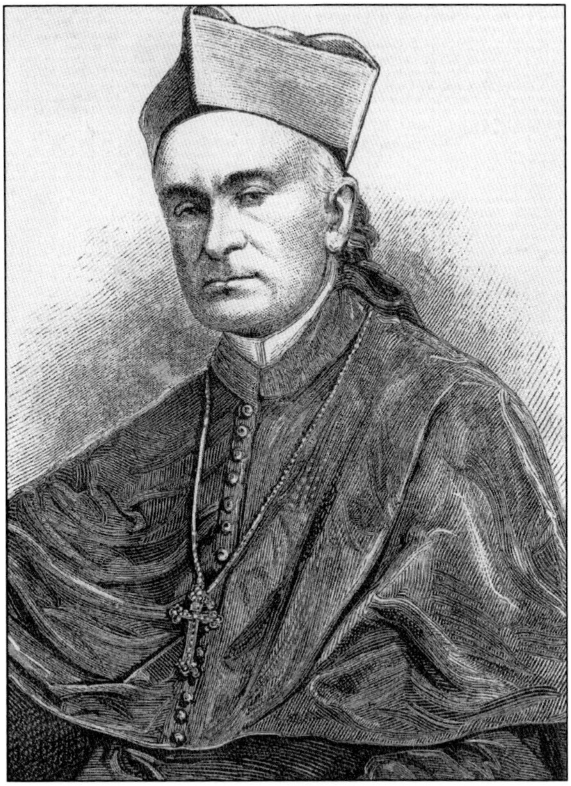

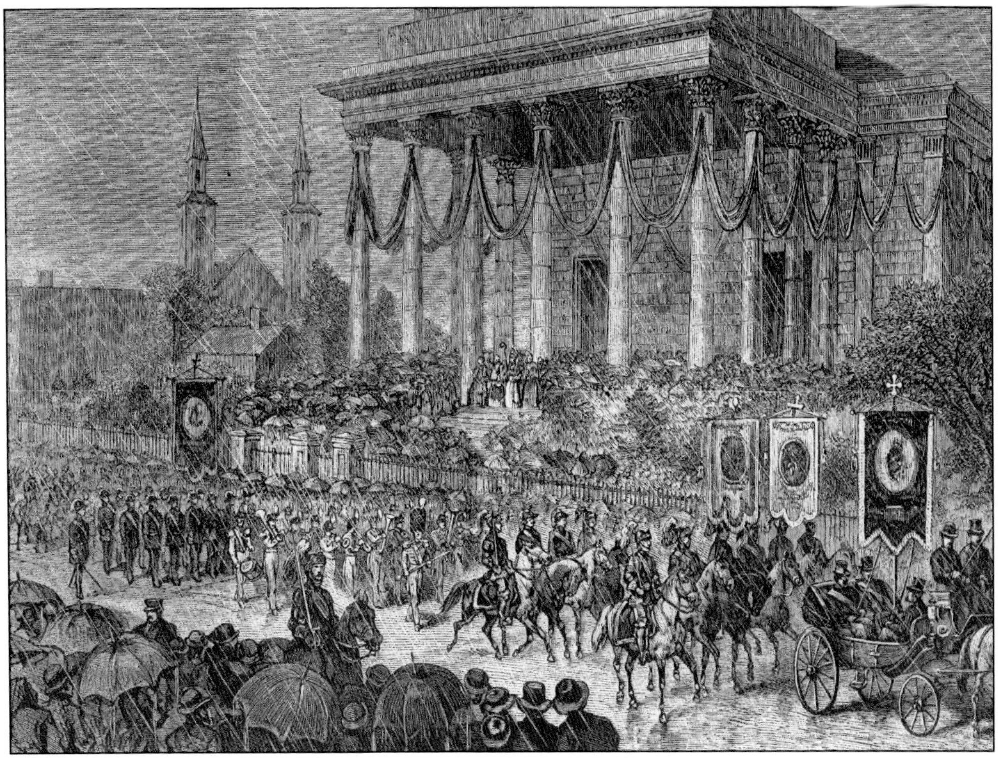

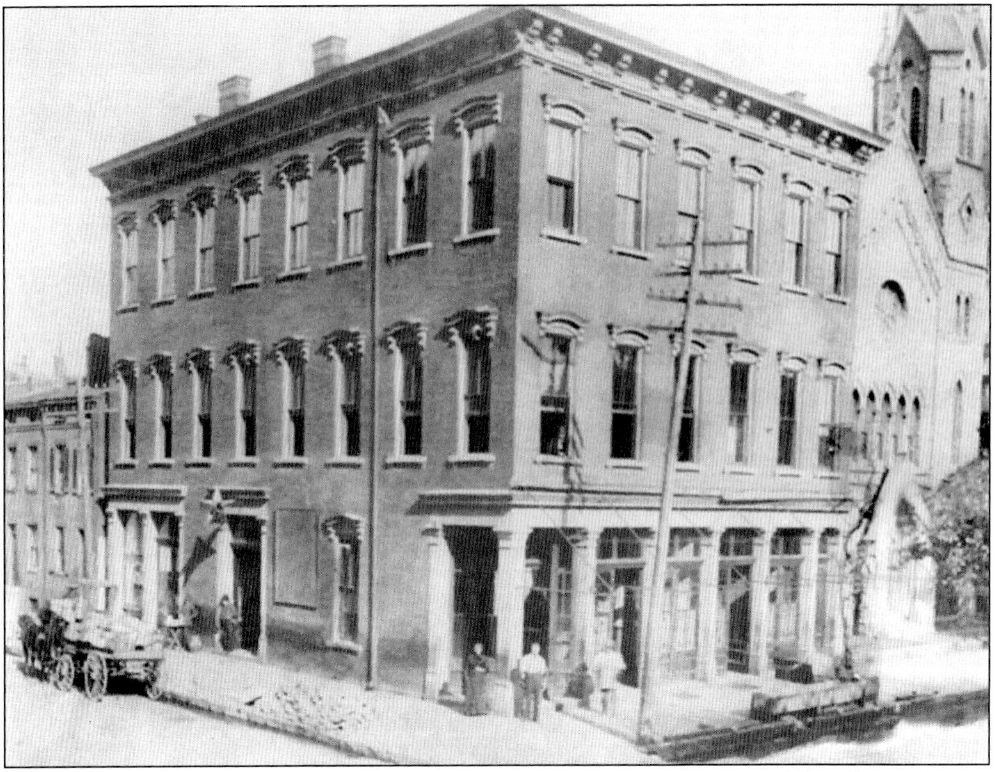

The date of construction is in dispute (some sources say 1873, others say 1880), but what is certain is that the building that was erected on Plum Street across from city hall became a monument to Irish pride. Originally, the Hibernian Building housed Henry Deters's saloon on the ground floor. Perhaps recognizing the mutual civic interests between two ethnic groups, but certainly not one to turn away some income, the German Deters leased the third floor to the Ancient Order of Hibernians in 1884 to be used as a meeting room. Thenceforth, the building was the gathering place for Irish interests and the departure point for parades and celebrations. The year after the Hibernians moved in, the saloon became a café and "sample room" under the name of Richelieu Hall. (Below, courtesy of Stacey Walsh.)

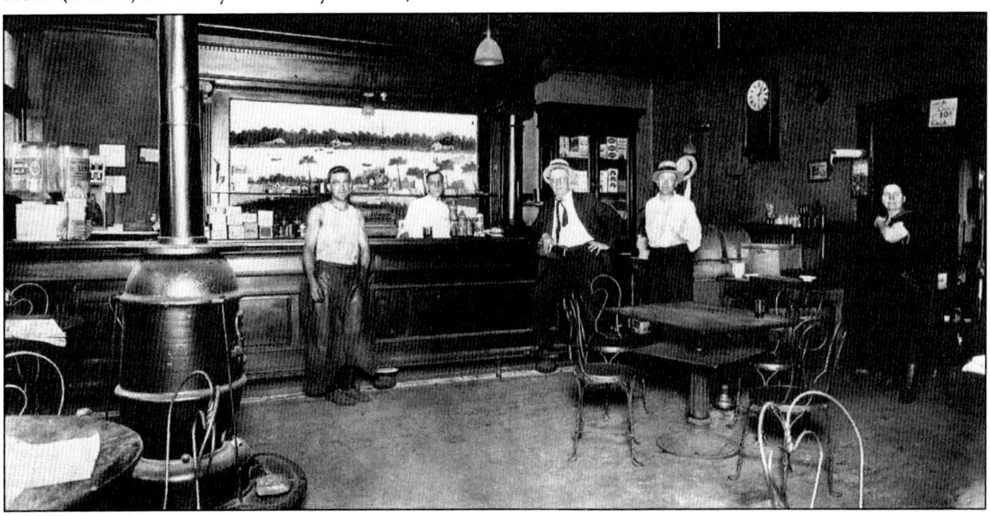

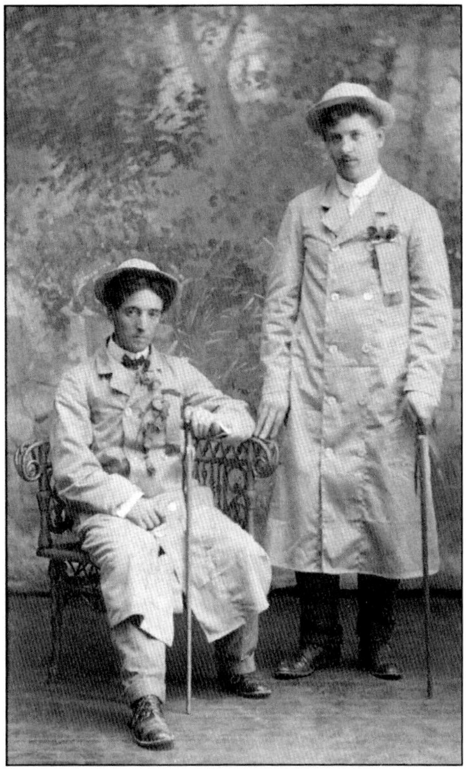

Decked out in their Irish celebration finery, Hibernians Michael Keating (sitting) and Barney McNamara (standing) pose for a studio photograph. The Hibernian ribbon was a typical adornment for the annual St. Patrick's Day parade. The American branch of the Ancient Order of Hibernians was formed in 1836 as an organization devoted to Christian charity, the preservation and expression of Irish culture, and the assertion of the rights of Irish Americans in the United States. The Cincinnati Hibernians made their first official appearance in the city when Archbishop John Purcell blessed their banners before the St. Patrick's parade in 1869. (Courtesy of Pat Mallory.)

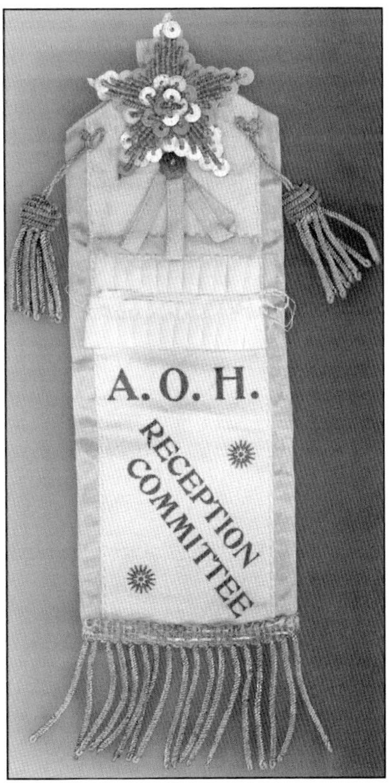

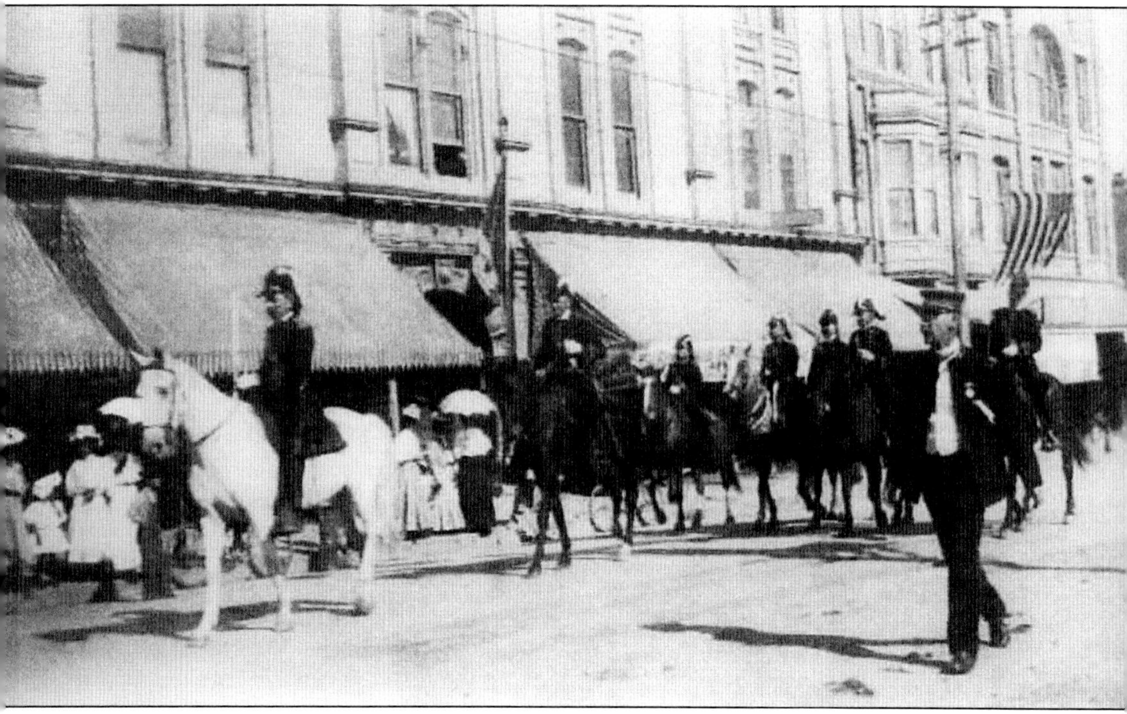

The celebrating of St. Patrick by the Cincinnati Irish dates back to the early 1840s when it was primarily a temperance parade. For example, in 1843 the *Catholic Telegraph* reported, "the eye glanced along the line of the procession, with banner and badge, proclaiming them defenders of the great cause, who could help rejoicing in the scene?" By the 1870s, the parade was more military in nature as a result of the Civil War and the Fenian cause. A recollection of one of those parades by Fenian George Sweeny noted: "The Fenians mustered at their armory . . . in the early morning, attracting the attention of the public in their neat uniforms, which consisted of a blue zouave jacket and pants trimmed with green." In the 19th century, the parade route was a long one. In addition to military groups, nearly every Catholic and Irish society marched along, coursing past the cathedral and city hall before crossing the river to Newport and Covington and wending its way back into Cincinnati. (Courtesy of Pat Mallory.)

John B. Morris was six years old when his parents moved the family to Cincinnati. Born in 1836 in Tralee, Ireland, Morris became one of Cincinnati's leading manufacturers. As a boy, he was apprenticed to a jeweler under Henry Clayton, and he worked as a gemologist until 1876 when he entered the hardware business, taking over the foundry built by Miles Greenwood, a notable proponent of mechanical education.

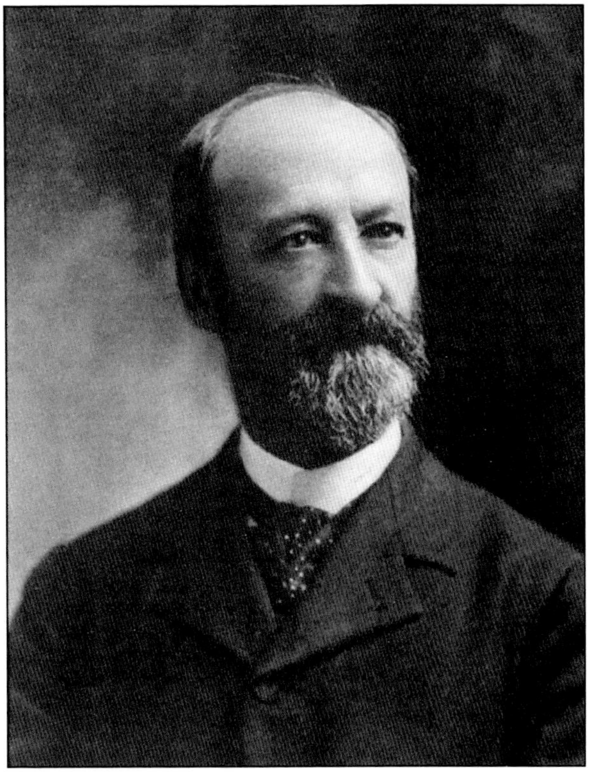

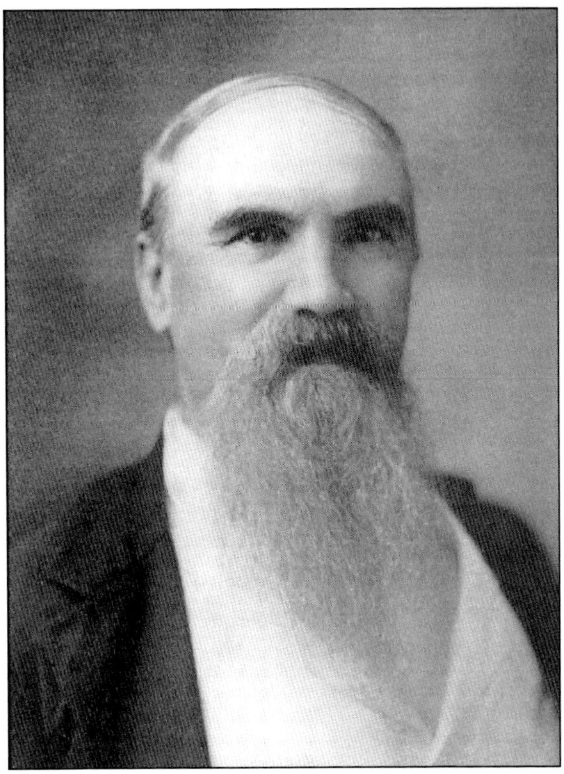

A native of County Kilkenny, Michael Ryan moved to Cincinnati with his parents in 1853 when he was eight years old. Following his father's trade as a butcher, Ryan eventually became president of the Cincinnati Abbatoir Company. He was very active in politics, but spurned the public arena when matters became increasingly corrupt in the 1880s. Still, when Gov. George Hoadly named his quartermaster-general on his staff, Ryan proudly bore the title of "General Michael Ryan" for the rest of his life.

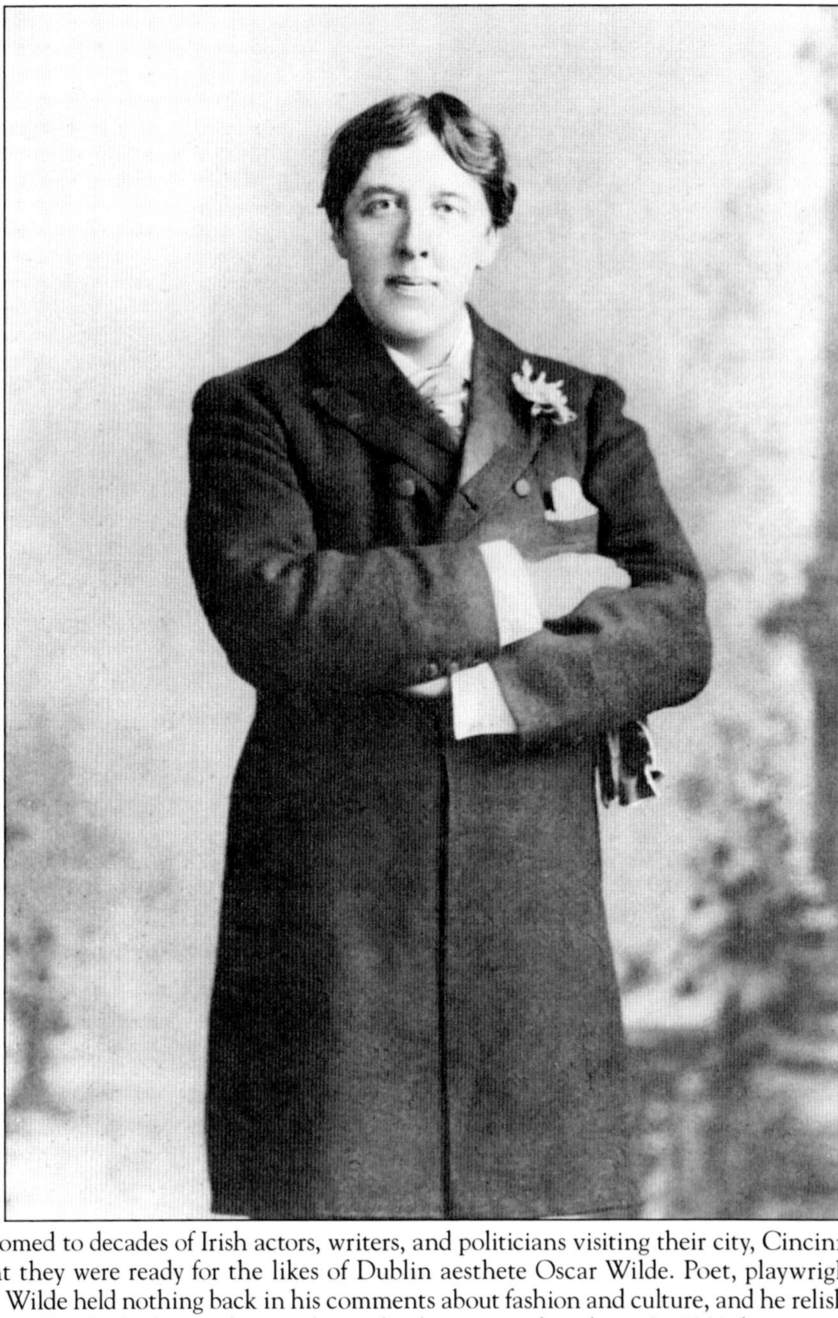

Accustomed to decades of Irish actors, writers, and politicians visiting their city, Cincinnatians thought they were ready for the likes of Dublin aesthete Oscar Wilde. Poet, playwright, and author, Wilde held nothing back in his comments about fashion and culture, and he relished the shocking effect he had on audiences during his lectures and readings. In 1882, he was on a tour of the United States, lecturing on "Beauty." His reputation preceded him, and the city was abuzz with anticipation as stores advertised Wilde-influenced clothing and jewelry. Passing through Cincinnati on his way to Louisville, Wilde stayed at the Burnet House and regaled local journalists with his opinions on style. On February 23, Wilde returned from Louisville for his lecture on "The Decorative Arts" at the Grand Opera House. His talk was received enthusiastically, but when he returned in June for another talk, he was considered tedious. However, Wilde considered Cincinnati one of the nicest stops on his American tour and his local hosts quite friendly.

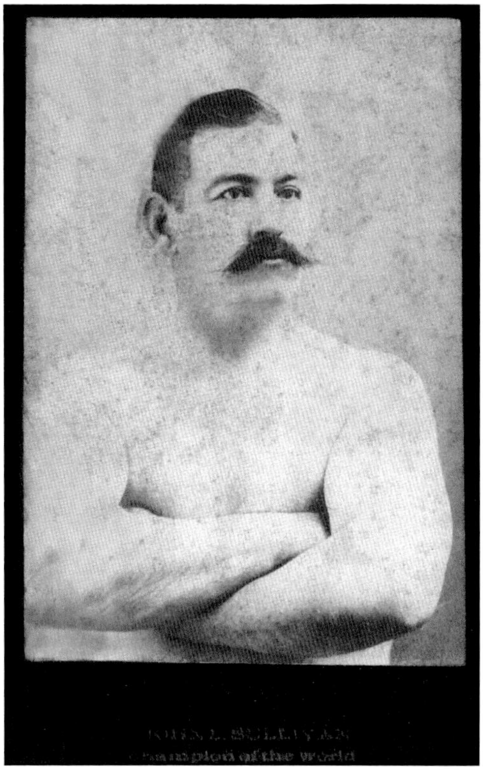

In 1885, Cincinnati's Chester Park was the site of the "Fight of the Century," a match between the Boston Strong Boy, John L. Sullivan (right), and Dominick McCaffrey of Pittsburgh (below). At the time, it was indeed the most important bout in a century of prizefighting because it would signal the coming end of bare-knuckle boxing. Theirs would be the first contended championship using gloves. On August 28, the day before the match, the hard-drinking Sullivan was arrested at the instigation of the Law and Order League. He secured his release in time for the bout, which drew 15,000 people to Chester Park, most of them Cincinnati Irishmen. McCaffrey entered the ring in red, white, and blue, stating, "I am of Irish descent, but I'm a true son of Ireland!" Sullivan, equally Irish, prevailed over McCaffrey in a disputed seven-round decision.

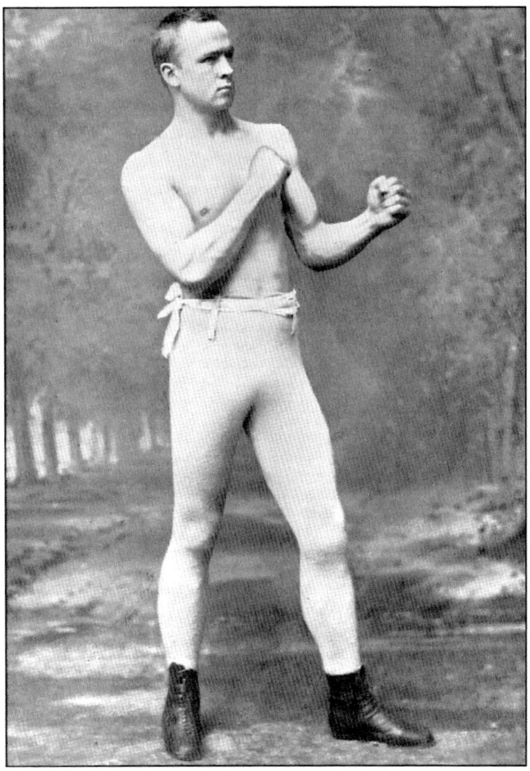

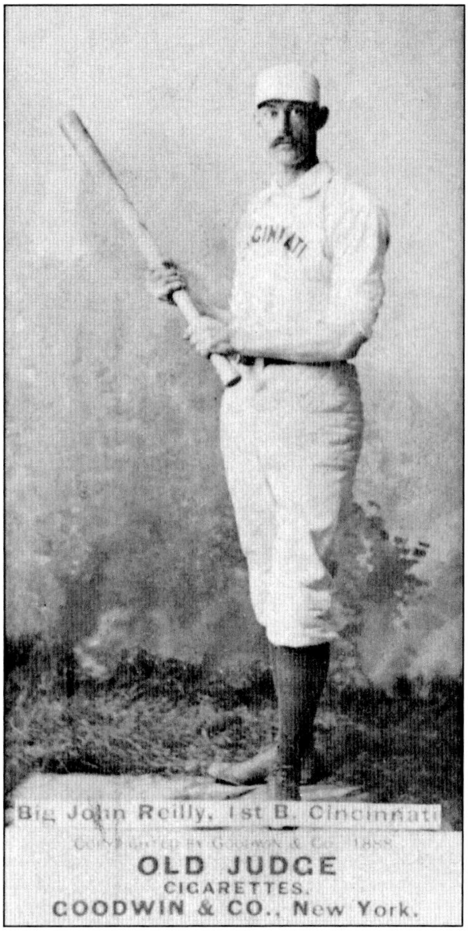

"Long John" Reilly (left) and Mike "King" Kelly were two of the many Irish ballplayers who would play professional baseball in 19th-century Cincinnati. Reilly was born in Cincinnati in 1858, where his father worked as a riverboat pilot. A talented artist, by the age of 15 he was working as an apprentice at the notable Strobridge Lithography Company and playing baseball for a local Irish team called the Emmett Greens. He went on to play for the Cincinnati Reds from 1880 to 1891. Kelly was a player of a different stripe. Although an outstanding ballplayer (and the inspiration for the vaudeville song, "Slide, Kelly, Slide"), he was a notorious drunk and bounced from team to team, debuting in his first major league season with the Reds in 1878 and coming back briefly in 1891 to head a rival professional team called Kelly's Killers.

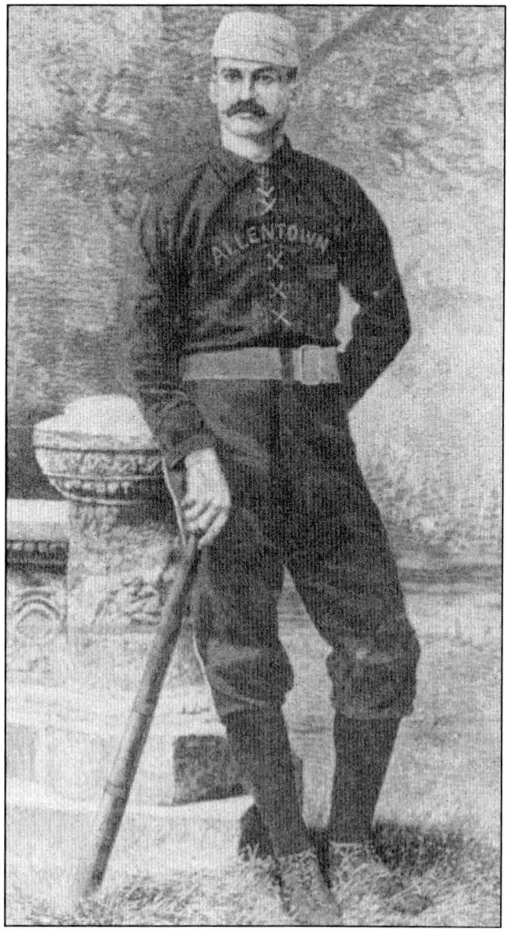

Four

"Killarney Moon, Please Shine Out Clear and Bright"

Irish societies flourished in Cincinnati as America barreled its way from the old 19th century to the halcyon years of the early 1900s. There were the Friendly Sons, the Hibernians (and the Hibernian Rifles, a group that would hold its military-like drills on Sunday afternoons following mass), and the Wolf Tone Club, named for Theobald Wolfe Tone, the 18th-century Irish revolutionary. There were also literary societies, such as the Grattan Club. Of the early-1900s Irish, Cincinnati writer Marianne O'Regan noted in a speech she made decades later about her heritage, there was still a strong feeling for the welfare of Ireland itself, and many prominent Cincinnati Irish Americans risked the disapproval of the Church as they advocated and celebrated any advance in Irish independence, including the 1916 Easter Uprising.

This affinity with Ireland was tantamount to the value of their lives here as Irish Americans, the Cassidys, the Sweenys (and the Sweeneys), the Murphys, the Deasys, the Ryans, the Keatings, the Cooneys, and on and on. It was a vital part of their identities and cultural validation, this maintenance of connections. Sure, there were the neighborhood saloons, the fraternal organizations, the parades, the Irish Days at Coney Island, the parish picnics and festivals, and the political clubs, but these were just the doors that opened something deeper within, a pride, a joy, and a spiritual tie to the history and lives on the other side of the Atlantic Ocean.

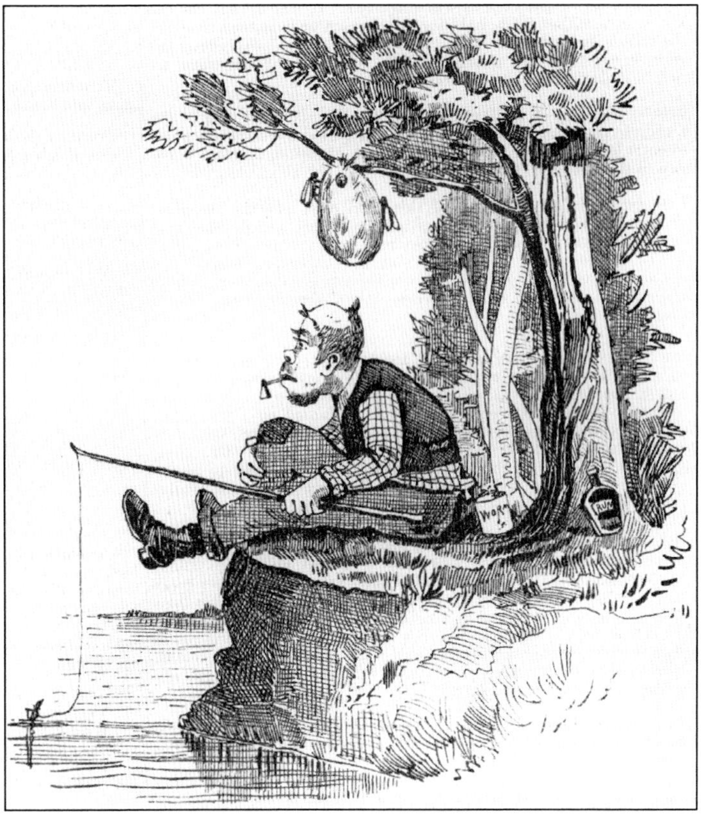

The Irish were widely caricatured by 19th-century British and American publications as brutish, slow-witted, and lazy. These stereotypes would continue into the 20th century, and though the graphic portrayal of the Irish with ape-like features faded away, the aspect of an Irish fondness for drink persisted. And though the Irish were making headway in city politics, in this 1885 Cincinnati cartoon, a councilman is drawn in tattered clothing, sitting on a riverbank with his jug by his side.

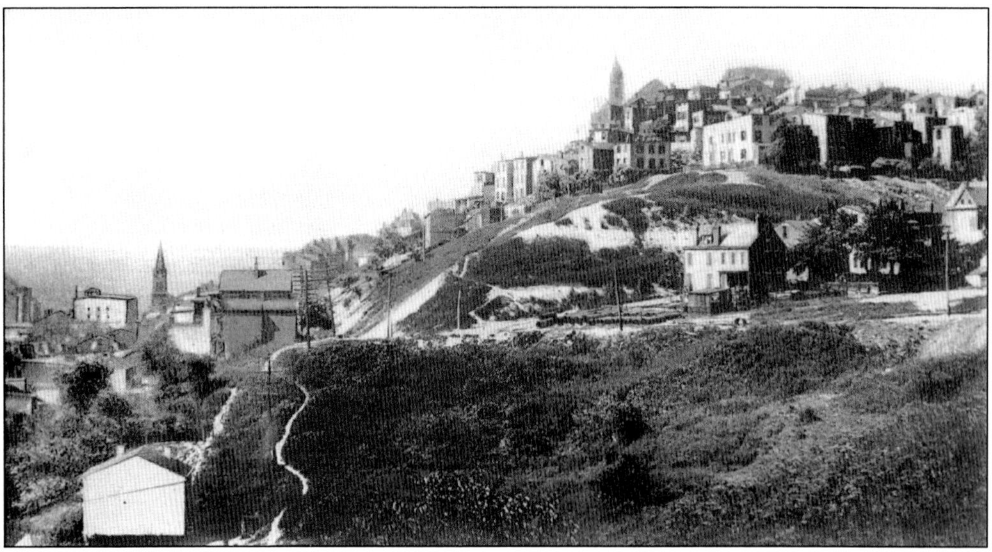

Many local Irish lived in Mount Adams in the late 19th century, and as a working-class neighborhood, the residents often found employment as gardeners and domestics in wealthier parts of town. There is an old joke told of the notable Judge Nicholas Longworth, who fancied himself a friend of the "sons of toil." One day as he drove his horse and cart through Eden Park, he picked up a laborer. "Pat," he said, "You'd be a long time in Ireland before you would be riding with a judge." The Irishman replied, "Yes, and you'd be many a day in Ireland before they'd make ye a judge!"

Erected in 1895, the Church of the Holy Cross (right) at the peak of Mount Adams was one of two Catholic churches in the neighborhood. Holy Cross Parish was established in 1873 to serve the Irish immigrants on the hill, and this church was constructed on the site of an earlier building. The Germans, on the other hand, worshipped in Immaculata Church (below), dedicated in 1860 in fulfillment of a promise Archbishop Purcell made when he safely made it through a storm at sea. While the church was being built, a dirt path was worn as people climbed to the top of the hill to pray at the site. After wooden steps replaced the path, a tradition was born in Cincinnati that is continued today: the pilgrimage of "praying the steps" on Good Friday. In 1977, Holy Cross closed and the German and Irish congregations were merged into the Immaculata Church. As a result, every year the Irish assert their own ethnicity by "stealing" the statue of St. Patrick from the church.

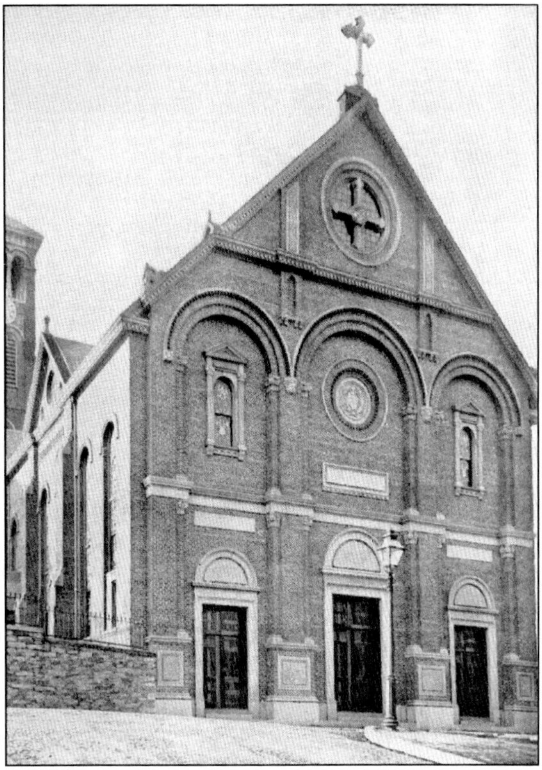

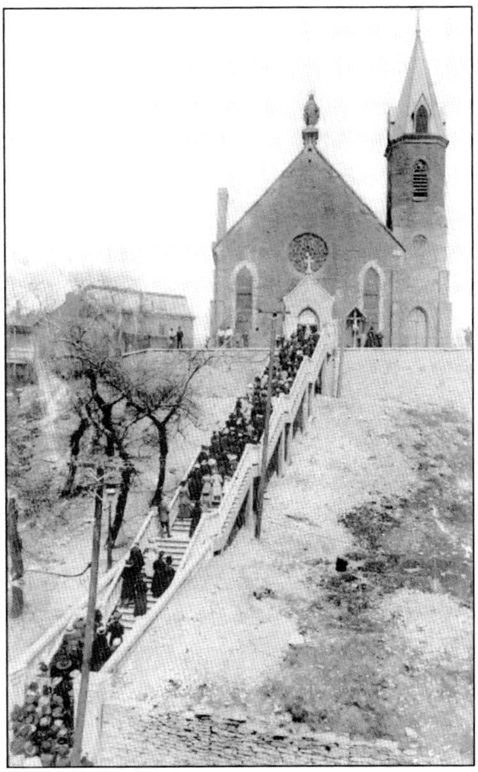

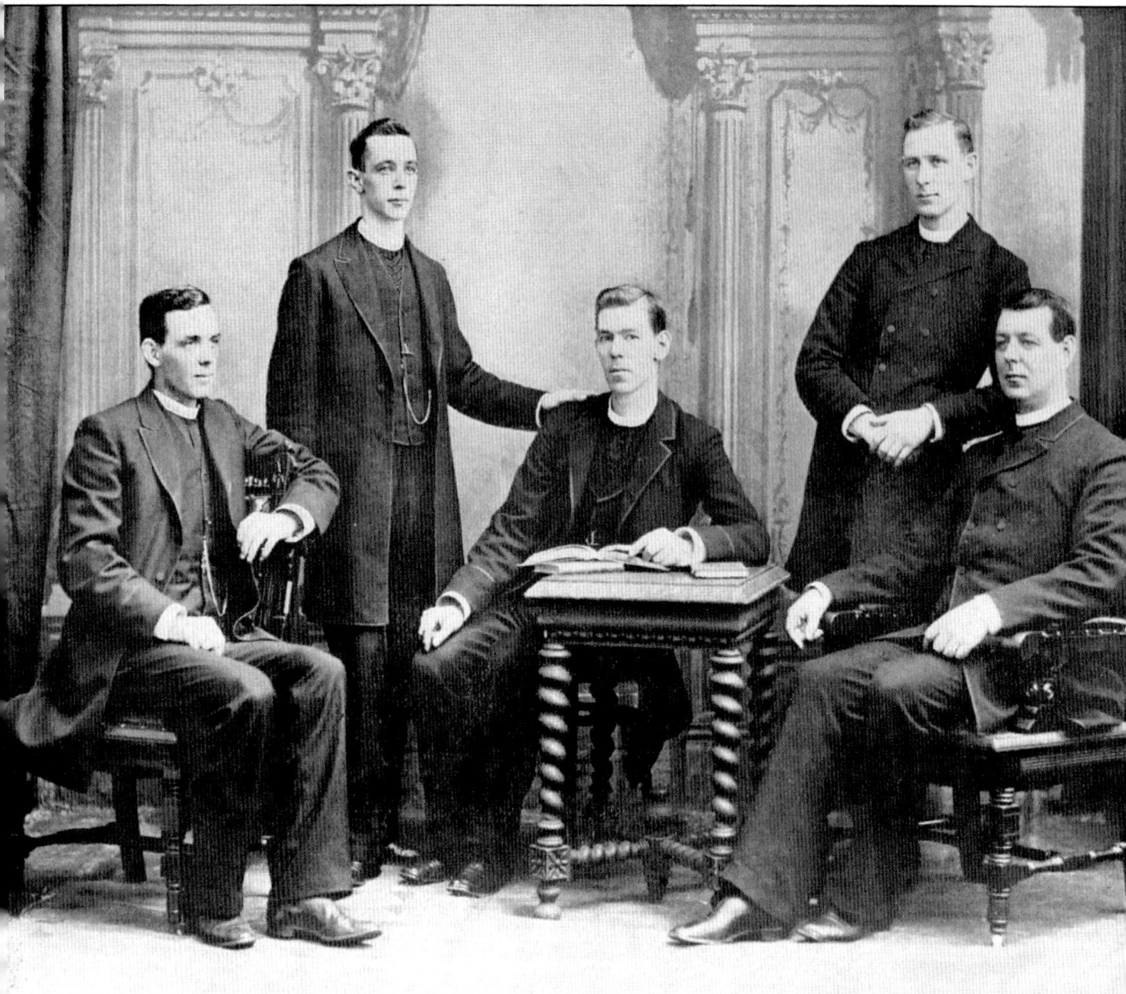

Having a son or daughter take a religious vocation in the 19th century was often proudly construed as a blessing by the family and an indication of their strong connection to the Catholic Church. In the case of the Hickey family, they were blessed many times over. Patrick Hickey and his wife boasted five sons in the priesthood in the 1890s: William, John, George, Edward, and Charles. All of them served parishes in the Cincinnati diocese, and one of their sisters became a nun in the Order of Notre Dame.

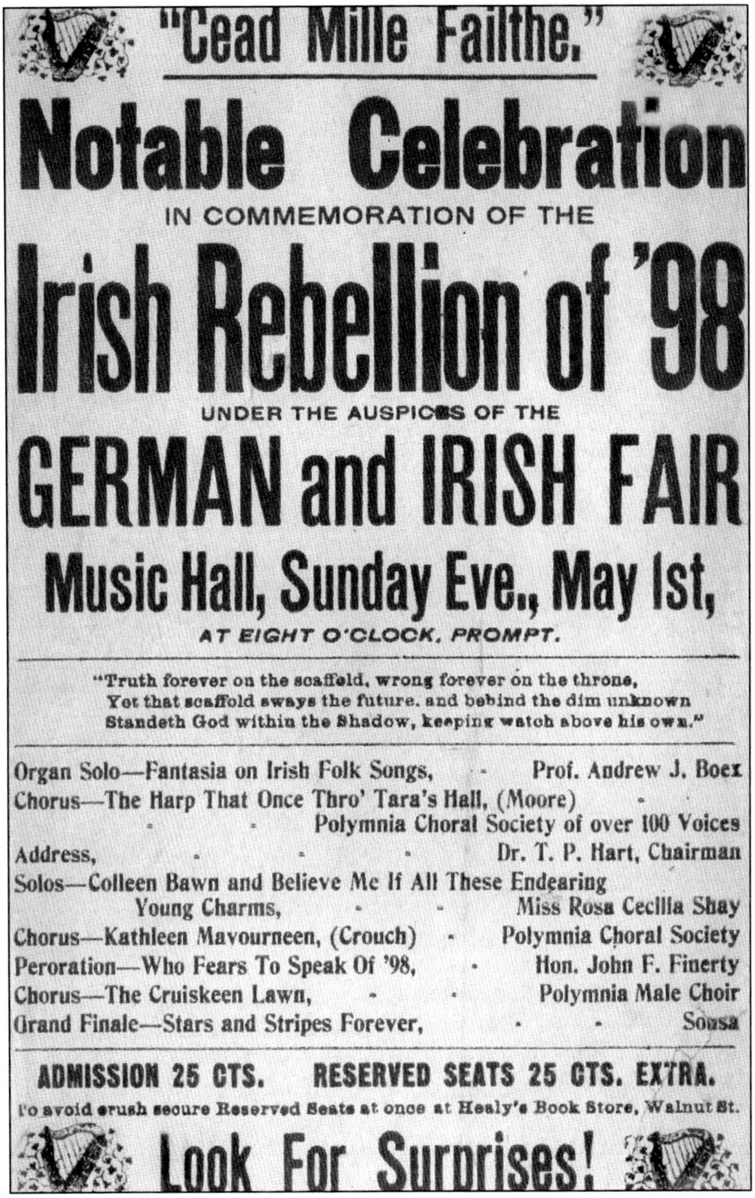

"Cead Mille Failthe."

Notable Celebration

IN COMMEMORATION OF THE

Irish Rebellion of '98

UNDER THE AUSPICES OF THE

GERMAN and IRISH FAIR

Music Hall, Sunday Eve., May 1st,

AT EIGHT O'CLOCK, PROMPT.

"Truth forever on the scaffold, wrong forever on the throne,
Yet that scaffold sways the future, and behind the dim unknown
Standeth God within the Shadow, keeping watch above his own."

Organ Solo—Fantasia on Irish Folk Songs, - Prof. Andrew J. Boex
Chorus—The Harp That Once Thro' Tara's Hall, (Moore) - - - Polymnia Choral Society of over 100 Voices
Address, - - - Dr. T. P. Hart, Chairman
Solos—Colleen Bawn and Believe Me If All These Endearing Young Charms, - - Miss Rosa Cecilia Shay
Chorus—Kathleen Mavourneen, (Crouch) - Polymnia Choral Society
Peroration—Who Fears To Speak Of '98, - Hon. John F. Finerty
Chorus—The Cruiskeen Lawn, - - Polymnia Male Choir
Grand Finale—Stars and Stripes Forever, - - Sousa

ADMISSION 25 CTS. RESERVED SEATS 25 CTS. EXTRA.

To avoid crush secure Reserved Seats at once at Healy's Book Store, Walnut St.

Look For Surprises!

It is commonly perceived that in Cincinnati, the Irish and Germans were allies in their battles against ethnic intimidation by the Know-Nothings and other anti-immigrant groups. And, that is certainly true. But not recognized as often is the antagonism between the two, especially in the matters of Catholic worship, education, and access to ecclesiastical authority. However, on one occasion the Germans and Irish came together in a notable fashion. In 1898, they presented the German & Irish Fair held at Cincinnati Music Hall. Two committees were established to organize the event on April 30, the Irish contingent headed by John Deasy, whose family would provide leadership in the local Irish community for several following decades. Intent on fostering nostalgic ties to the respective countries, the committees promised fairgoers the display of soil samples from each Irish county and each German state, 300 feet of paintings of Irish and German scenery, along with a facsimile of Blarney Castle and "Colleens dressed in the picturesque costumes of 100 years ago." (Courtesy of Pat Mallory.)

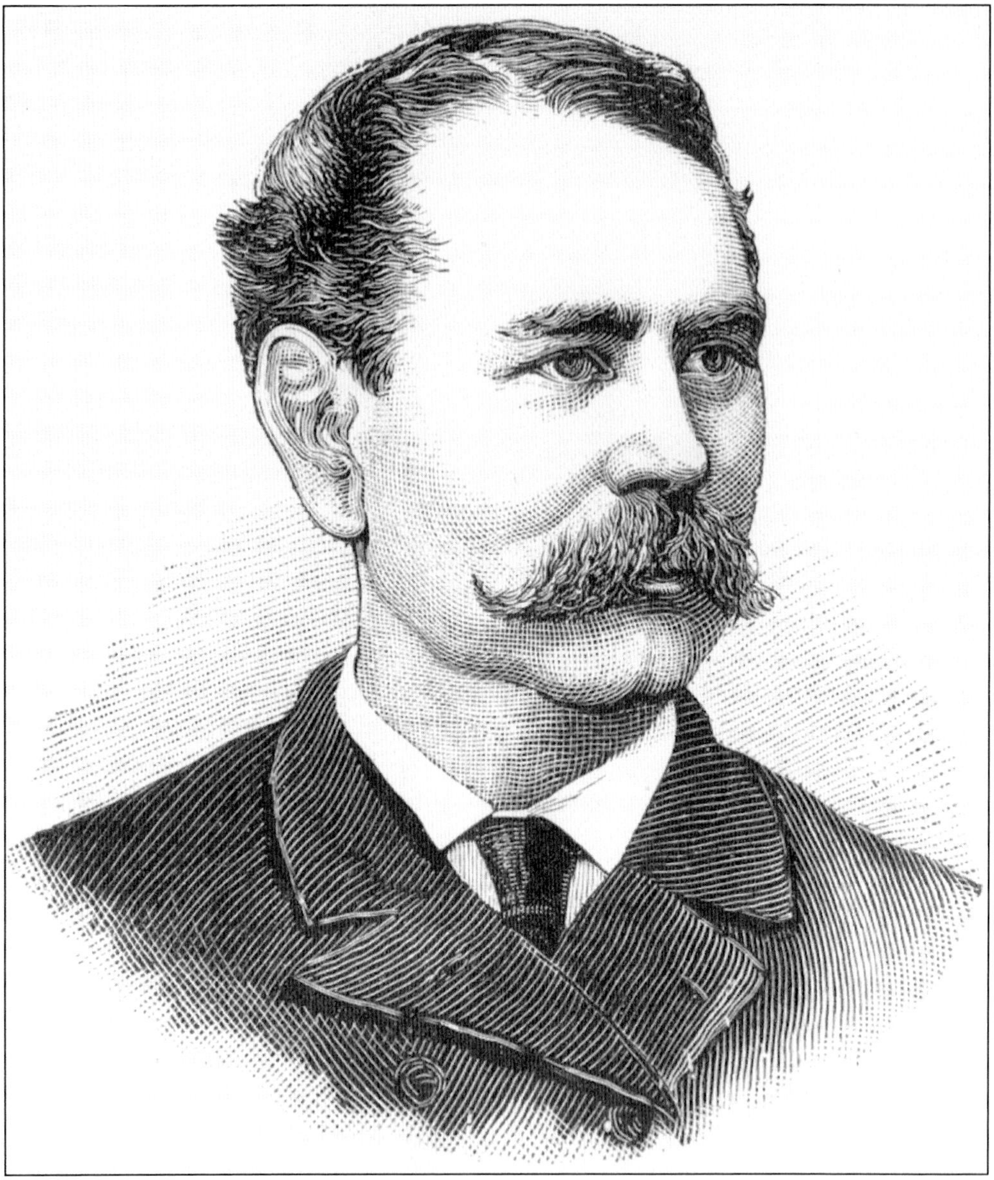

Beginning his career in the 1880s with Cincinnati's famous US Playing Card Company under legendary founder A.E. Russell, Irishman Robert Morgan headed the firm before being named to the Board of Police Commissioners, becoming president of the commission in 1886. The Cincinnati Civil Service Commission was established in that year as well, and as part of this reform movement, police affairs were controlled by the mayor and four commissioners, two from each political party. In just a few years, the Irish presence in the police ranks was considerable, mirroring the same trend in other major American cities. The Irish were becoming enfranchised in public affairs. A Walnut Hills resident, Morgan also led the way to hiring African American policemen, and as president of the police commission he created the "Morgan Medal" to acknowledge the outstanding work of officers.

Cincinnati's police department began its existence with the simple passing of an ordinance in 1803, which required men over 21 years old to register as a rotating group of night watchmen. Over the next few decades, the police would become a force of paid, professional officers stationed in precincts throughout the city. However, throughout the riots over race, ethnicity, and immigration in the 1840s and 1850s, the Irish were conspicuously absent from the police force despite their growing numbers in the city's population. By the 1870s, as more Irish became elected judges and commissioners in Cincinnati and Hamilton County, more of their brethren were welcomed into the police department. In the tabloid cartoon, Irish policemen are shown leading a St. Patrick's Day parade in 1885, and the early 1900s postcard view is of a police revue at the Cincinnati Reds' ballpark, the Palace of the Fans.

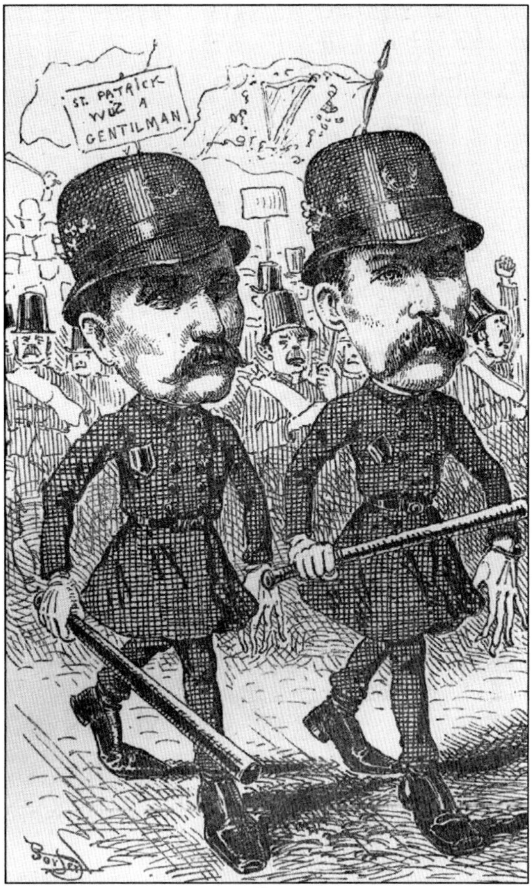

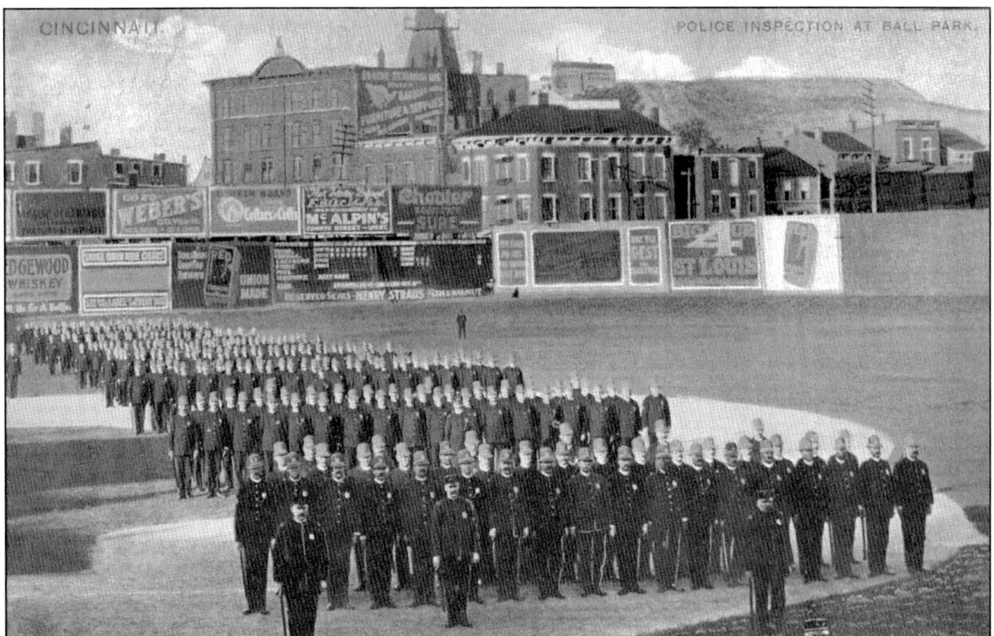

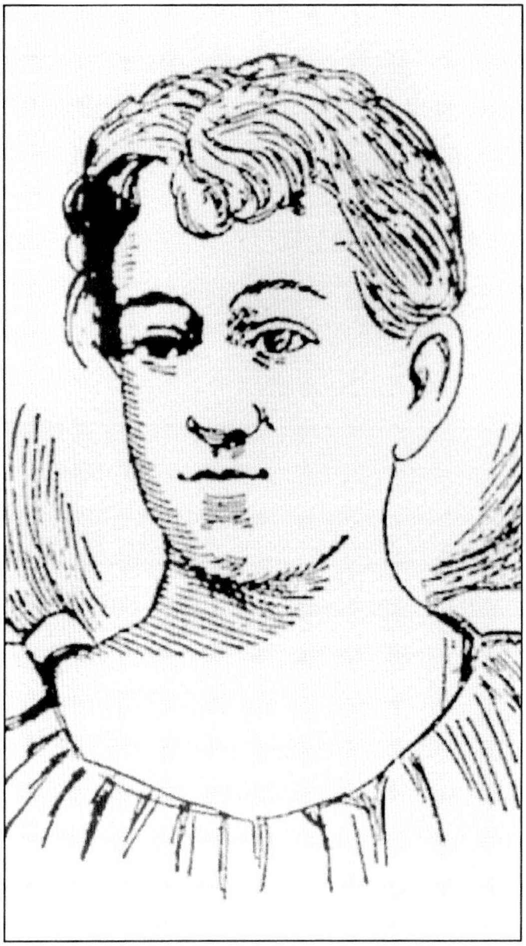

The story of Mollie Gilmartin is a very sad tale. Born in County Sligo, Mary "Mollie" Gilmartin was the object of affection from her family's parish priest, Dominick O'Grady. Seeking to end the unwanted attention, her family sent Mollie to Chicago in September 1893, where her brother, Michael, was a priest. But O'Grady followed her to America, and there was, in fact, some exchange of sentiment between the two, as O'Grady and Mollie exchanged several letters. Sent to Cincinnati in January of 1894 to her cousins on Chestnut Street, again, O'Grady followed. One April morning as she left for her job with the Pulvermachers Galvanic Belt Company, the spurned priest caught up to her, pulled a revolver, and fired several shots. Mollie died on the street. Soon arrested by the police, O'Grady first gave his name as George Reed, but soon confessed. In jail, he tried to commit suicide by drinking poison, but failed. At his trial, he was found insane and committed to the Longview asylum, but four years later was reinstated as a priest. Dozens of Irish attended her funeral, but for decades, Mollie lay in an unmarked grave. In 2011, a relative came from Ireland to place a headstone for her and a memorial service was held in Sligo.

Gilmartin, Mary C.

F W S 19 Yrs. 4-25-94

28 Chestnut St. 409

Ireland

Gunshot wound - Homicide

Dr. L.A. Querner

Sullivan & Co. St. Joseph New

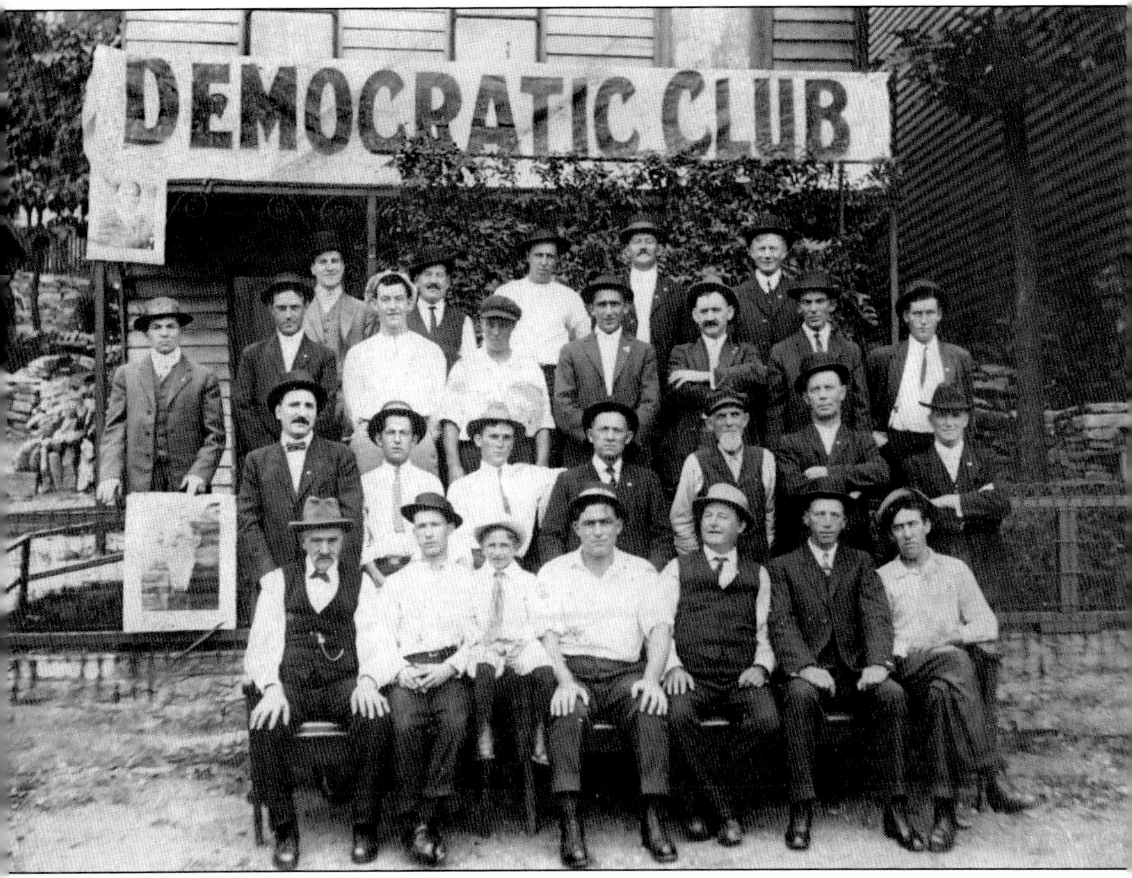

The Democratic Club of Cincinnati's First Ward was the political base for many of Cincinnati's Irish in the 19th century. It was the First and Third wards, along the river east of the city and extending into the basin along Deer Creek and up the hillside to Mount Adams, where the Irish first established their presence in the city. Including the river settlement of Fulton that later was incorporated as a township, the eastern wards were home to roustabouts, domestic workers, and the proprietors of small neighborhood businesses. The democratic club worked to enfranchise the Irish vote in the 1870s, 1880s, and 1890s in order to secure a measure of influence in local machine politics and to garner patronage for city jobs. (Courtesy of Pat Mallory.)

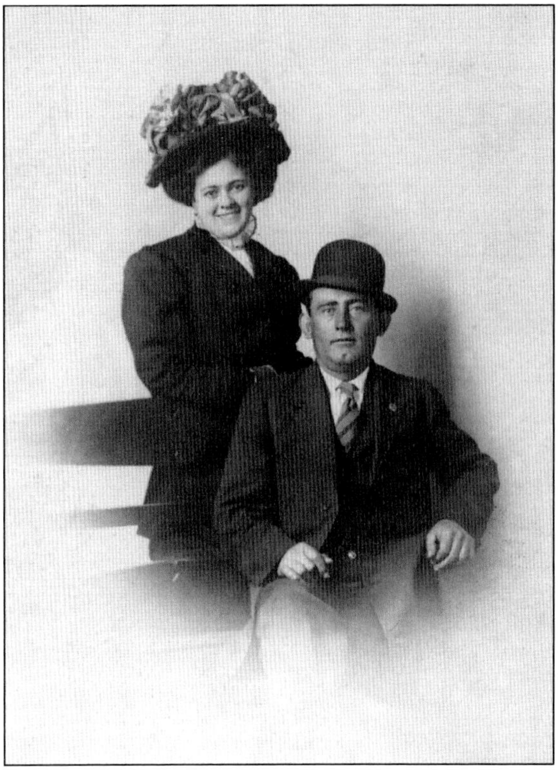

In the photograph at left, Paddy Keating sits posed with his wife for a formal studio photograph. Keating was an active member of the Knights of Labor, organizing the hod carriers into a union, which in its earliest days was comprised mainly of Irish workers. It is said by family members that after Paddy died, Aunt Nellie McNamara kept his bedroom just as he had left it, down to his revolver placed on the bureau. Another photograph dear to her descendants today in the Mallory clan is that of Kate McNamara, below, shown in a tintype taken by her employer, who was an amateur photographer. Kate, who died of cholera in 1874, worked as a maid for a Mount Auburn family. (Courtesy of Pat Mallory.)

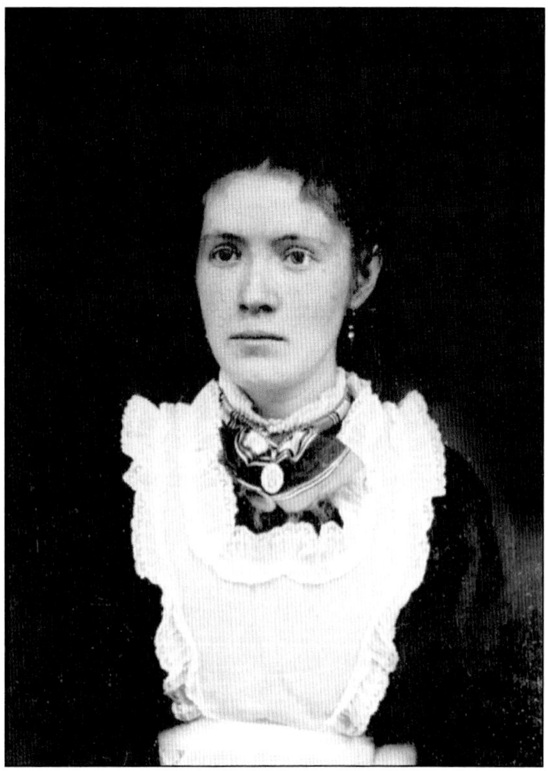

The daughter of Irish immigrants Nathan and Sara Earl, Virginia Earle was destined for the stage. She was born in Cincinnati in 1873, where both her parents and her brother worked for the city's several theaters in bit acting parts and in set design. After the family moved to Chicago, where Nathan Earl found work as a machinist, Virginia began her acting career in 1887 and added an "e" to the family name to appear more sophisticated. Her work in light opera and vaudeville continued for three decades.

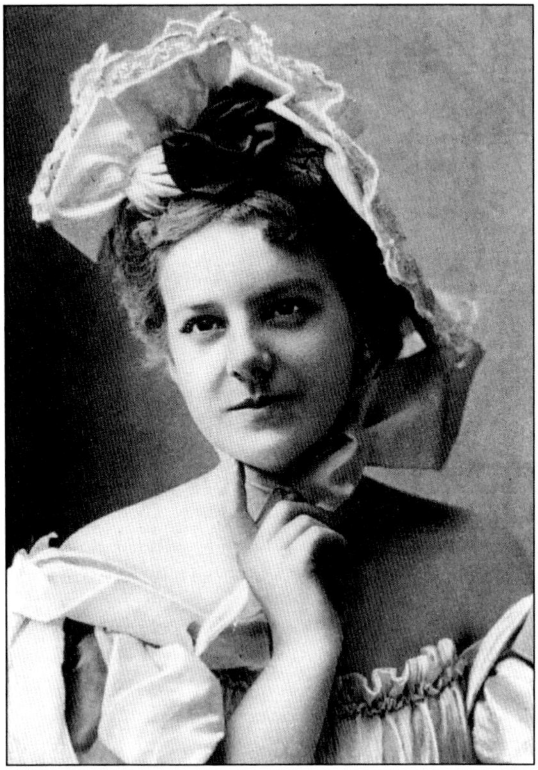

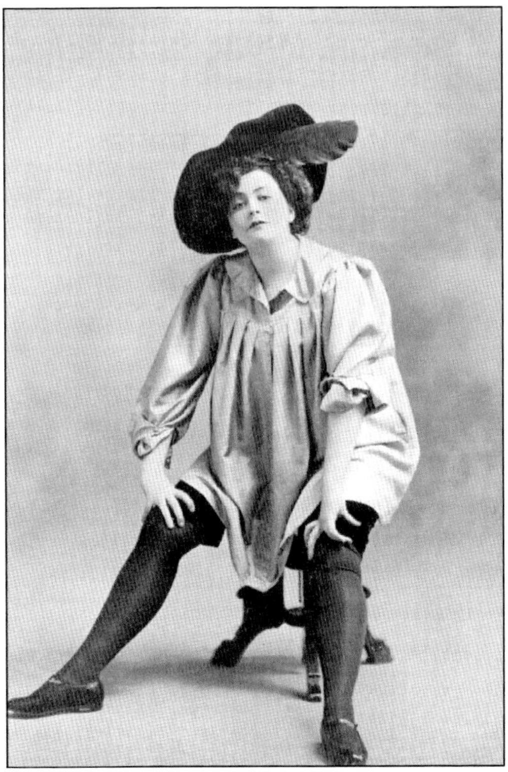

Born in 1870 to a Spanish mother and an Irish father, Delia O'Callaghan was raised in Cincinnati and educated at St. Patrick's School. As a teen, she became a chorus singer in traveling comic operas, taking the name "Trixie Frigenza" so she would not embarrass her family. As Trixie, young Delia would go on to become one of the great vaudeville stars in the early 1900s. Offstage, she was devoted to Catholic education and to women's rights. A committed suffragette, she once said, "I do not believe any man is better fitted to form a political opinion than I am."

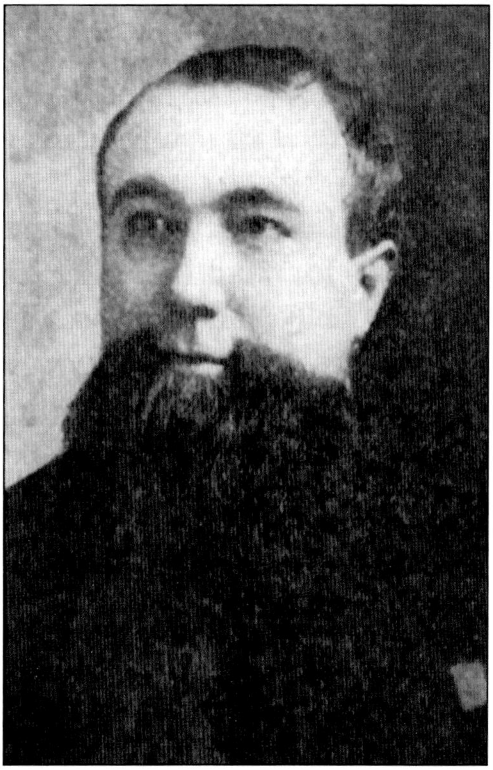

Andy Gilligan was the proprietor of one of Cincinnati's most popular taverns for the theater crowd in the late 19th century. Born into the trade in Riverstown, County Sligo, Ireland, where his father ran the Ten Mile Tavern, young Gilligan came to Cincinnati in 1862 in the midst of the Civil War. He first worked as a grocery clerk near the National Theater, but by 1868 he was running his own billiard parlor near Race and Vine Streets. In 1880, he opened Gilligan's Café on Vine Street, and over the next few decades, Gilligan's was the hangout for touring actors and bohemians, a welcome spot filled with an immense collection of theater photographs and memorabilia. Amidst the raucous conversation inside the café, the frequent Irish fiddle music spilled out the doors to the neighboring streets.

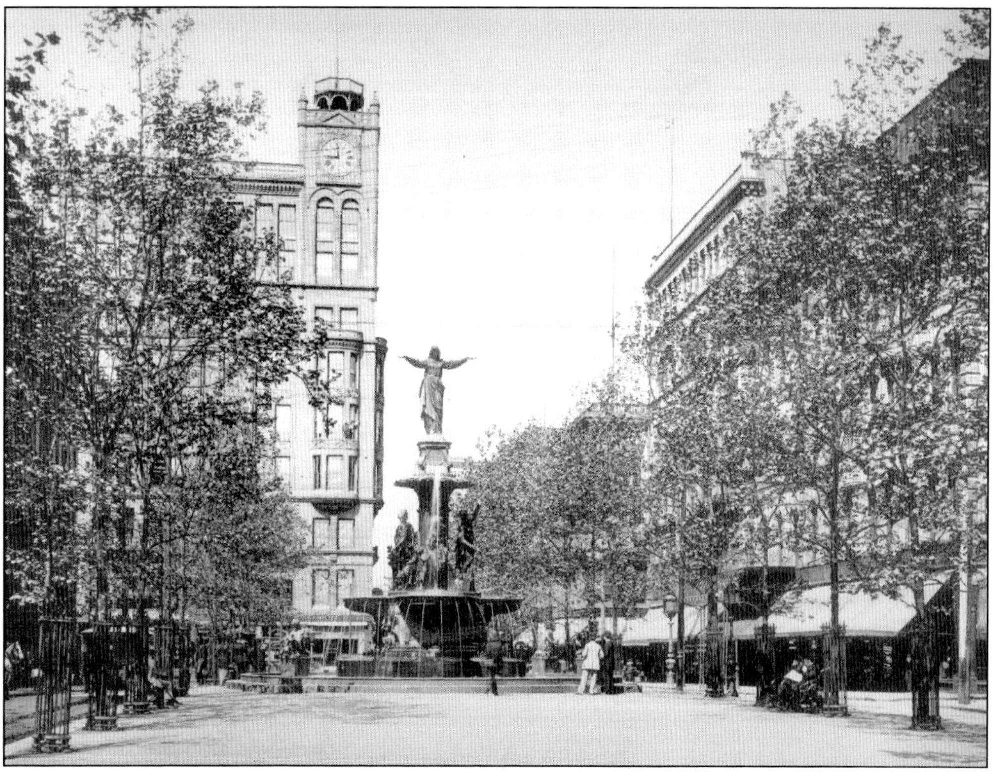

Five

"Oh, a Credit to Ould Ireland, Boys, is McNamara's Band"

The identification with Ireland by Irish Cincinnati would take the same form as it did for the rest of America in the first decades of the 20th century. While Irish immigrants were still coming to the United States, there was now over a century of the Irish presence in this country, and third, fourth, and fifth generations of the early immigrants. Naturally, the separation in time gave rise to a somewhat romantic and maudlin view of the "ould sod." And at the same time that many Irish Americans would still struggle in the city to make ends meet, there was a sense of a Golden Age that may have had the hat of truth knocked off and sent spinning away. Amidst the political upheaval of Ireland itself, it was easy to claim patronage and a sense of ownership of the changes there.

This romanticized view of a verdant, traditional, lilting-of-speech Ireland was not a bad thing necessarily, especially as it was tempered by several Irish American leaders in Cincinnati who fought hard for Irish independence and appreciated the bloody struggles engendered by the Irish Civil War. On the contrary, it proved to be beneficial in that it sustained a community of like interests. The traditional Irish organizations in Cincinnati were even bolstered by such entities as the Cincinnati Celts, an athletic club that held track meets at the old Armory in the West End and sponsored basketball teams. The Celts also fielded a team in the nascent days of professional football in the late teens and early twenties. The team was led by Mel Doherty, a Cincinnatian who graduated from Marietta College and came home to Cincinnati to work as a bandleader and to play football. His "bunch of wild Irishmen," as they were called, were not all that good and did not last very long, but they represented a new aspect of Cincinnati Irish culture.

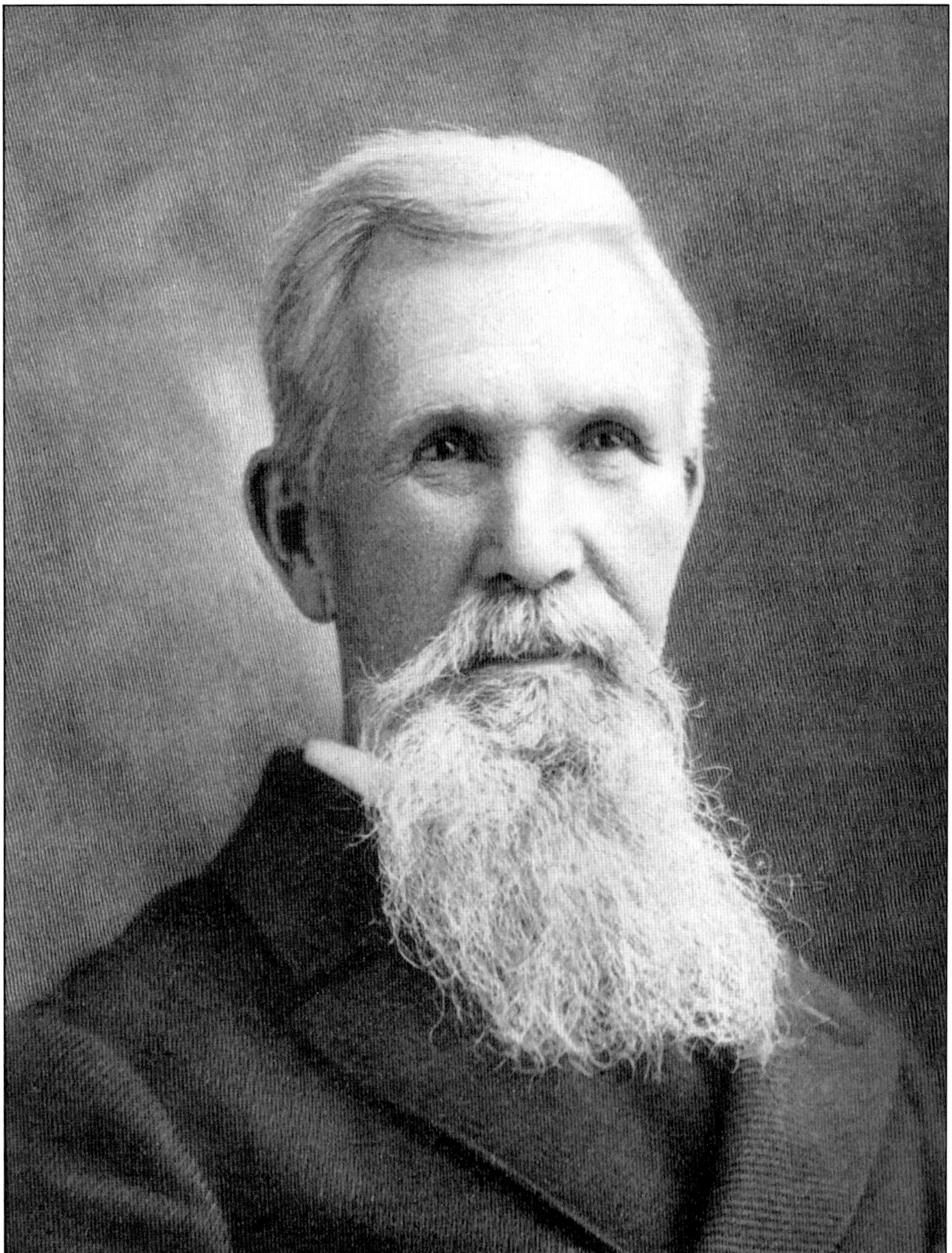

Michael Ryan had somewhat of a morbid occupation but one that he faithfully fulfilled for over 50 years. Ryan served as the morgue keeper in Cincinnati, handling all the cases of murder, mayhem, mysterious accidents, and misfortunate deaths. He started as an assistant to the city undertaker, but his discretion in celebrity cases and his forthright manner in what was, for many of his friends and acquaintances, a macabre practice, kept him employed until he was 83 years old. Four years after his retirement from the morgue, Ryan died at the age of 87. His funeral service was held in St. Peter in Chains Cathedral, with burial in the Irish section of St. Joseph's Cemetery.

As is the case with many long-established funeral homes in America, their history often begins with the livery business or the carpenter trade, building coffins and carrying the deceased to the graveyard. The Gilligan Funeral Homes in Cincinnati were formed in 1877 after Patrick Gilligan, an immigrant from County Sligo, began a livery trade upon his arrive in 1857 and then expanded it into an embalming and undertaking business as P. Gilligan and Sons. One of the sons, John J. Gilligan (pictured here), took over the business in 1905 after his two brothers died and was later joined by his son Harry. The Gilligan clan was the first to use a motorized hearse in Cincinnati, and today, the fifth generation of the family continues to operate the business under the direction of Harry J. Gilligan III and Peter J. Gilligan. (Courtesy of Gilligan Funeral Homes.)

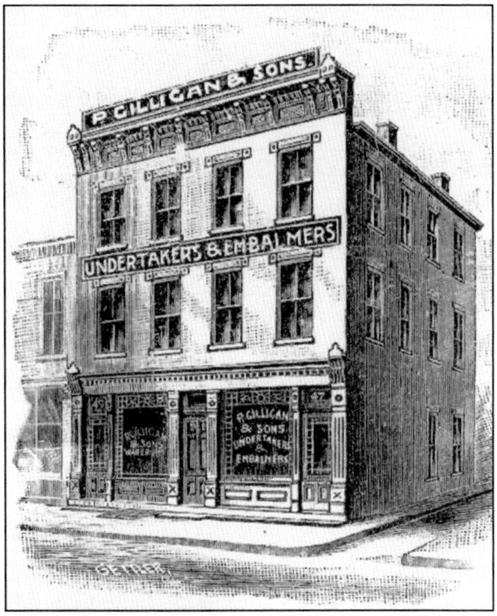

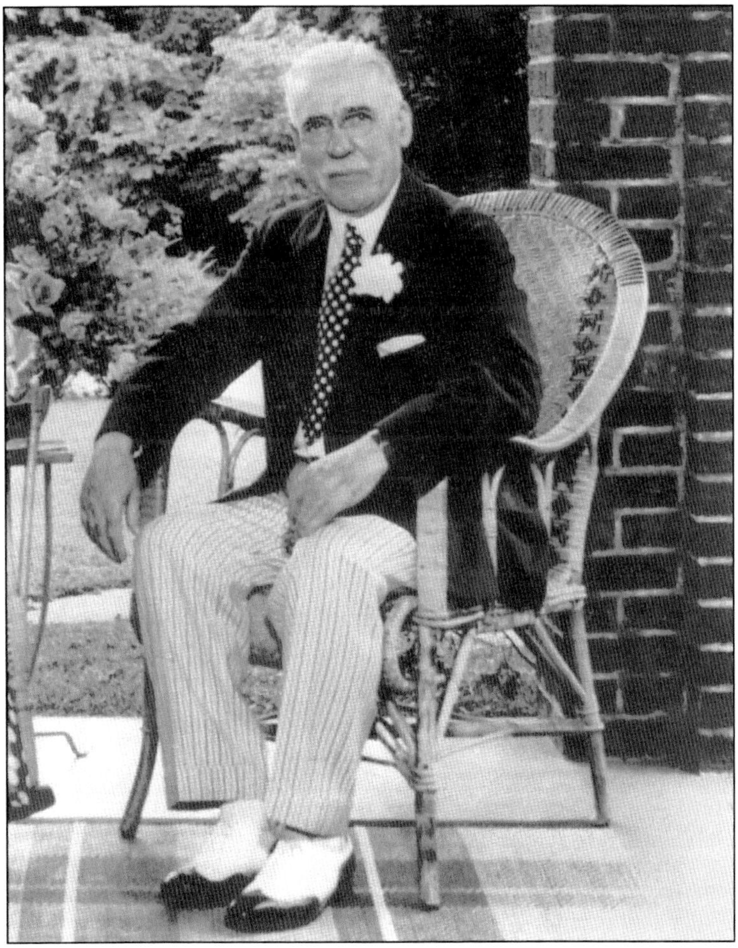

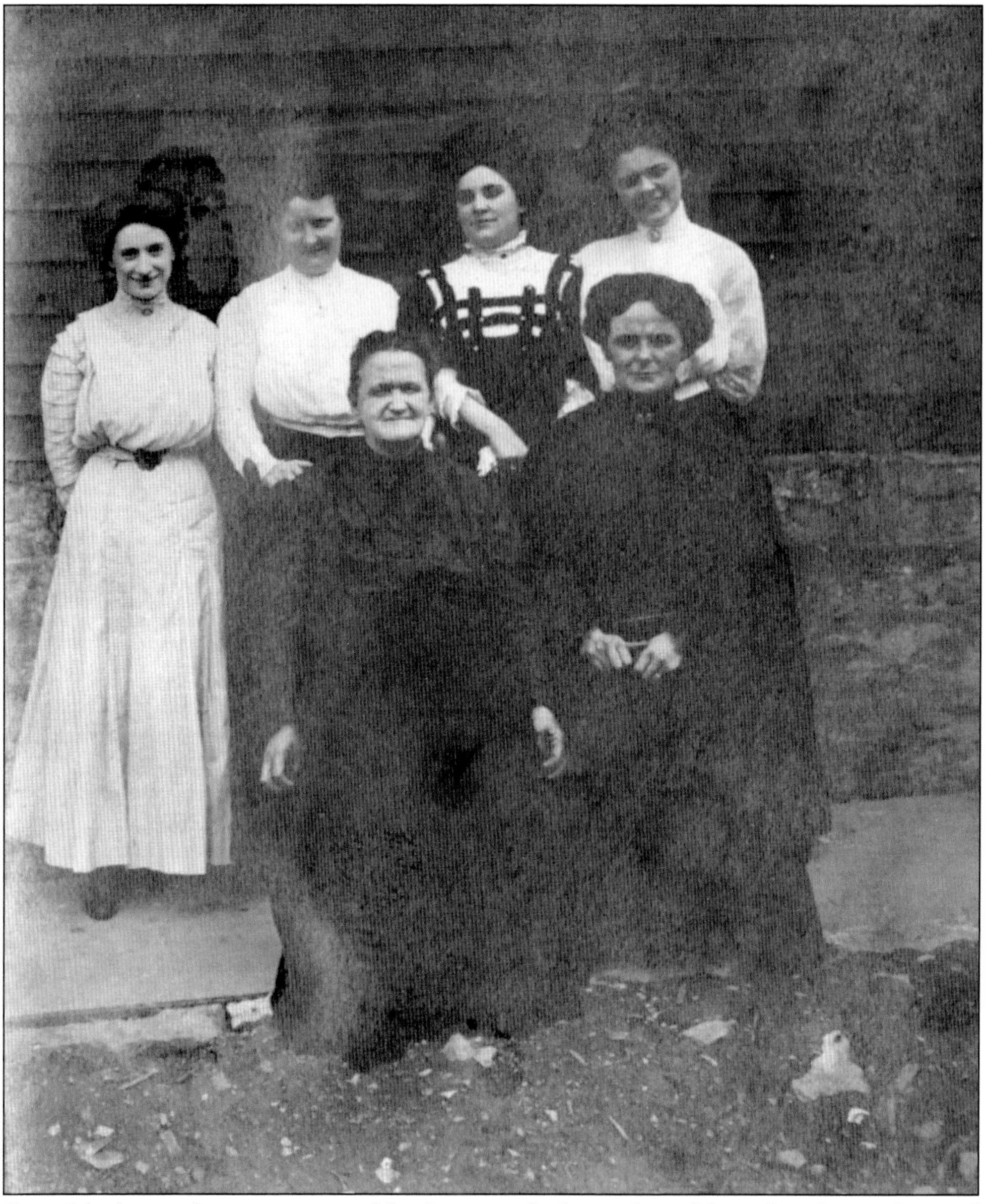

One of the longest lasting customs of the American Irish was that of the wake, where a deceased family member was laid out at home. Friends and relatives were invited in to pay their respects, laugh and cry over memories of the dead, and offer some comfort to the family. Candles were lit and prayers said, and close relatives sat next to the body, keeping vigil throughout the night. And there may have been some drinking and singing, all intended to mark the passing of a beloved one and send him or her off to eternity in fine form. The day after, the undertaker would arrive to take the body to the church for the funeral. In this 1914 photograph of Pat Mallory's Keating relatives, the women wait outside for the hearse from Gilligan's Funeral Home to arrive and gather the body of Michael Keating. (Courtesy of Pat Mallory.)

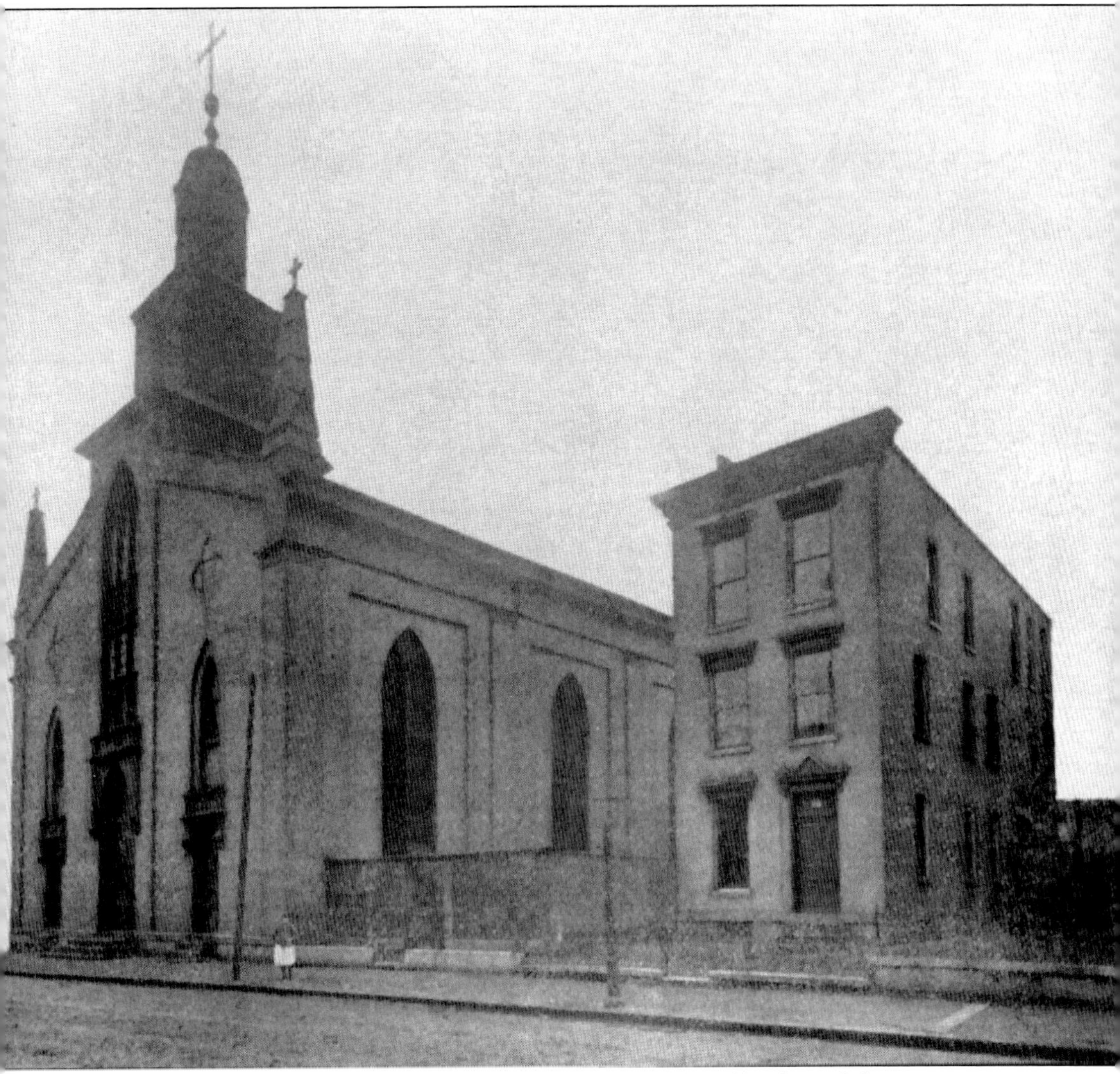

Located at Third and Mill Streets, St. Patrick's Church was established by the archdiocese to serve the growing Irish population. The congregation was formed in 1849, with the church constructed a year later and the dedication held on November 24, 1850. Staffed throughout its history by Irish priests, the parish counted 500 families at its peak in the late 1800s.

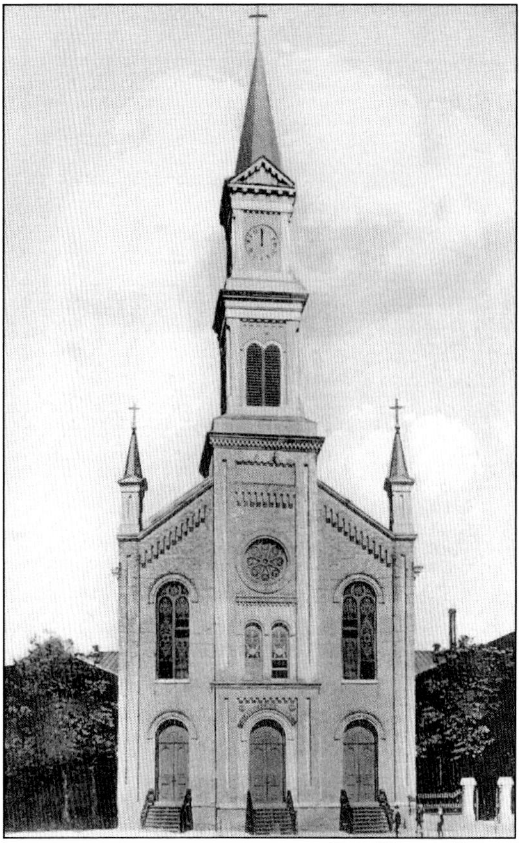

As was the case throughout most of the archdiocese's early history, German and Irish Catholics found it difficult to get along when they shared a church. The disputes were expressed in many ways, but for the most part it came down to pride in their respective ethnicities. Both Irish and German wanted priests from their own heritage and homilies directed at their particular concerns. Such was the case in the neighborhood of Cumminsville. The German congregation of St. Boniface (left) separated from the Irish when both shared a church and the latter group thrived in another St. Patrick's (below), constructed in 1873 and the only Cincinnati church with both a dome and a steeple in the cruciform center.

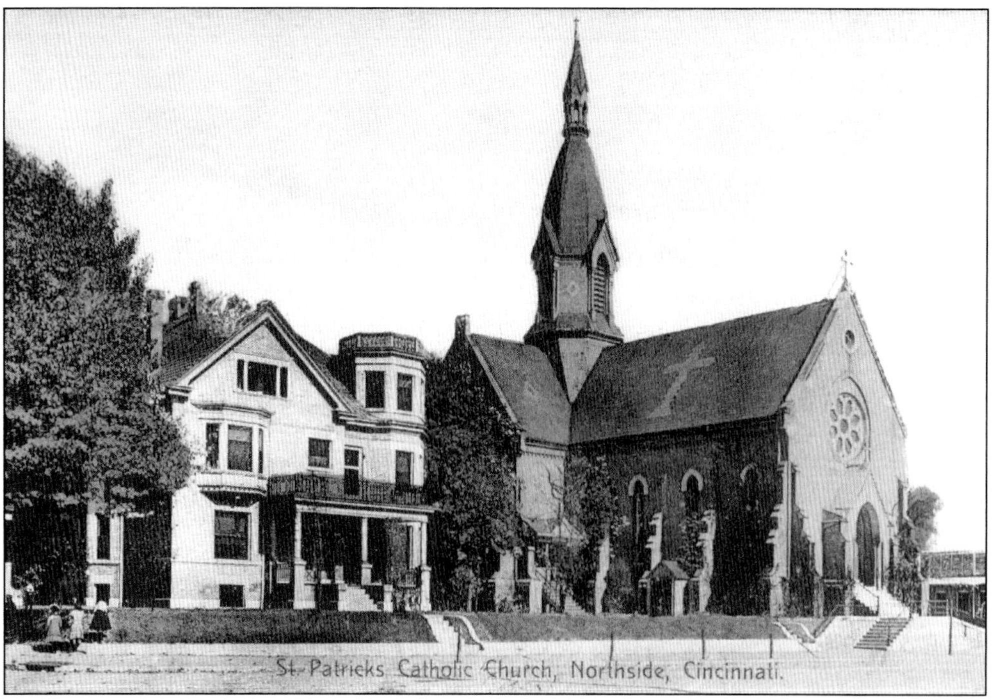

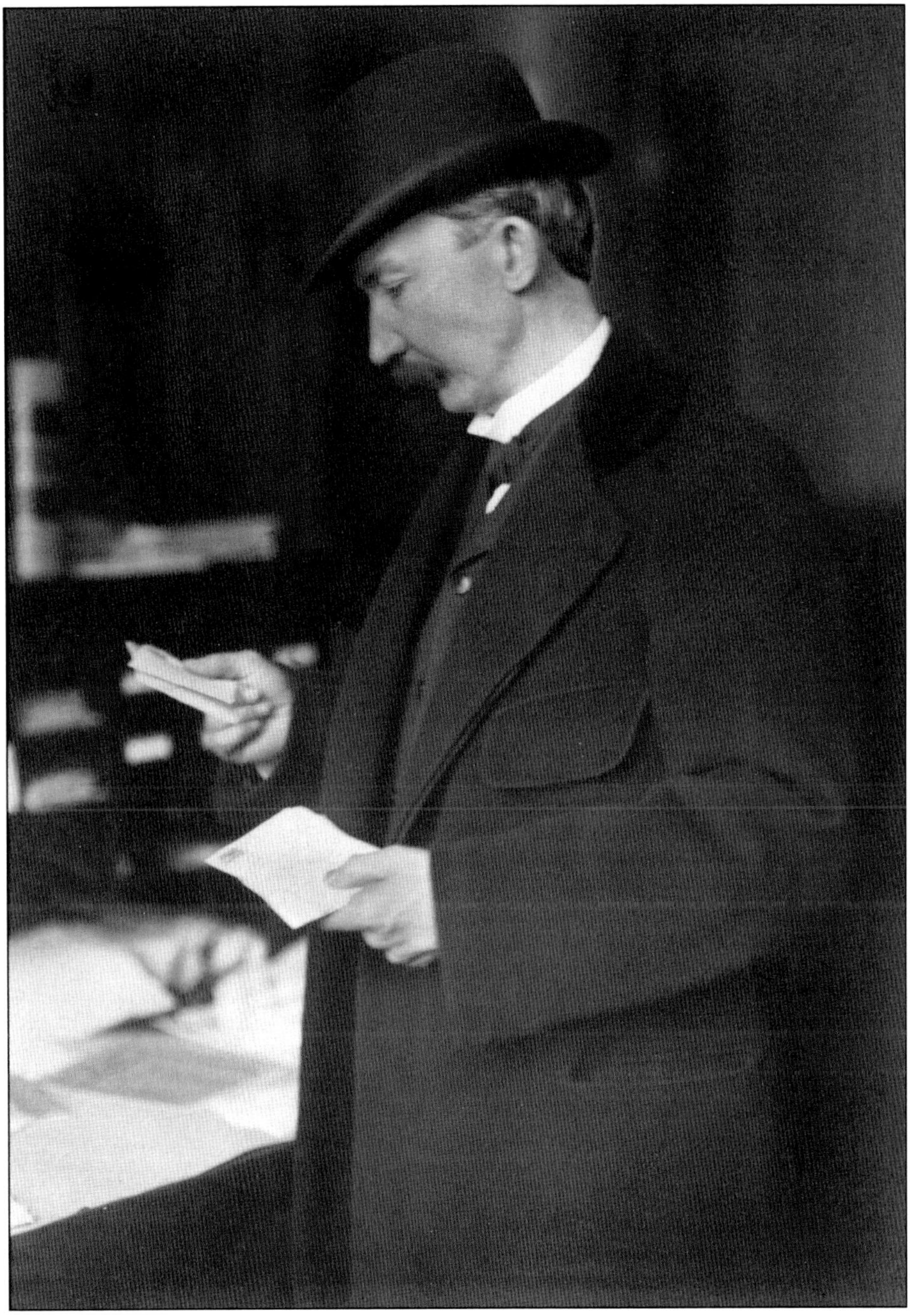

Democrat Edward J. Dempsey served as Cincinnati's mayor for two years, from 1906 to 1908. Born in 1858 to Irish parents, Dempsey was educated in the parochial school system before attending Cincinnati Law School. After admission to the bar in 1879, he became increasingly involved in the city's politics and became a superior court judge in 1898. Dempsey campaigned for Democratic presidential candidate William Jennings Bryan, who faced off and lost to Cincinnatian William Howard Taft in the 1908 election, but his most notable participation in local politics came when he served on the charter commission in 1917, successfully reforming party structure in Cincinnati. Dempsey Park in Price Hill is named for him. (Courtesy of Pat Mallory.)

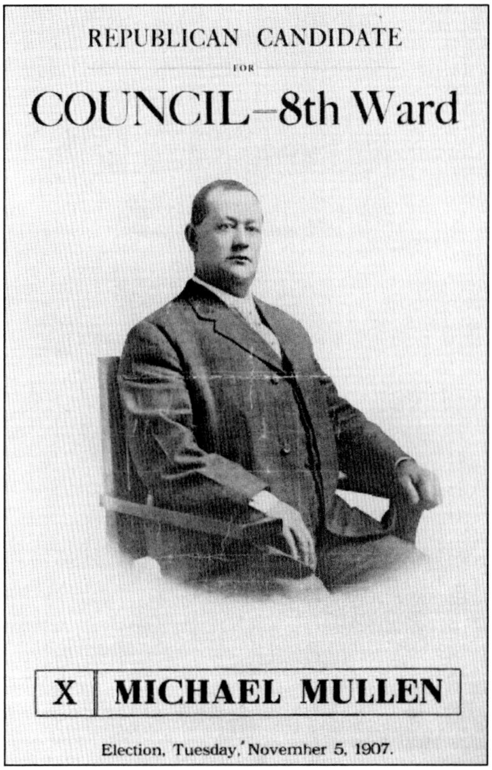

"Politics are said to be inborn in an Irishman, but at this time, in Cincinnati, he had not shown in any distressing degree this aptitude." Expressed in 1870, this sentiment was changed by Mike Mullen, the influential ward healer. As the Eighth Ward captain, he controlled dozens of patronage jobs, all of which went from Democrats to Republicans when he bolted to the machine politics of George B. Cox. The son of Irish immigrants, Mullen was beloved in his ethnic community, helping his constituents through bad times and holding a massive "Irish Day" picnic every year. He was Cox's man on city council, running his business from city hall and his private detective agency (pictured here). After he died in 1921, his loyal Irish constituents raised funds for a memorial bandstand in Lytle Park, where a marker to Mullen now stands.

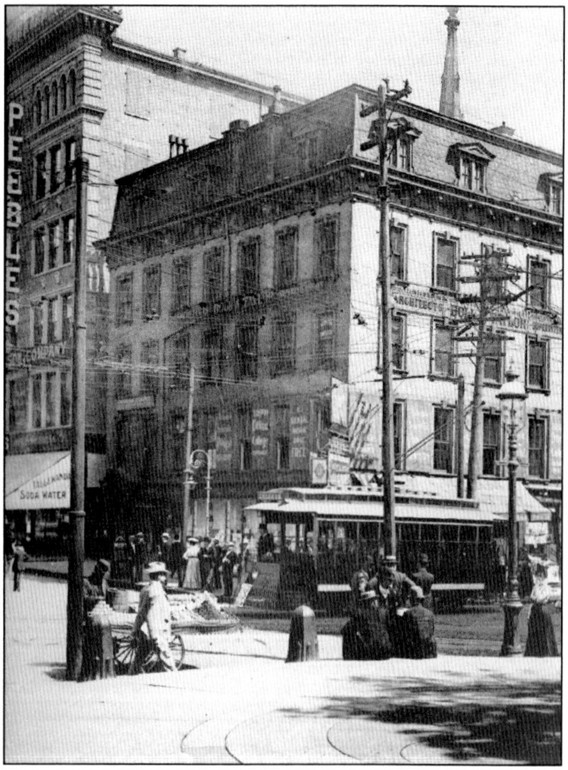

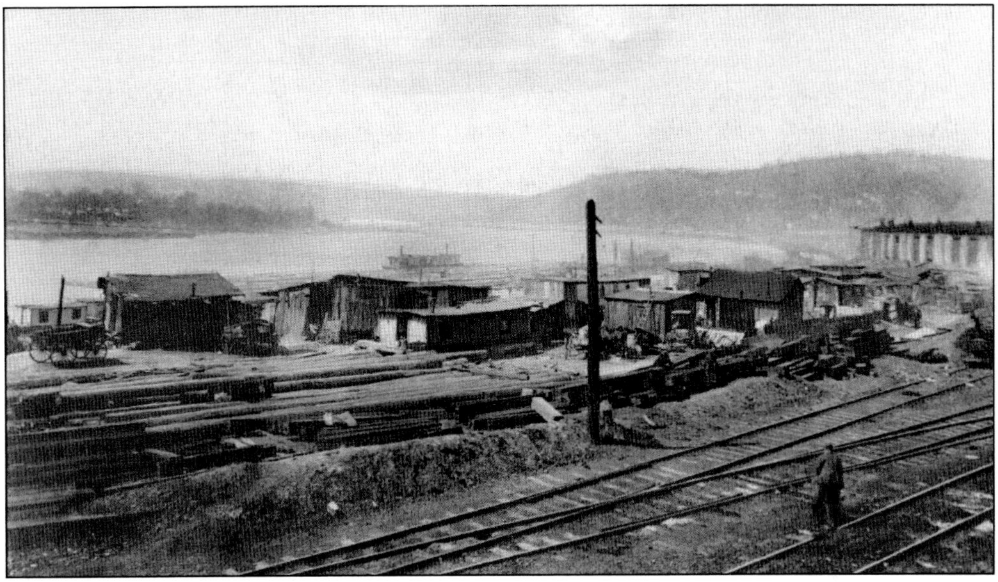

Throughout the 1800s and well into the early years of the 20th century, the Irish shantytowns existed along the Ohio River, both east and west of downtown Cincinnati. Those shanty neighborhoods were called by such names as Rat Row, Sausage Row, and Bucktown, and they were filled with the poorest of the city's population. Crime and destitution were a part of life around the shacks. The Irish poor sometimes found work on the docks or in the produce houses, lifting cargo and loading goods onto wagons and steamboats and later, freight trains. For the shanty children, the rail yards and river were their playgrounds, and any unwary visitor was an easy mark for picking pockets.

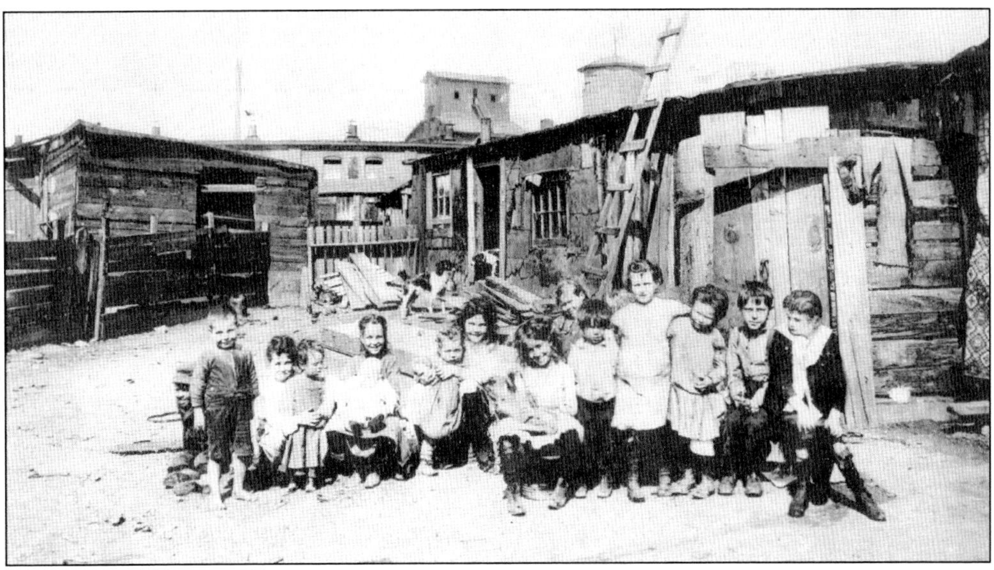

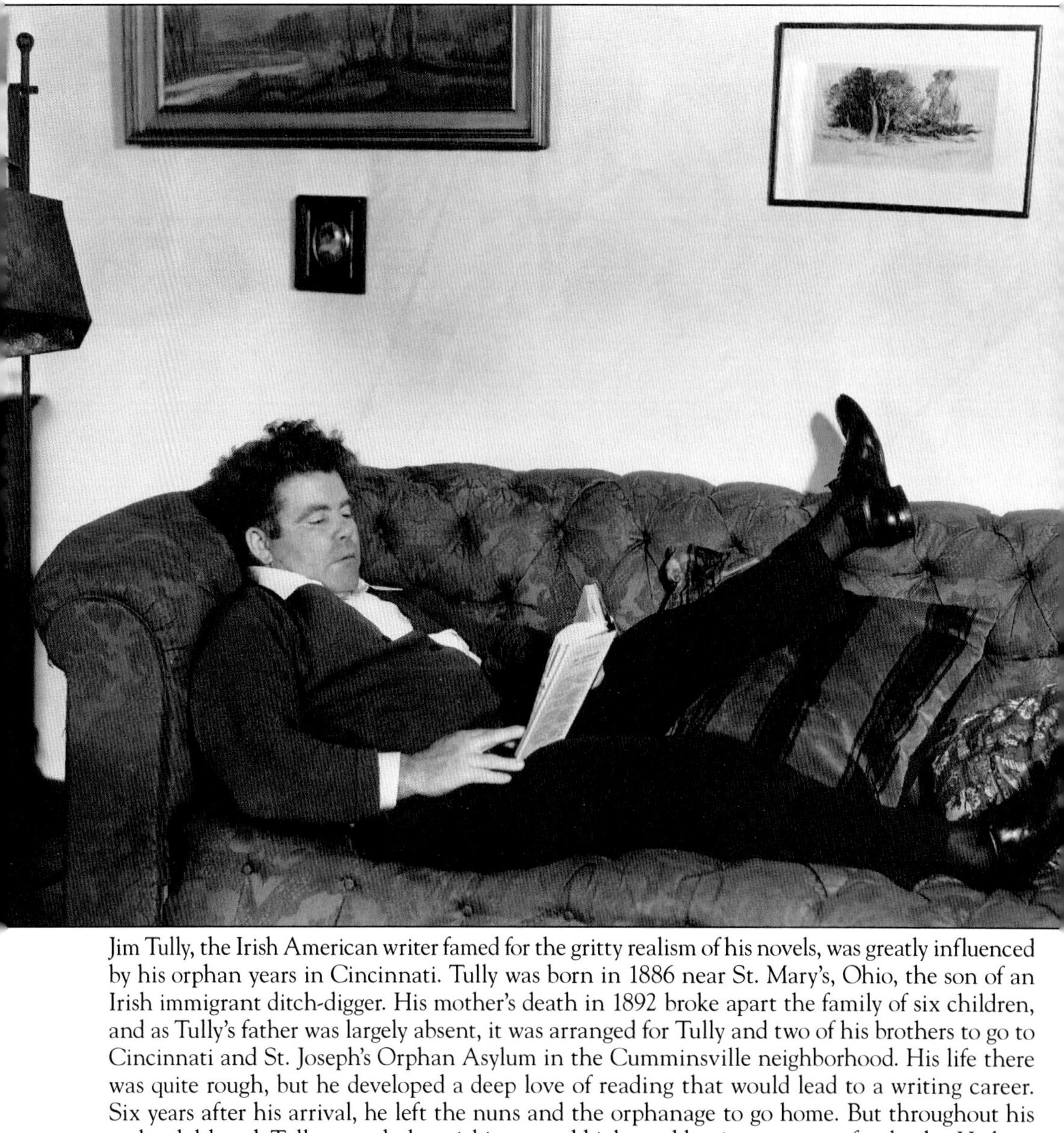

Jim Tully, the Irish American writer famed for the gritty realism of his novels, was greatly influenced by his orphan years in Cincinnati. Tully was born in 1886 near St. Mary's, Ohio, the son of an Irish immigrant ditch-digger. His mother's death in 1892 broke apart the family of six children, and as Tully's father was largely absent, it was arranged for Tully and two of his brothers to go to Cincinnati and St. Joseph's Orphan Asylum in the Cumminsville neighborhood. His life there was quite rough, but he developed a deep love of reading that would lead to a writing career. Six years after his arrival, he left the nuns and the orphanage to go home. But throughout his early adulthood, Tully was a hobo, picking up odd jobs and boxing to earn a few bucks. He kept writing, however, and by 1912, he was working in Hollywood as a reporter. By the 1920s, he was a celebrated author and screenwriter, his novels often depicting the lives of hardscrabble vagabonds. In particular, his books *Shanty Irish* and *Biddy Brogan's Boy* drew upon his Cincinnati years. (Courtesy of Jim Tully Papers, Department of Special Collections, Charles E. Young Research Library, UCLA.)

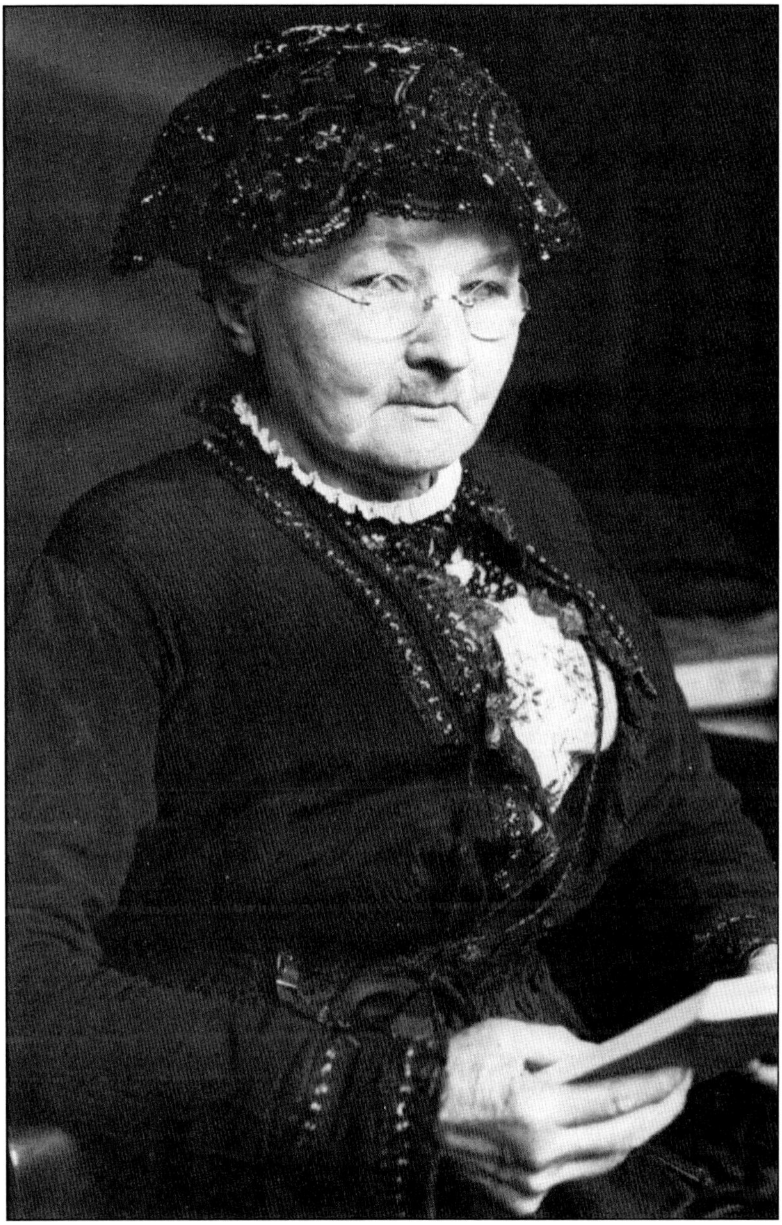

Mary Harris Jones, known in American history as "Mother Jones," and once labeled as "the most dangerous woman in America," was born in County Cork to a tenant farmer. Her birth date has been variously given as 1830 or 1837, but what is definitely known is that when she was 15, her family immigrated to Toronto, where she was educated. After coming to America, she married George Jones, a labor activist. After she lost her husband and four children to a yellow fever epidemic in Tennessee, Mother Jones moved to Chicago where she became a dressmaker and labor organizer. In the early 1900s, she organized against the use of children in textile mills and fought to organize coal miners in Appalachia and Colorado. Recognizing Cincinnati as key to workers' interests, she came to Cincinnati in 1902 to meet with the Central Labor Council for support of the United Mine Workers and again in 1910 to speak about her "Children's Crusade" against unsafe working conditions.

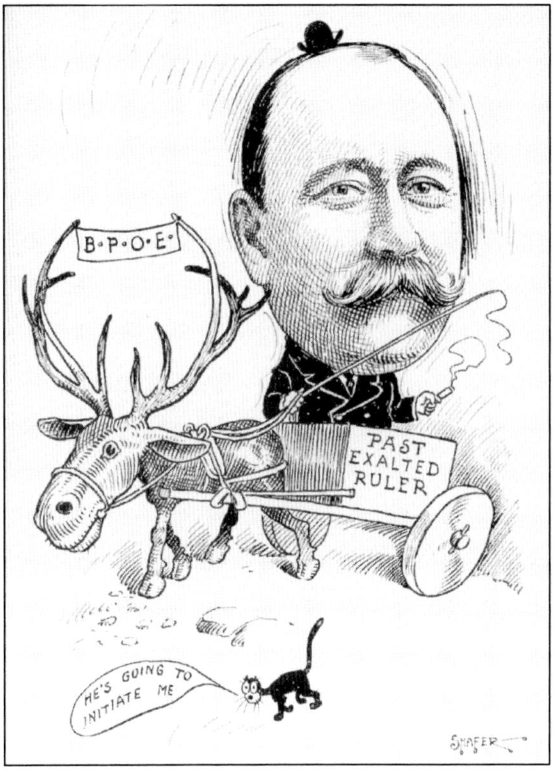

Cincinnati's Friendly Sons of St. Patrick (FFSP) was formed in 1868, only the third such chapter in the United States, following the first one organized in Philadelphia nearly a century prior, in 1771 and the second in New York in 1784. For Cincinnati, the creation of the chapter signified a distinct change in the image of the Irish in the city. The FFSP welcomed everyone who had an affinity for Ireland or hereditary ties. But the fact that a large part of the membership was composed of professional men such as judges, educators, industrialists, and business leaders was important in determining how the Irish were regarded. And, as a mover and shaker in Cincinnati in the early 1900s, you were entitled to be caricatured as some FSSP officials were: Thomas Cogan (left), who served as president in 1893, and Thomas Shay (below), president in 1897.

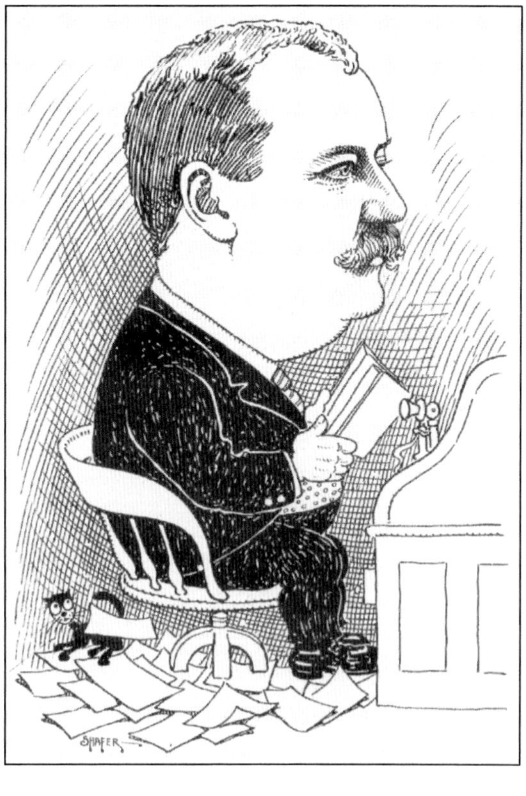

As with the FSSP presidents portrayed on the facing page, the 1911 book of caricatures attempted to capture most of the city's leaders. Right is Norman Kenan, president of the Cincinnati Gas & Electric Company and head of the Friendly Sons in 1900, and below is Judge John G. O'Connell, who served as president of the organization in 1904, and who was also an influential member of the Cincinnati Board of Education. From its founding a few years after the Civil War to the present, the Friendly Sons of St. Patrick have worked to benefit the city, with a charitable foundation today and sponsorship of the annual Celtic Festival. The Cincinnati FSSP currently has more than 500 members, and every year it holds a formal banquet on March 17, of course.

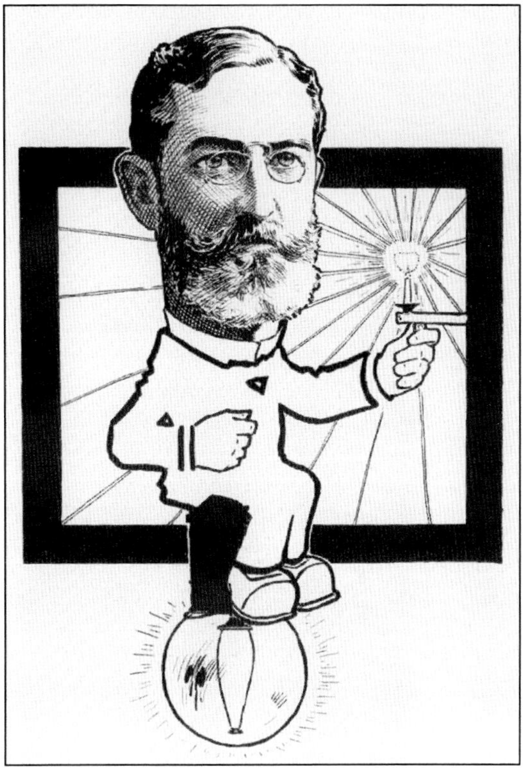

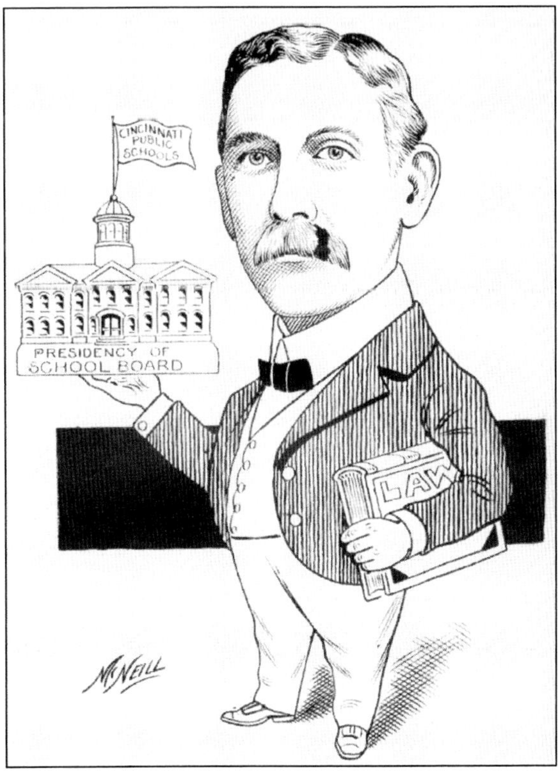

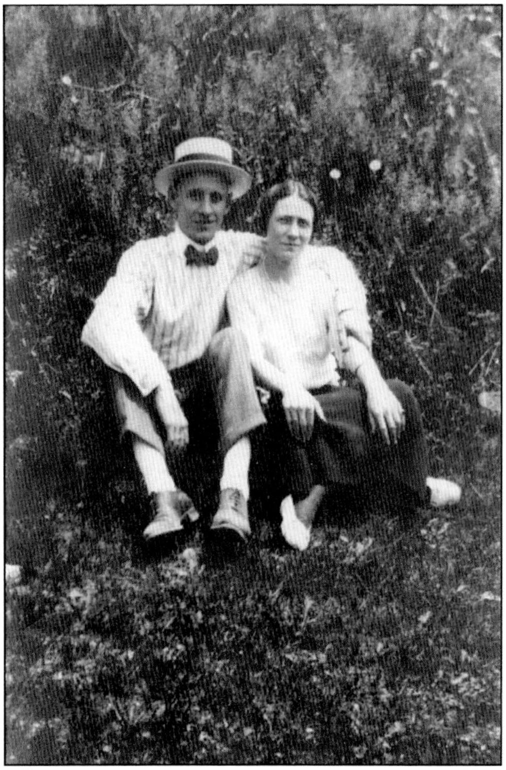

John Warnock, pictured left with his bride, Louise Krone, around 1910, had an Irish mother in O'Bryonville. Shortly after the Warnock's daughter Mary Louise was born in 1913 (she is pictured below as a young child, with a neighbor boy), Louise died and Mary Louise was raised by her grandmother Bridget and her two aunts, Minnie and Madeleine. Her father's German name notwithstanding, the upbringing was decidedly Irish with a strong household brogue. O'Bryonville began as an Irish area settled in the 1830s by Laura O'Bryon, who purchased 72 acres along Madison Pike. Other Irish followed, and though her husband, Edward, would lose part of the land in a card game to a man named Edwin Morris, the property would later be deeded back to the O'Bryons. In 1870, O'Bryonville was annexed by the city of Cincinnati. (Courtesy of Susie Kauck.)

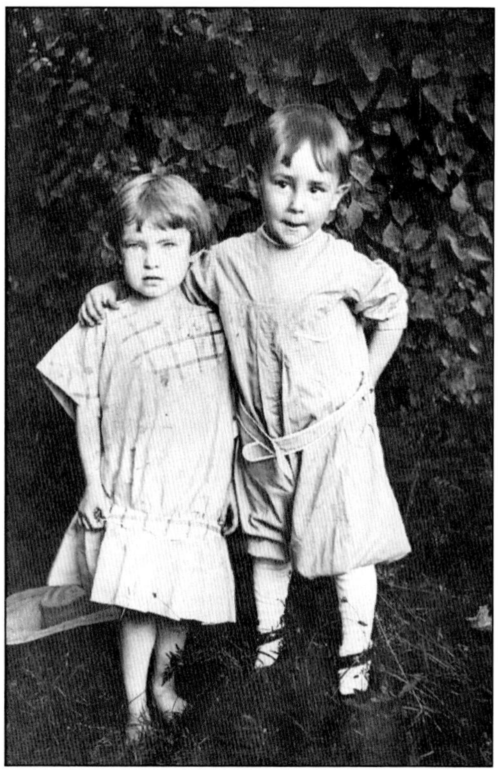

As a young woman, Mary Louise Warnock was strongly influenced by the neighborhood culture. Though her grandmother raised her on a day-to-day basis, her father was always present, working hard as a groundskeeper for the Charles A. Phelps family. He had remarried after the death of Mary Louise's mother, and had three additional children. During the hard times of the Great Depression, he gave up his job so that another worker, who had nine children to feed, could keep his. Mary Louise's daughter Susie Kauck tells of the little pieces of life that made up her mother's heritage in O'Bryonville, how her grandmother would give Mary Louise a hot baked sweet potato to eat (and to keep her hands warm) on the way to school on a cold winter morning, and the family's summer trips taking the steamboat *Island Queen* to Coney Island for "Irish Day." (Courtesy of Susie Kauck.)

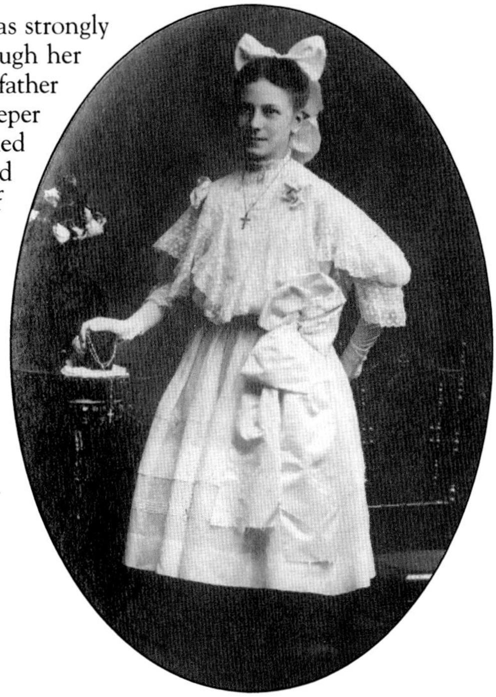

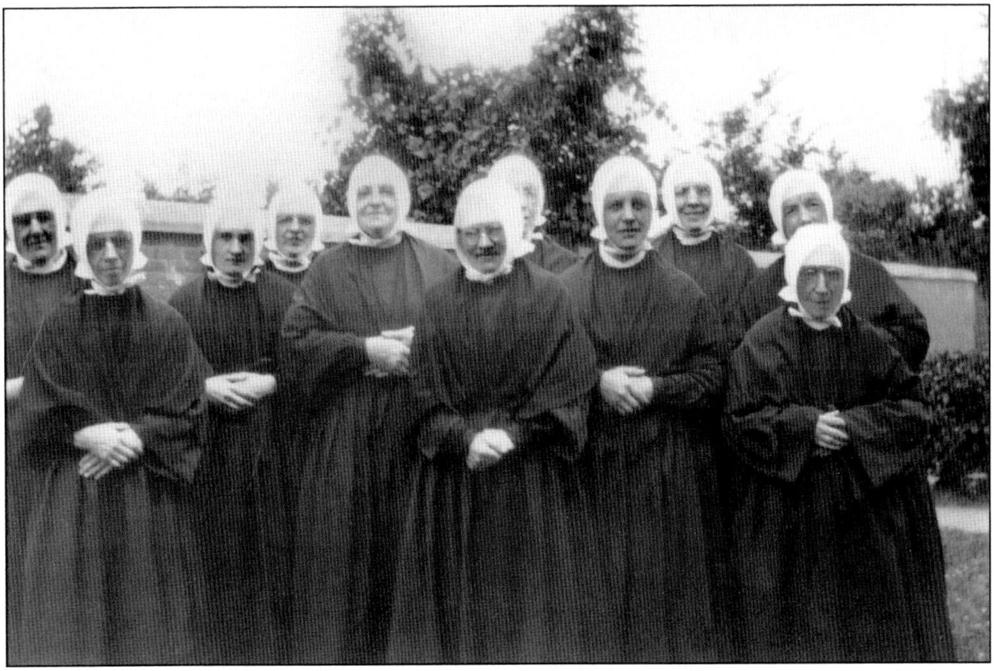

Though young Irish women in Cincinnati who were called to a religious vocation could choose from two orders that had a strong Irish heritage, the Sisters of Mercy and the Sisters of Charity, one who decided to forego the ethnic connection was Sister Marguerite, who joined the Little Sisters of the Poor, a Cincinnati order with its origins in France. Raised in an O'Bryonville Irish household, Sister Marguerite is part of this 1939 centennial photograph of the nuns. (Courtesy of Susie Kauck.)

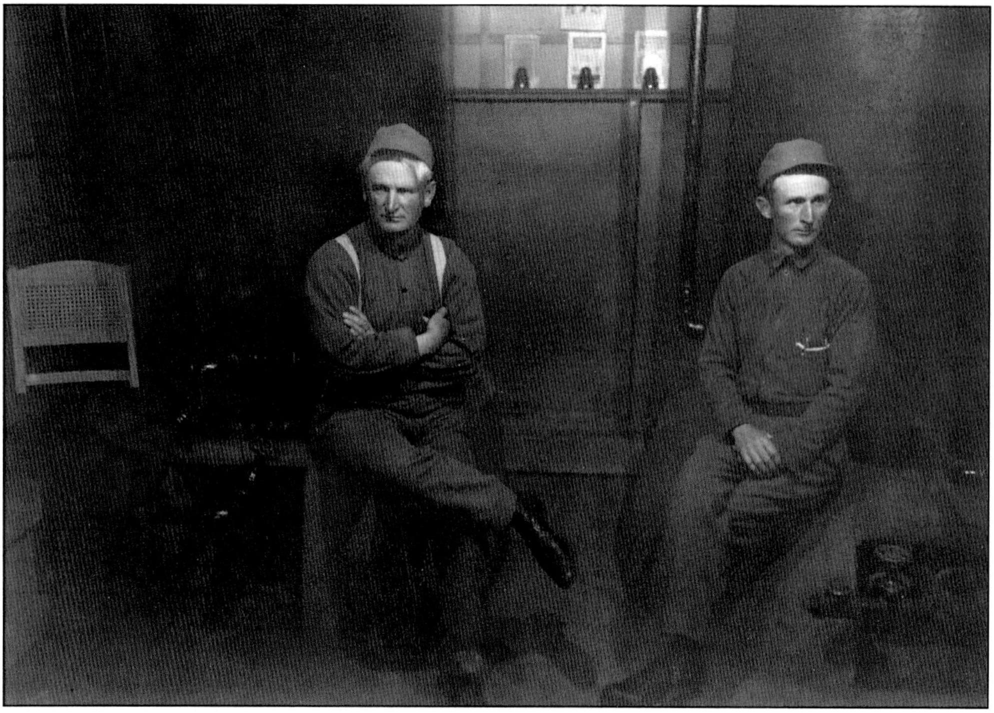

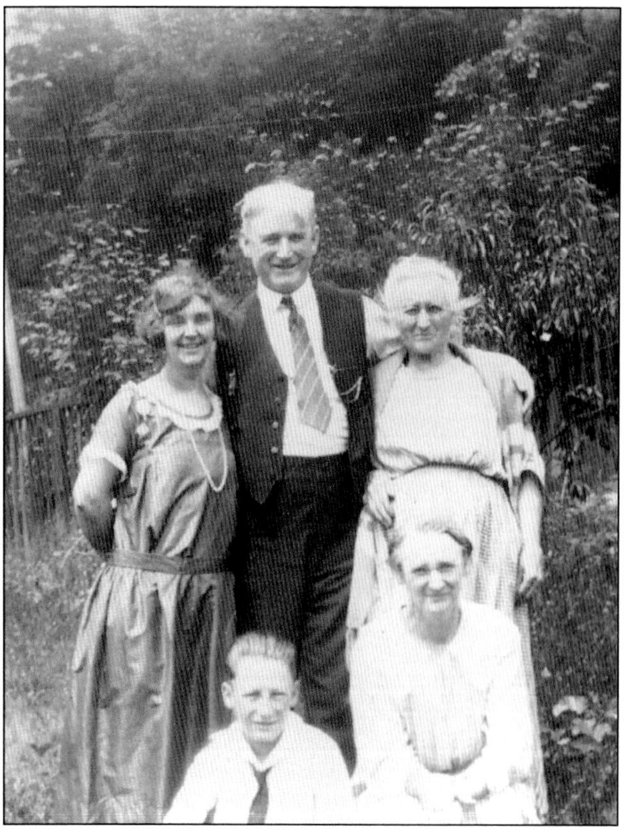

Two of Cincinnati's most notorious Irish were the McNamara brothers, John and James, who were raised in the Northside neighborhood. Both were union men as ironworkers and became involved in labor politics. In 1910, as a protest against union busting in California, the McNamaras dynamited the Los Angeles Times Building. Their defense attorney was the redoubtable Clarence Darrow, but despite Darrow's skill in the courtroom, the brothers were convicted and sent to San Quentin Prison. Above, the brothers are pictured together in prison, John on the left and James on the right. James would spend the rest of his life in jail, and John was released after 10 years, standing with his mother, sister, aunt, and nephew after his return home to Cincinnati. Both brothers died within months of each other in 1941.

"IRISH DAY"

"THE DAY WE CELEBRATE"

THURSDAY, AUGUST 17th, 1911.

Come up and help the Irish celebrate at the Cincinnati Shoe 'en's Camp, on the Little Miami River—Stop No. 7, New Richond Pike.

Take New Richmond or Bethel Black Car, Sycamore St., at 6:30, 7:30, 10, 9:00, 9:45 and 11:15 A. M.

P. S.—In case of rain will ave wagons to take you ver

COMMITTEE { *JAS. COWEN, WM. DOHAN, WM. HENNESSY, JESSE MacDONALD, HARRY O'HAM.* }

Numerous organizations held "Irish Days" in the late 1800s and the early decades of the 1900s. Most often these picnics and fairs were sponsored by politicians or fraternal organizations to foster ethnic pride and identity, just as they were for the Germans or Italians. Some stores or factories held Irish Days as well, as much to provide recreation for their employees as to, perhaps, encourage some trade from the local Irish population. As this postcard shows, the Cincinnati Shoe Company held a picnic upriver in New Richmond, and as the names indicate, the picnic organizers were all of an Irish bent.

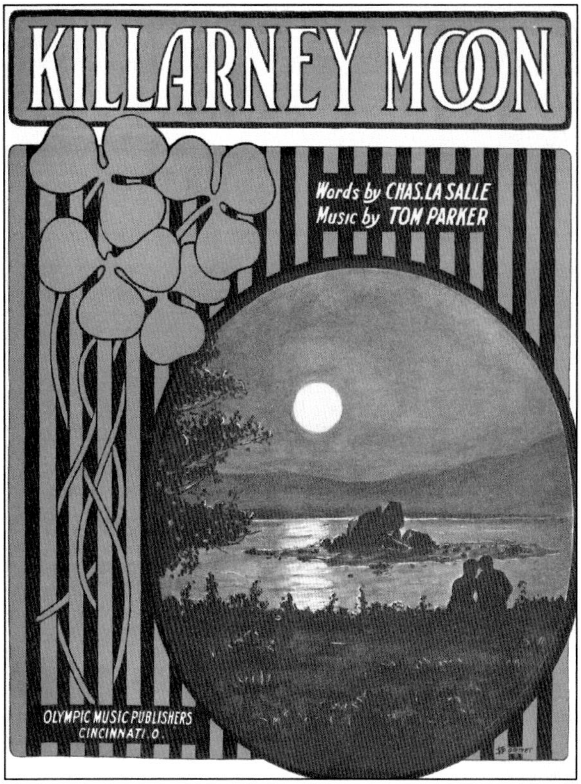

By the late 1800s, the Irish American experience fully entered popular culture with the burgeoning publication of sheet music. A great many of the songs were maudlin and nostalgic longings for the "ould sod," but they indicated a real desire to maintain some connection to Ireland as American life, in its bustle and mobility, threatened to obscure its heritage. And most often, it was the second and third generations of Irish who dominated the buyer's market. Tin Pan Alley in New York City, fostered by vaudeville and stage shows, produced song after song after song, but Cincinnati had a share of the sheet music business as well, and several popular songs and light operas were published here as illustrated by the two images here.

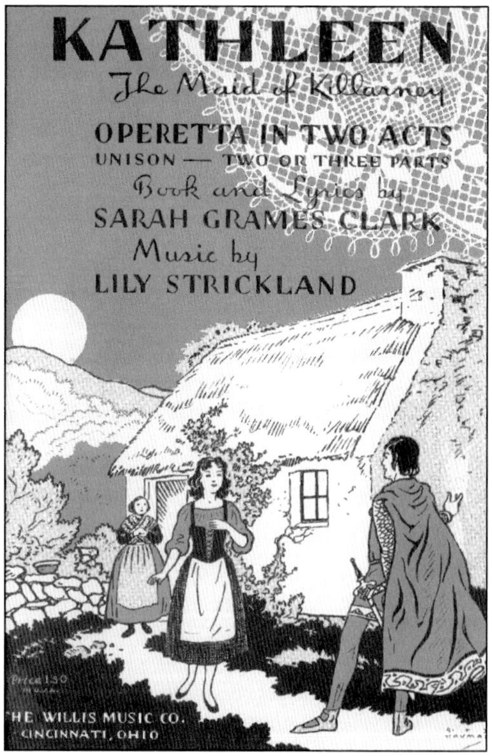

Capt. George Sweeny (right) was one of the great old Irish patriots in Cincinnati, who carried his struggle for a free Ireland up until his death in 1932. Sweeny was born in Dunmore, Ireland, in 1844 and came to Cincinnati in 1861. He enlisted in the Union army the following year, mustering out when the Civil War ended. Sweeny then joined the Fenian movement and took part in the ill-fated invasion of Canada in 1866. Throughout the rest of his life, he would fight for Ireland and worked to bring Irish American factions together in support for his native land. In the 1919 photograph below, he is pictured second from right, next to Eamon de Valera in the middle. At the time, de Valera served as prime minister in the Irish independence government and spoke in Cincinnati Music Hall as part of his American visit to raise funds and political support. (Both courtesy of Andrew Sweeny Jr.)

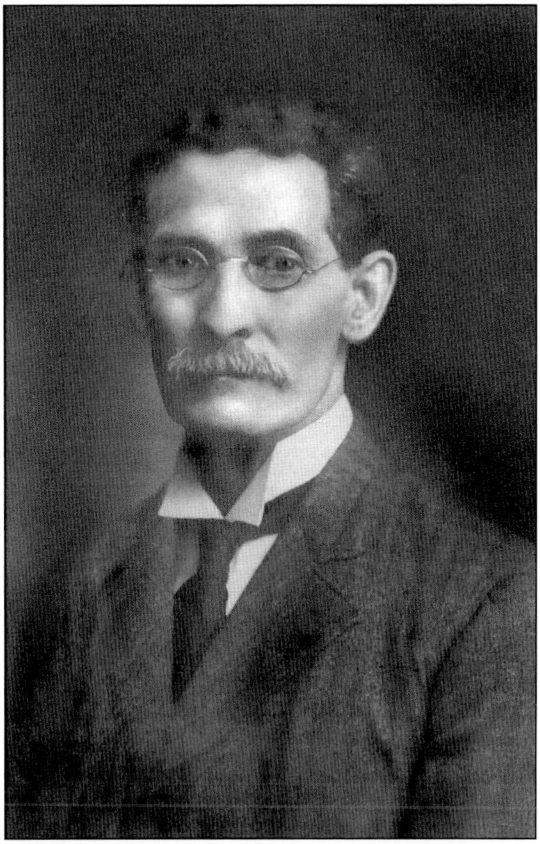

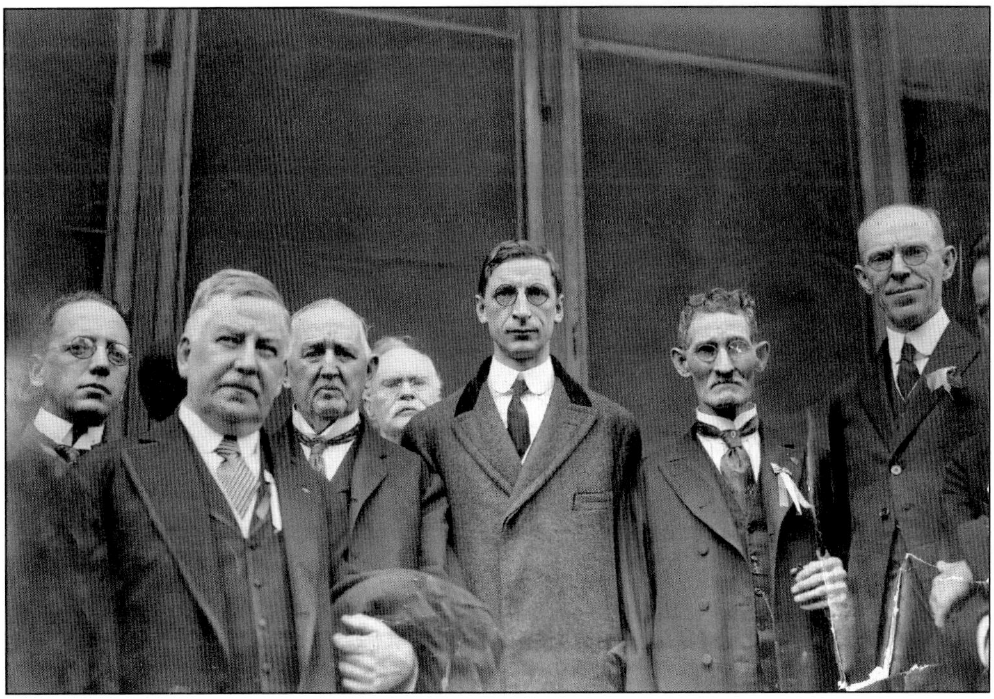

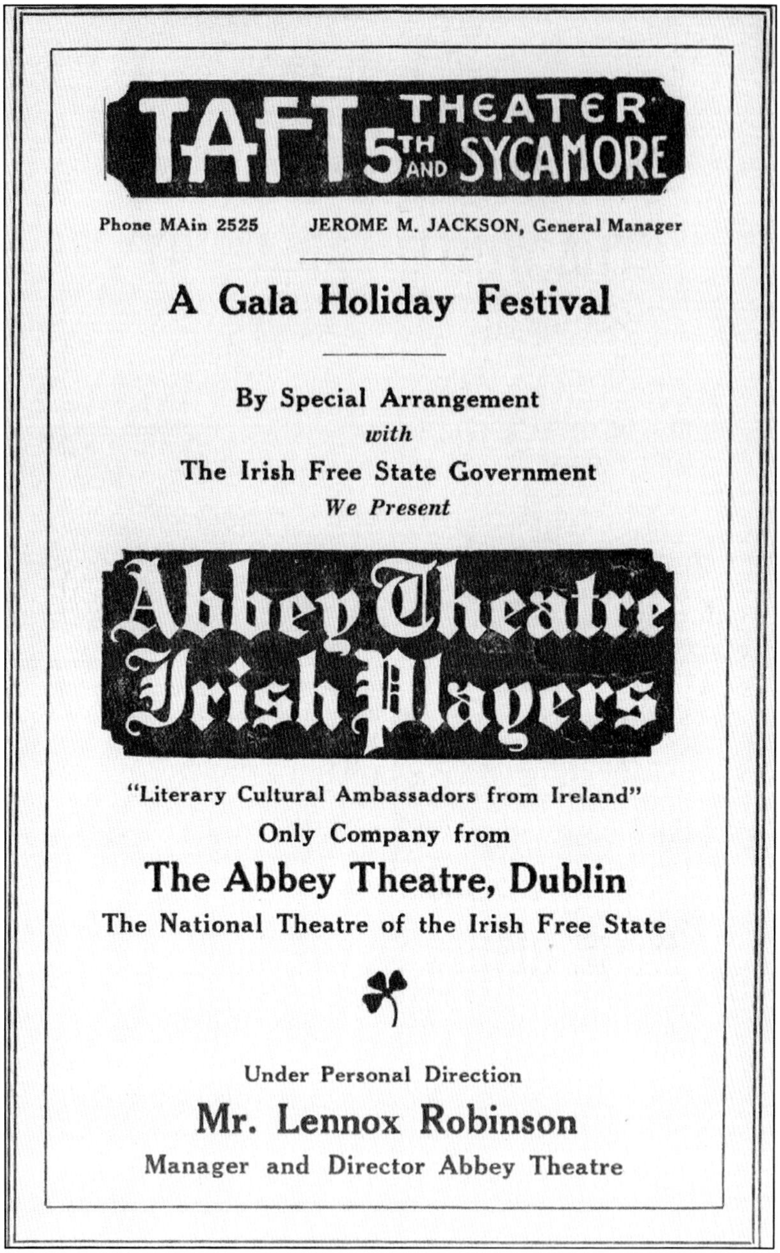
TAFT THEATER 5TH AND SYCAMORE

Phone MAin 2525 JEROME M. JACKSON, General Manager

A Gala Holiday Festival

By Special Arrangement
with
The Irish Free State Government
We Present

Abbey Theatre Irish Players

"Literary Cultural Ambassadors from Ireland"
Only Company from
The Abbey Theatre, Dublin
The National Theatre of the Irish Free State

Under Personal Direction
Mr. Lennox Robinson
Manager and Director Abbey Theatre

Ever mindful of their American countrymen, especially those who provided financial and political assistance to the cause for freedom from England, Irish literati, actors, singers, and performers toured the United States in the 1920s and 1930s to cement ties with their supporters. The tours were little different from the frequent ones produced for the previous 100 years, but after Ireland obtained semi-autonomy for itself, there was a change to government sponsorship. In this flyer for a performance at the Taft Theatre, the Irish Free State government arranged for the Abbey Theatre players to perform during the Christmas season of 1931. Dramatist and poet Lennox Robinson was a long-standing figure in the abbey. Known as a nationalist, his first play, *The Cross Roads,* was produced there in 1909, five years after its opening as part of the Irish Literary Revival under W.B. Yeats and Lady Gregory.

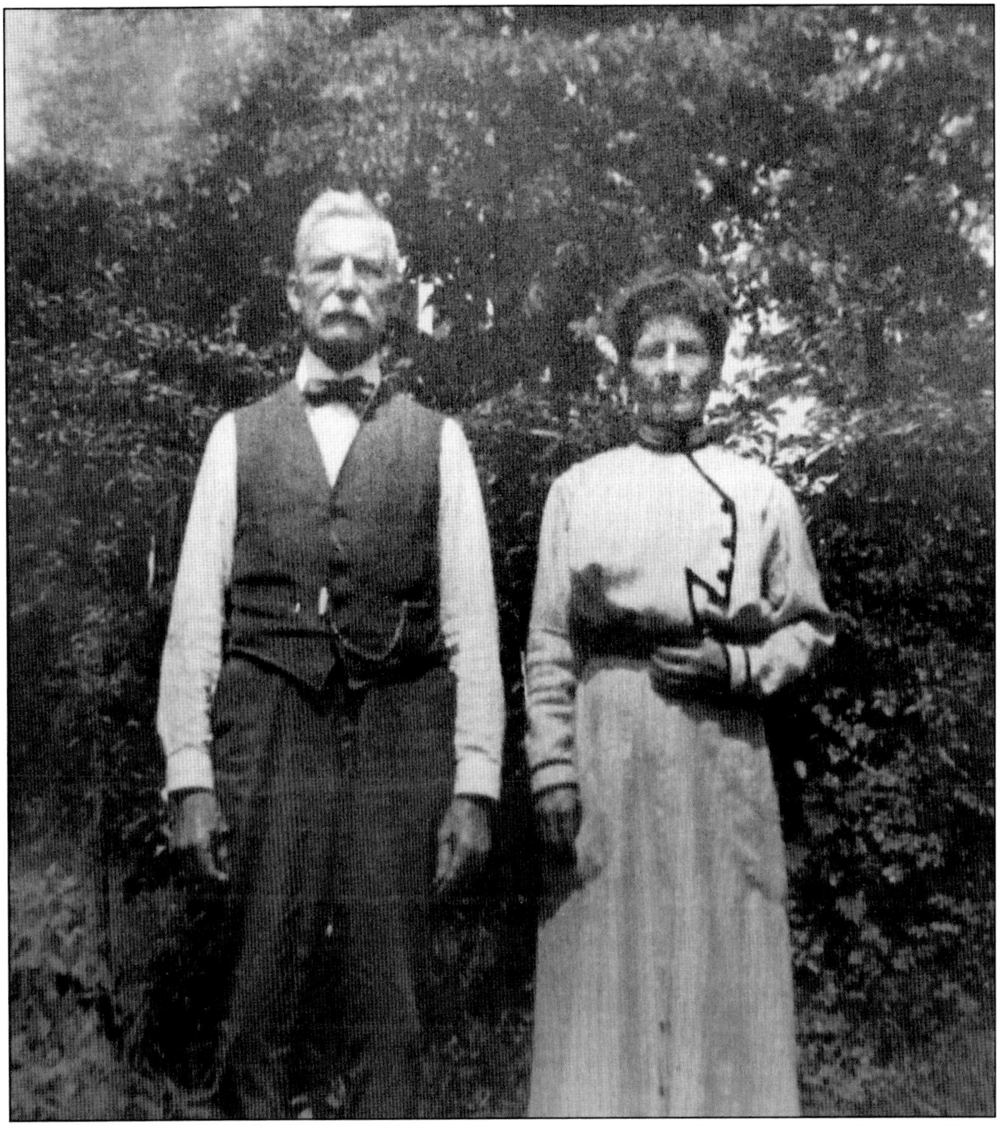

Ring Place in Price Hill is a circular street that at one time was home to several related Irish families. In fact, the name of the street derives as much from the view as it does from its direction. In this photograph of the Regan family, patriarch John Regan stands with his wife in their front yard. Regan was born in Ireland in 1843, and after coming to America, he settled in Cincinnati and worked downtown as a clerk. Up in Price Hill, a neighborhood that was home to many local Irish, Regan thought the view from the hilltop was much like that of a "ring" in his home county back in Ireland. So, he petitioned the city to rename the street. In 1897, the street's original name as Neff Road near Grand was changed to Ring, and in 1911, that name was continued with the renaming of part of Fairbanks Avenue. (Courtesy of Stacey Walsh.)

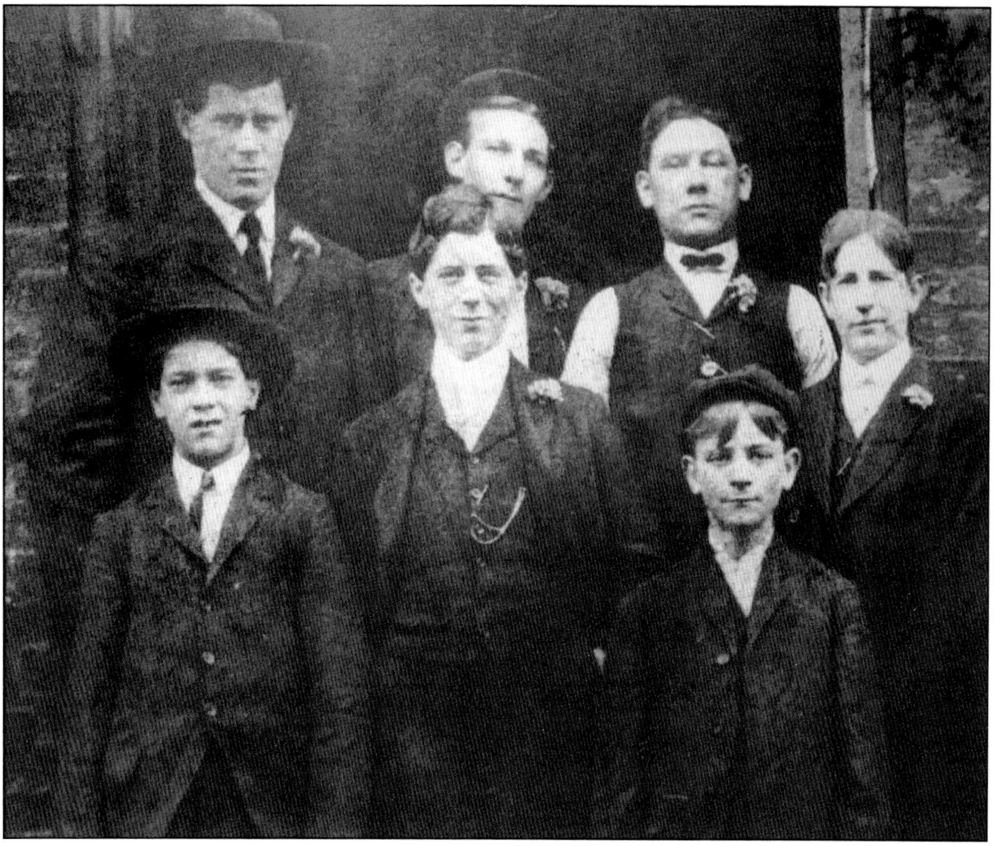

ANNUAL ELECTION
OF THE
Irish Building and Loan Company
Thursday, January 31, 1929

VOTE FOR 15 DIRECTORS

No. Shares........	No. Shares........
☐ Timothy Deasy	☐ Geo. Brown
☐ John B. Doyle	☐ W. J. Carter
☐ James Corcoran	☐ James Finley
☐ Wm. Coguill	☐ Michael Sullivan
☐ Thos. Fay	☐ T. J. Kenealey
☐ Thos. McGowan	☐ Louis Kull
☐ Geo. Nicholas	☐ Robt. Lanigan
☐ Dan C. Sullivan	☐ Jos. McGarr
☐ John C. Thompson	☐ Paul Sweeney
☐ Walter Walsh	☐ D. Byrns
☐ Florence Hahn	☐ Ed. Hackett
☐ Mike Grady	☐ F. Contadino
☐ Dan. L. O'Bryan	☐ John Elias
☐ Lawrence Frede	☐ M. J. Malloy
☐ F. J. Beutel	☐ Mary Rooney

Nominating Committee: DAN SULLIVAN, G. NICHOLAS, W. WALSH, JOHN CORCORAN, THOS. McGOWAN

In 1863, Joseph P. Carbery and Charles E. Callahan formed the Irish Building and Loan Company in Cincinnati, the first savings and loan established in the state of Ohio. Because banks would not lend money to many Irish, this new company was created to provide loans for building or purchasing homesteads. The first loan was made to John Donheen for $408, to be repaid at $1.05 per week and six percent interest. Pictured above in the early 1900s is Walter Walsh, standing in the middle front with his friends at a West End candy store. Walsh would become a director of the company, his name showing on the other image of a 1929 election ballot. The company was eventually acquired by Tri-State Building and Loan, and ultimately the assets were taken over by Chase Manhattan Bank as a result of the savings and loan crisis in the 1980s. (Above, courtesy of Stacey Walsh.)

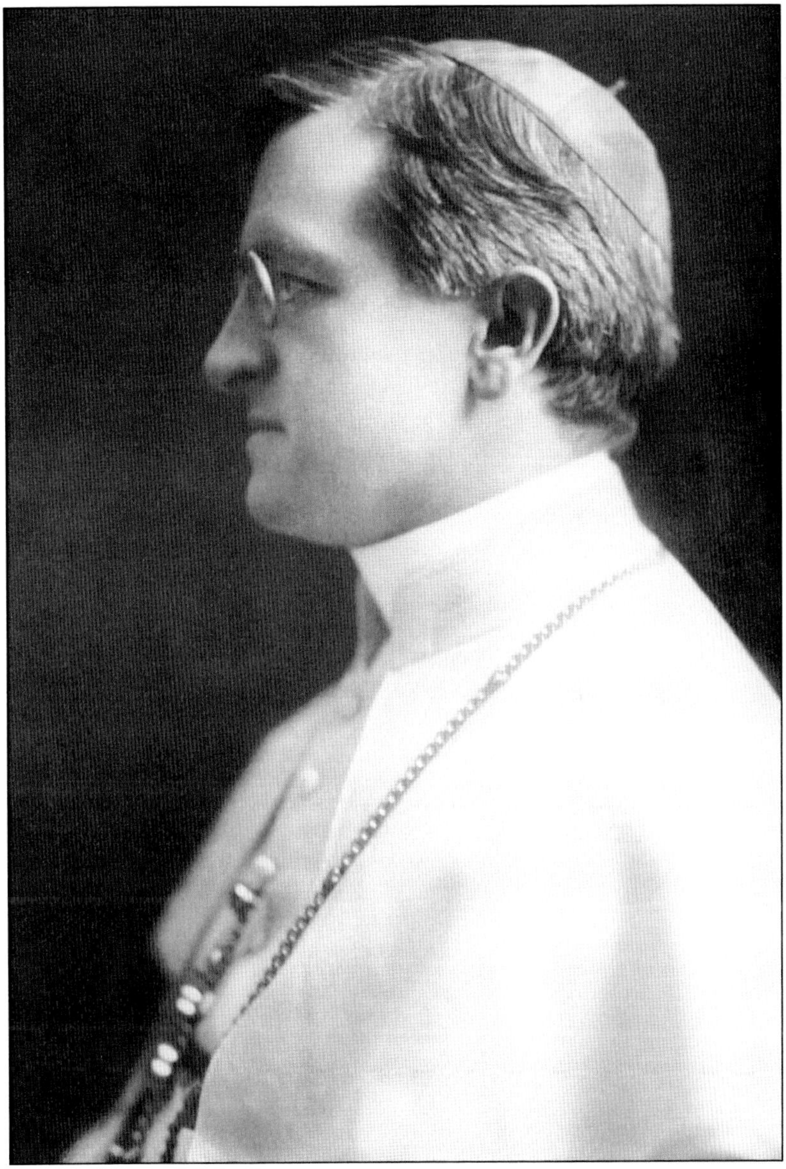

Archbishop John Timothy McNicholas was born in County Mayo in 1877 as plain "Timothy." When he was four years old, his family immigrated to America, landing in Philadelphia where he was educated in local parochial schools. After his ordination to the priesthood in the Dominican order in 1901, he took "John" as his religious name, and left for studies in Rome, where he earned his doctorate in sacred theology. Back home in America, McNicholas quickly rose through the ecclesiastic ranks, and in 1925 he became the fourth archbishop of Cincinnati and was installed at St. Peter in Chains Cathedral. McNicholas was a formidable clergyman with wide-ranging national influence. He emphasized social justice and during the Great Depression, denounced the unmitigated concentration of wealth as a crime. McNicholas also founded what would become the Catholic organization, the National Legion of Decency, and worked to raise the levels of parochial education. His early and outspoken condemnation of the persecution of Jews by Nazi Germany in the 1930s won him a diverse following throughout the country. He served the Archdiocese of Cincinnati until his death in 1950 at the age of 72.

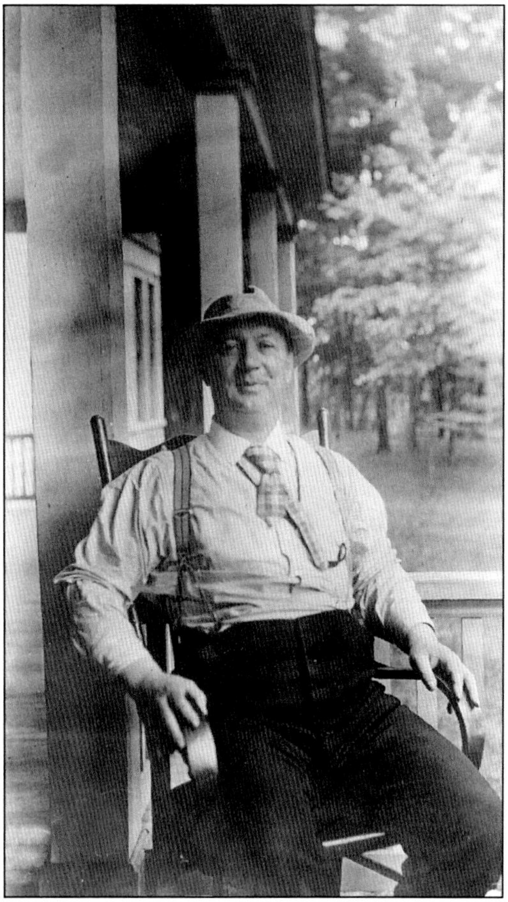

Born in St. Louis, the son of Irish immigrants, Francis J. Finn would make his mark in Cincinnati as a Jesuit educator and the author of more than two dozen juvenile Catholic novels. After graduating from Saint Louis University, Finn became a priest and began his teaching career in parochial boarding schools. While teaching at Marquette University, he began writing what would become his most famous novel, *Tom Playfair*, which was published in 1890, the year he came to Cincinnati to teach at St. Xavier College (pictured here). Finn's intent in his novels was to provide uplifting works for the typical American, Catholic boy. In fact, *Tom Playfair* was so influential that a teenager in Cincinnati took it as his pen name when his essay earned him the title of valedictorian of his Woodward High School class. He was the first African American to have that honor, and Theodore Berry would go on to become the first African American mayor of Cincinnati and a notable civil rights leader. (Courtesy of Xavier University Library.)

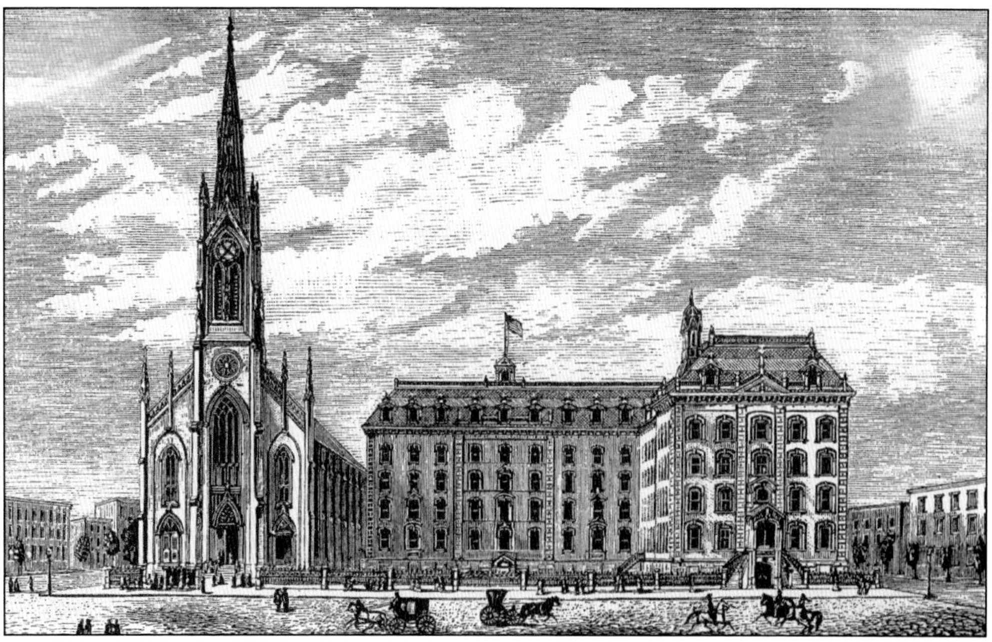

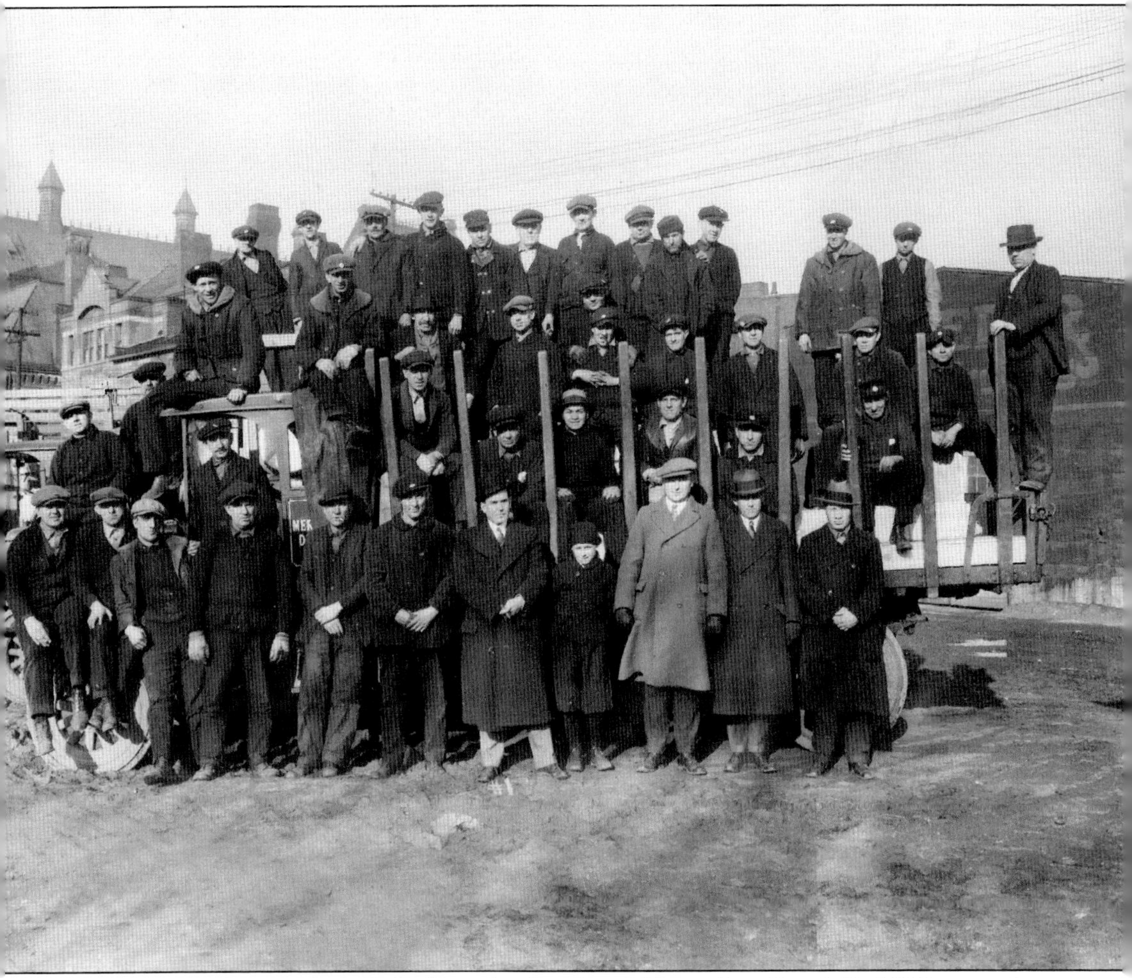

Pictured near Cincinnati Music Hall along the abandoned Miami-Erie Canal, Neil O'Brien and his employees at the Merchants Drayage Company pose before beginning work on what would be Cincinnati's ill-fated subway project. Since its completion in 1845, the canal had carried decades of people and goods down to the Ohio River. In the bed of the drained canal in 1920, O'Brien's firm helped excavate and haul away the dirt for the construction of the tunnels. Eight years later, the subway was shelved due to engineering and financial problems, and Central Parkway now covers the old path of the canal. The workers for the Merchants firm were continuing a long line of Irish workers in America's tunnels, railways, and canals over the previous century. It was always dangerous work. In digging the Whitewater Canal tunnel in the 1840s in nearby Cleves, for example, four Irishmen were killed in a wall collapse. It is said they were taken to a high spot and buried in unmarked graves, an area that now lies beneath Taylor High School. Whether their ghosts are active there or not is for the students to say. (Courtesy of Pat Mallory.)

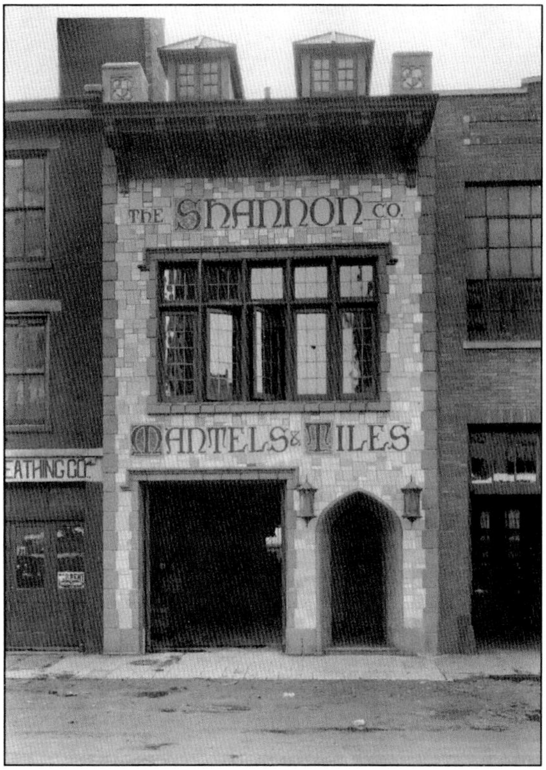

During the course of the subway project in the 1920s, the Rapid Transit Commission of Cincinnati hired a photographer to document the work. Several times throughout every day, photographs were taken of the construction progress, as well as the damage caused to homes and buildings along the route. Developed from 8-inch-by-10-inch negatives, the photographs provide remarkable detail and clarity of the city from Fairview Heights through Over-the-Rhine. As the subway construction passed such landmarks as the Windisch-Muhlhauser brewery and Cincinnati Music Hall, it gave the photographer the opportunity to create images that now preserve a view of long-forgotten, everyday, family-run businesses. In the left photograph, the Shannon Company that produced decorative fireplace mantels and tiles—very popular in a city that embraced Rookwood-style ceramics—shows a bit of Celtic design on the front of the building.

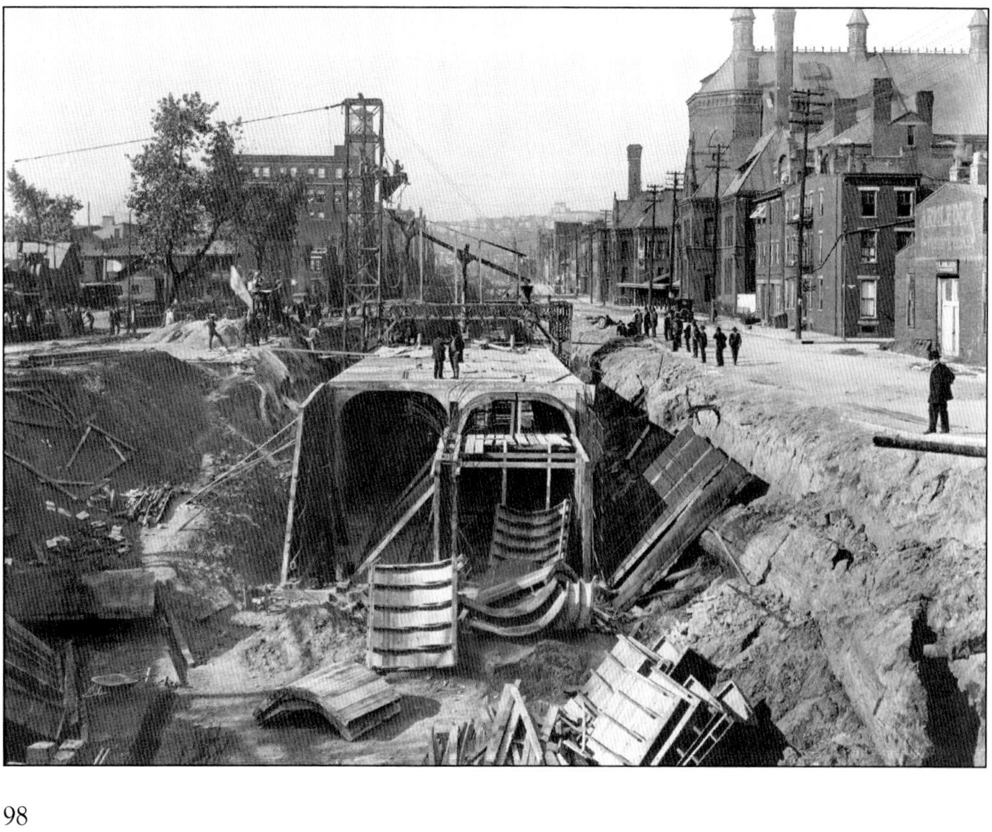

Six

"But We Dance to the Music, and We Dance"

The vitality of Cincinnati Irish culture over 200 years can not be minimized, but it has been especially vibrant since the 1950s. Individuals such as Dick Ormond, Bob Castellini, Tommy Hogan, Bob Fitzpatrick, Robert Smith, Ray Carr, and dozens of other men and women help form Irish life in the Queen City as time has moved to the 21st century. Performers like Patrick Quinn, the Bloody Tinth, the students in the Riley School of Irish Music, Ceol Mhor, Dark Moll, Silver Arm, and the Unlucky Charms, as well as the annual Celtic Festival enliven the arts, as do writers like Cathal Liam, Jinny Powers Berten, Norah Holt, and Michael McEvilley.

For every ethnic group, their culture consists of ideas, ideals, and artifacts that are created and preserved, all to pass down to the next generation. It is the continuing celebration of culture that keeps it alive, whether it is an artifact like a Hibernian parade ribbon, an idea, song, poem, or organization manifesting pride or the ideal that there is human experience worth preserving, that in moving across the ocean to a new land, opportunities, and the maintenance of a community will result. The Cincinnati Reds may don green caps and shamrock emblems now and again, and the beer may flow and the green, orange, and white may wave every St. Patrick's Day, but it is the intangible things such as the core family sense of "Irishness" like that of Anne Keehan Sullivan's family on the West Side, or the joy in hearing a family story that marks the legacy of the Cincinnati Irish.

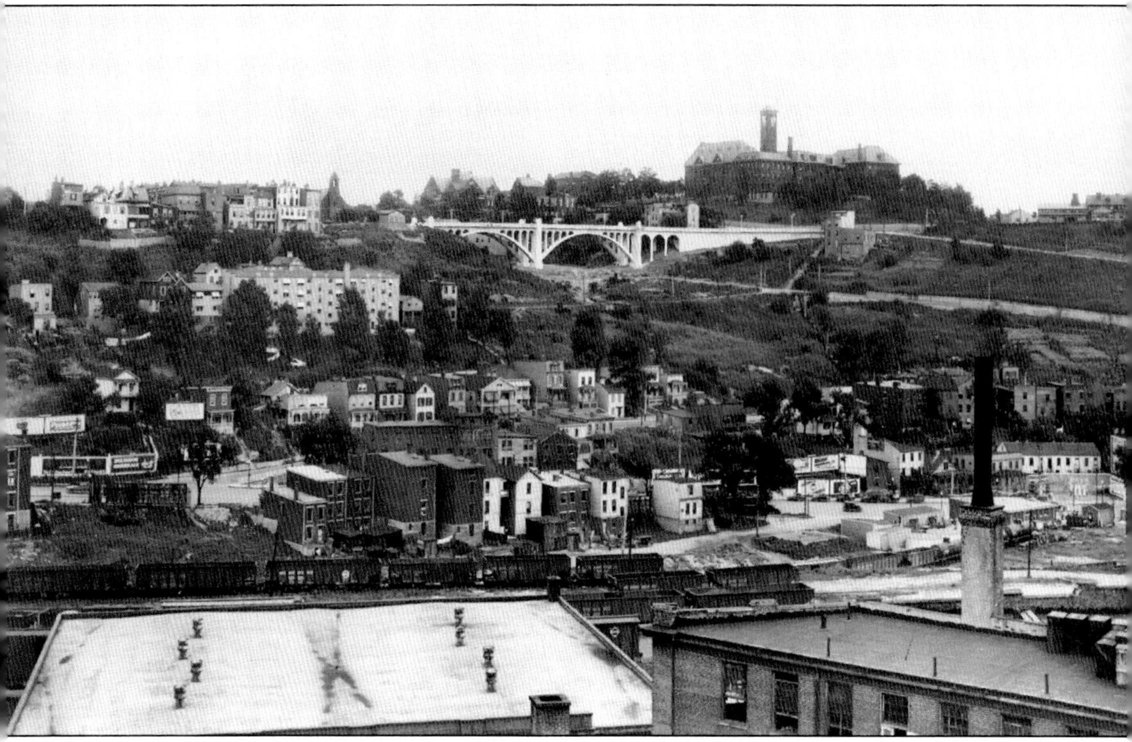

Viewed from a downtown rooftop, the neighborhood of Mount Adams in the late 1940s is still very much a working-class enclave of Irish and Germans. The Holy Cross monastery can be seen rising above the Ida Street bridge, along with Cincinnati's ubiquitous row houses. At the time this photograph was taken, Mount Adams was the typical urban neighborhood: schools, stores, and saloons were just a short walk from home, and work was found either right there in the neighborhood or down the inclined railway to the basin of Cincinnati. By 1950, the Irish had lived there for nearly a century, but over the next few decades, Mount Adams would undergo dramatic change. Families moved to other neighborhoods, and the infrastructure and real estate declined. By the 1970s, though it was still a modest neighborhood, revitalization was in the works to the point that Mount Adams today is an affluent place to live. Still, it retains its traditional architecture and there remain small pockets of the original ethnic atmosphere.

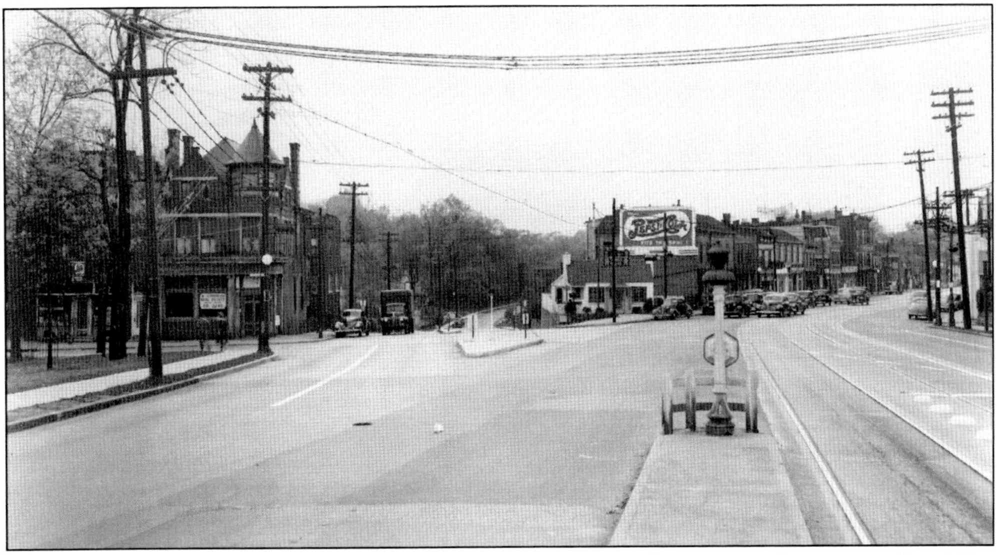

Once a traditional Irish and German neighborhood, O'Bryonville also was changing in the 1950s. Street improvements to Madison Road that bisected the neighborhood invited changes to the traditional businesses. O'Bryonville would lose its Irish character as the older families died out or moved away, but its rebirth as a shopping destination would keep the neighborhood's name alive. In 1994, four decades after this photograph was taken, O'Bryon's Irish Pub would even revitalize that local Irish heritage.

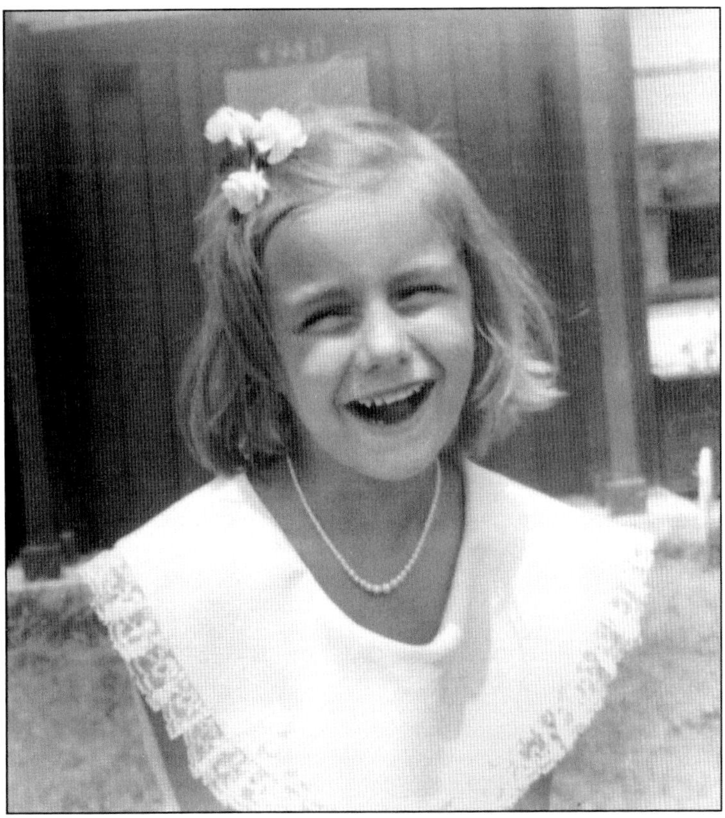

Susie Kauck recalls that as a child in the 1950s, her mother would sometimes entertain her with impromptu performances of Irish dance. Kauck's mother was raised in O'Bryonville, and in the days before there were schools in Cincinnati that formally taught such dancing, children learned them from their families. As her mother jigged about the room, young Susie clapped in time and laughed along with her mother while attempting a few steps herself. (Courtesy of Susie Kauck.)

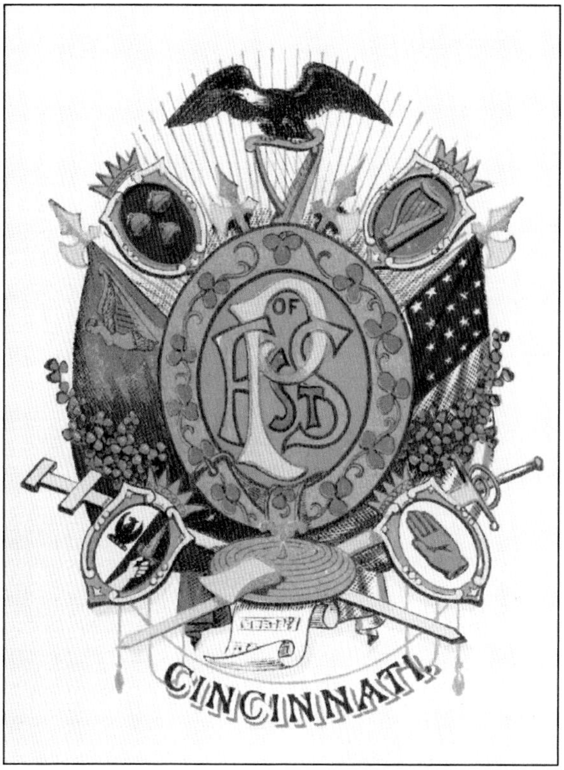

By the mid-20th century, the Friendly Sons of Saint Patrick were solidly established in Cincinnati as a society devoted to the appreciation of Irish heritage. In 1943, Judge William J. Dammerell served the organization as president. A longtime member of the Friendly Sons, Dammerell brought a sense of his judicious temperament as well as a strong measure of conviviality. Rarely equaled in his embrace of the good life, Dammerell maintained a brood of Irish wolfhounds to which he was completely devoted. In fact, when one of his favorites died, he took pen to paper in lament: "To numb too weep, too desolate for tears or pain-releasing sight. A puppy stumbles up to us—Kings do not die!" Dammerell (right) is pictured below in the 1950s with two German American friends, noblemen Klemens von Staffenberg (left) and Carl Alexander von Volborth (middle). (Below, courtesy of Christopher von Volborth.)

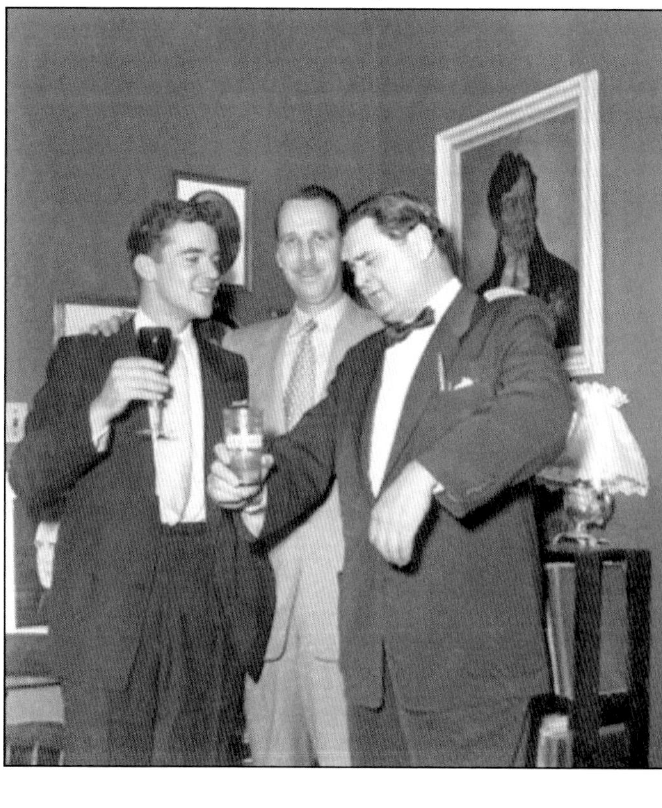

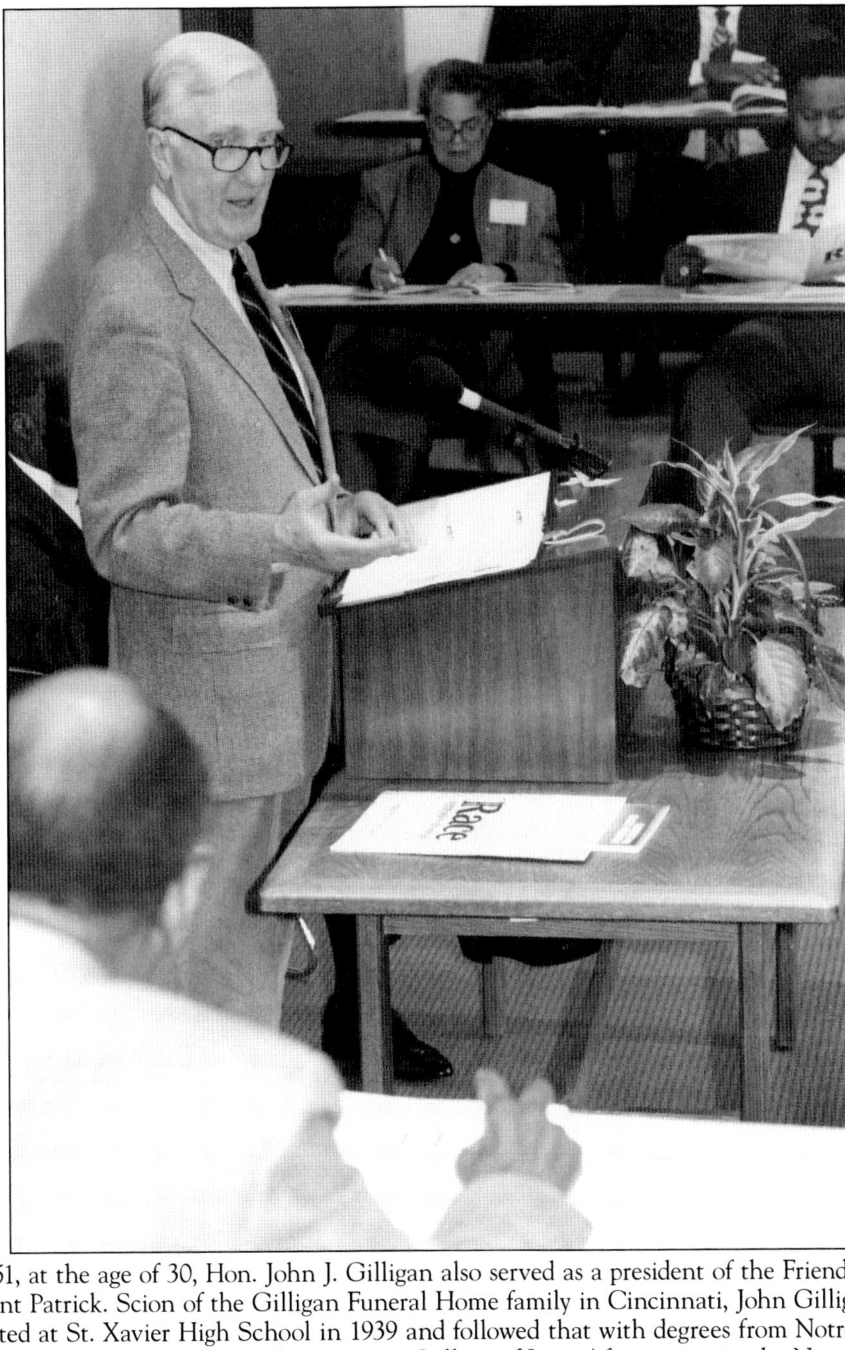

In 1951, at the age of 30, Hon. John J. Gilligan also served as a president of the Friendly Sons of Saint Patrick. Scion of the Gilligan Funeral Home family in Cincinnati, John Gilligan was educated at St. Xavier High School in 1939 and followed that with degrees from Notre Dame University and the University of Cincinnati College of Law. After a stint in the Navy during World War II, he taught at Xavier University before entering politics, becoming successively a Cincinnati councilman, a US congressman, and the governor of Ohio from 1917 to 1975. His public service continued after his years of elective office as he was named to the United States Agency for International Development and the Institute for Public Policy. Closely tied not only to Cincinnati's Irish community but to the welfare of the entire city as well, John Gilligan also was a member of the Cincinnati Board of Education from 1999 into the 21st century.

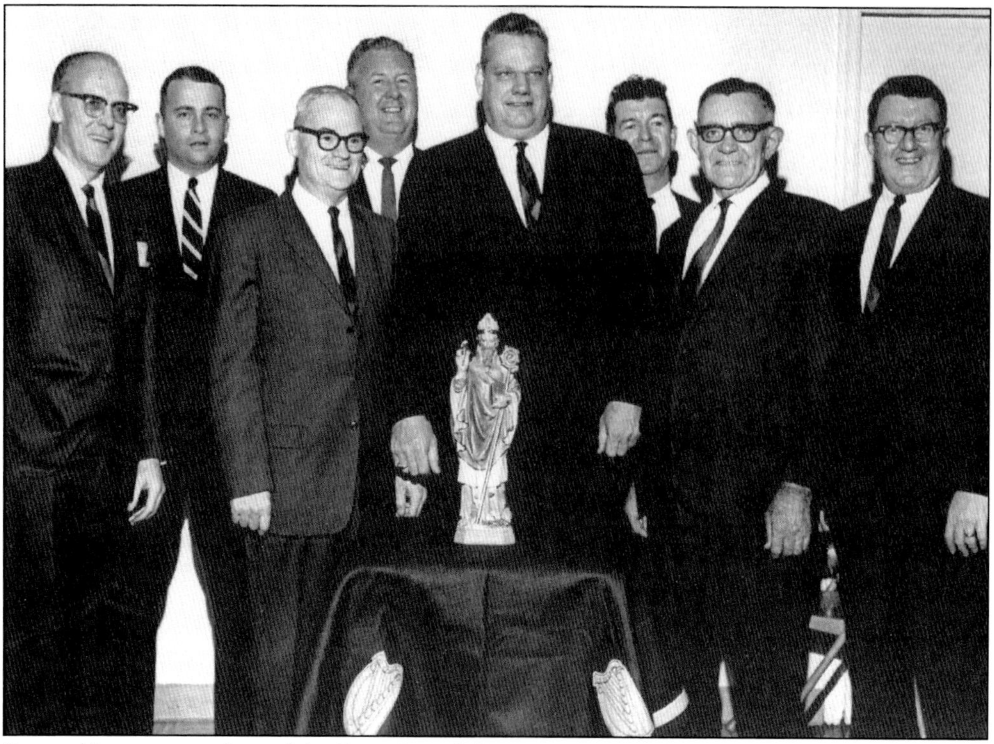

Pictured here are members of the Saint Patrick Division No. 1 of the Ancient Order of Hibernians (AOH) in Cincinnati. From left to right are Bill McCluskey, Frank Geary, Joe Keane, Tom O'Brien, Jim Murphy, Hal McKenzie, Jim Kearney, and Jack Tracey. The AOH, with the leadership of O'Brien, Murphy, R. Murray Fogarty, and another member, Michael Murphy, would lead the effort to restart the city's St. Patrick's Day parade in 1967. (Courtesy of Pat Mallory.)

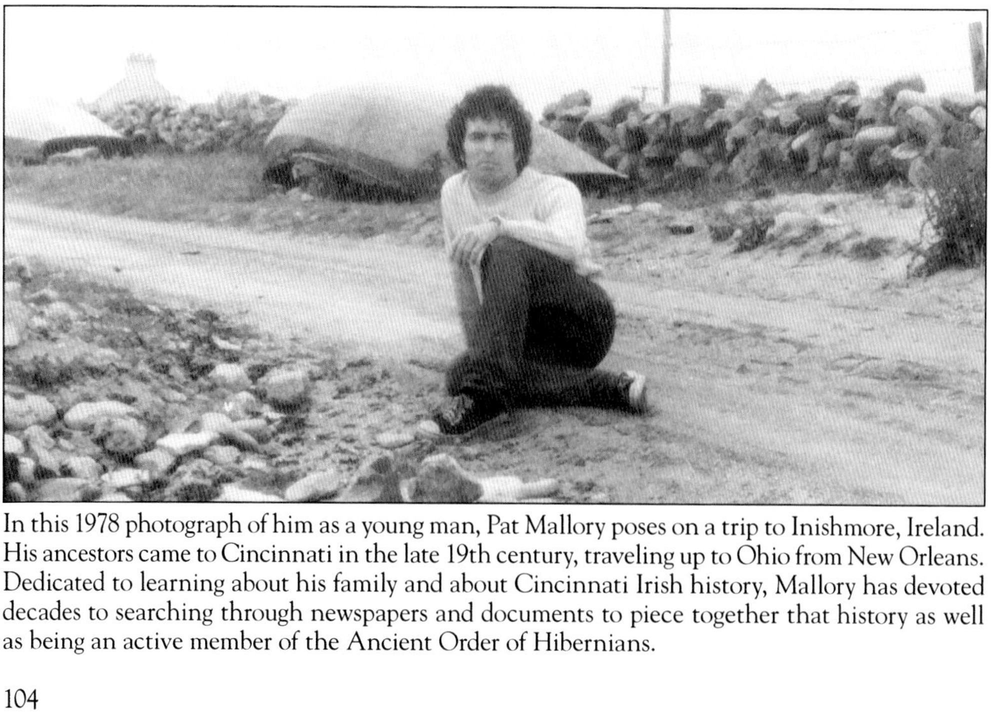

In this 1978 photograph of him as a young man, Pat Mallory poses on a trip to Inishmore, Ireland. His ancestors came to Cincinnati in the late 19th century, traveling up to Ohio from New Orleans. Dedicated to learning about his family and about Cincinnati Irish history, Mallory has devoted decades to searching through newspapers and documents to piece together that history as well as being an active member of the Ancient Order of Hibernians.

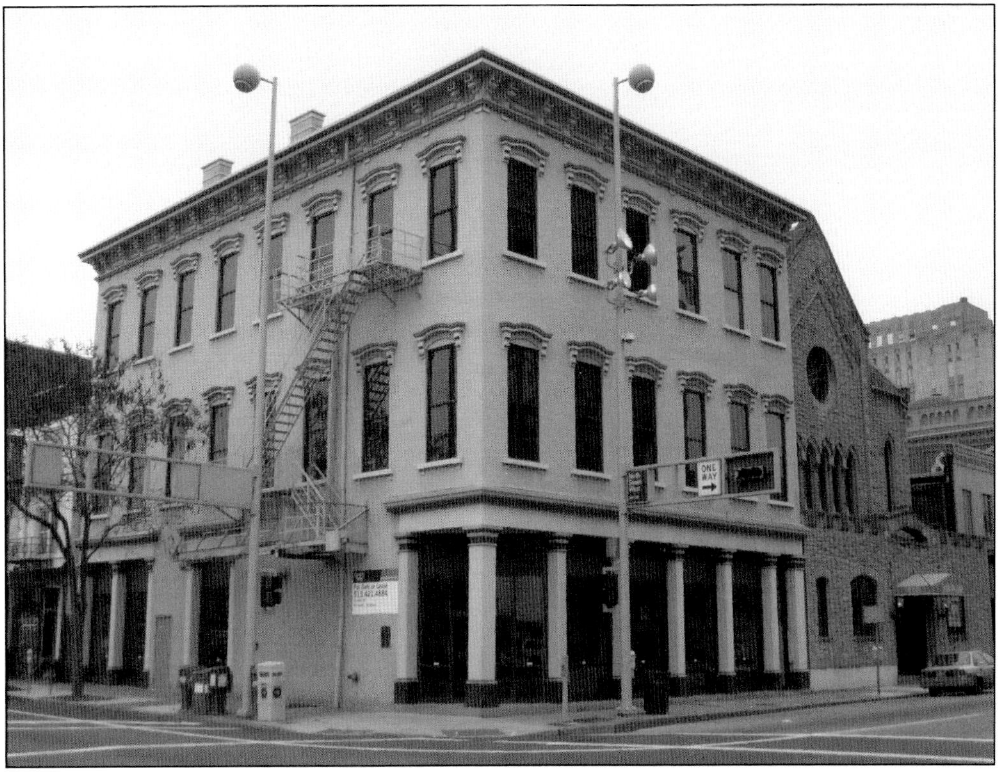

As it stands today, the Hibernian Building at 814 Plum Street is a physical reminder of the city's early Irish days. The three-story structure, also called Hibernia Hall, was designated as a historic property on Friday, March 12, 2004, as a kick-off to that year's St. Patrick's Day celebration. The ceremony included the dedication of a plaque that was mounted on the West Ninth Street side, the text indicating the building's importance. At the time, the Hibernian Building housed the Freedman, Gibson & White advertising and communications agency, but on November 17, 2011, the Hibernian Building was sold at auction.

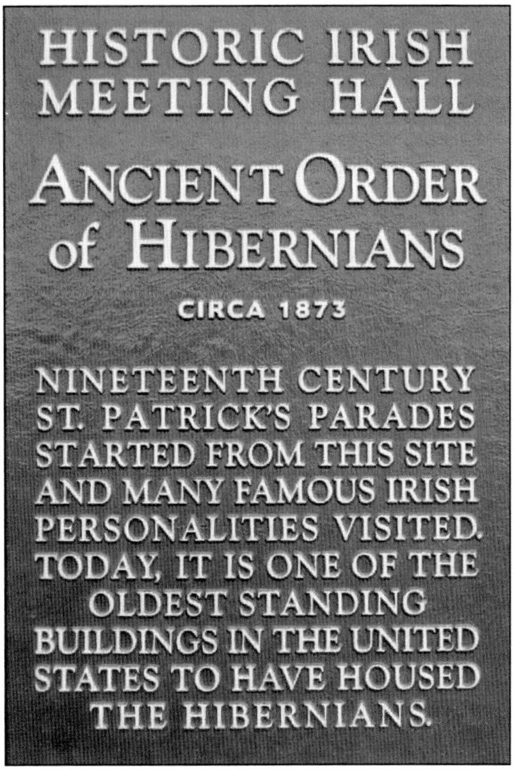

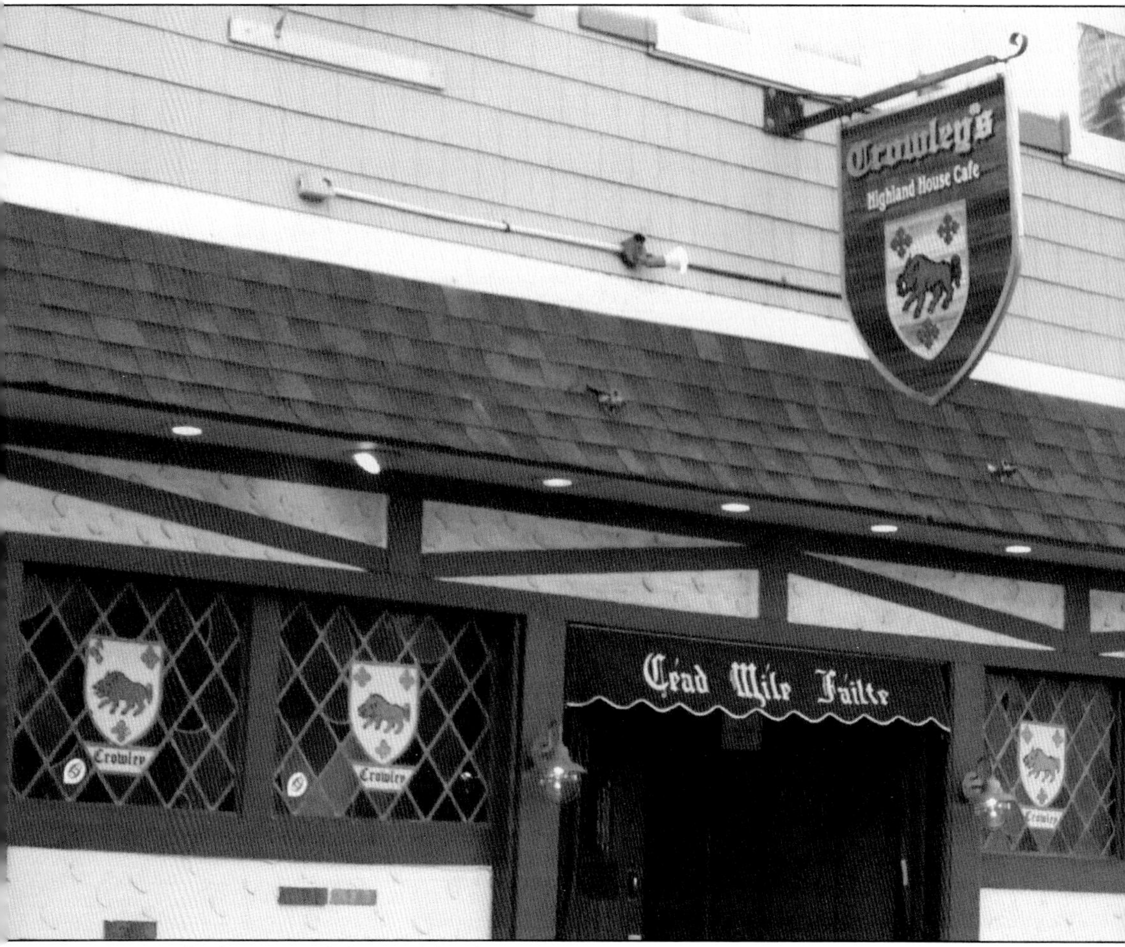

Once the location of the Highland House Café (and the Highland House Social Club inside), Crowley's is the oldest Irish pub in Cincinnati. William Crowley opened its doors in 1937, and throughout its history, the hilly, narrow streets of Mount Adams made every house within walking distance of the bar. It was the quintessential neighborhood tavern, a place for the Irish and German working class families to enjoy a few beers and a lot of good company. It has always sat nearly cheek to jowl with Holy Cross-Immaculata Church across the street, which is fitting considering the strong Catholic clientele who crossed its threshold over the years. And, for the annual Praying of the Steps each Easter season, it is said that more than one pilgrim climbing up the hill prefers to slip into Crowley's for a bit of refreshment.

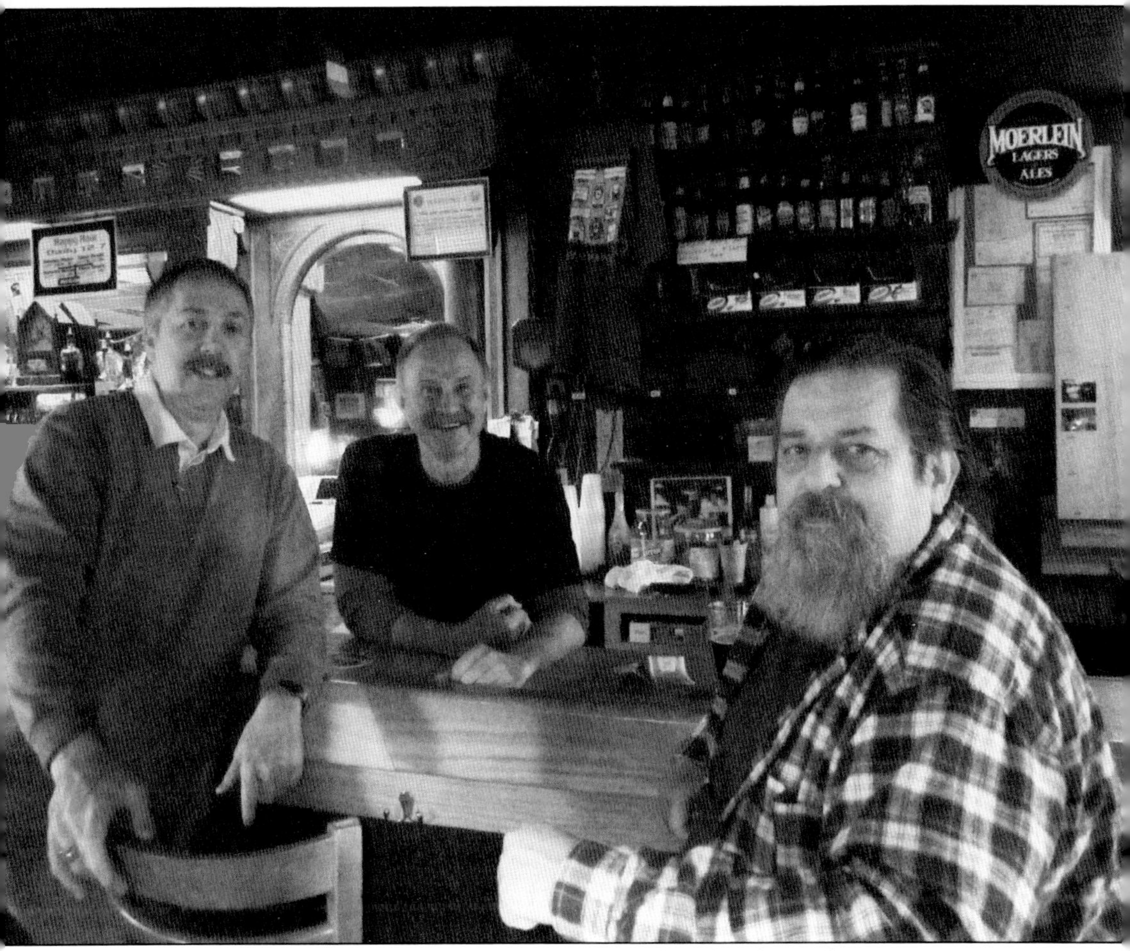

Crowley's Irish heritage has withstood the changes in the neighborhood over the past generation, as has the ownership. Whether it has been David, Tim "Bebo," or Kevin, the Crowley clan still calls the pub home, as do a score of extended relatives. The decor, the tap offerings, and the close relationship it has to the annual stealing of the St. Patrick statue from the church is a vital part of the city's Celtic heritage. And while tourists, college students, and people throughout the city tend to flock to Crowley's in the evenings and on weekends, the afternoon crowd still maintains the old family atmosphere of the neighborhood. Many of the longtime residents have moved away, but they often return for a few beers. In this photograph on a typical afternoon, Andy Clepper, who grew up in Mount Adams and attended parochial school there, Mike Bucke, and bartender Steve Beverage hold down the bar and tell a few stories.

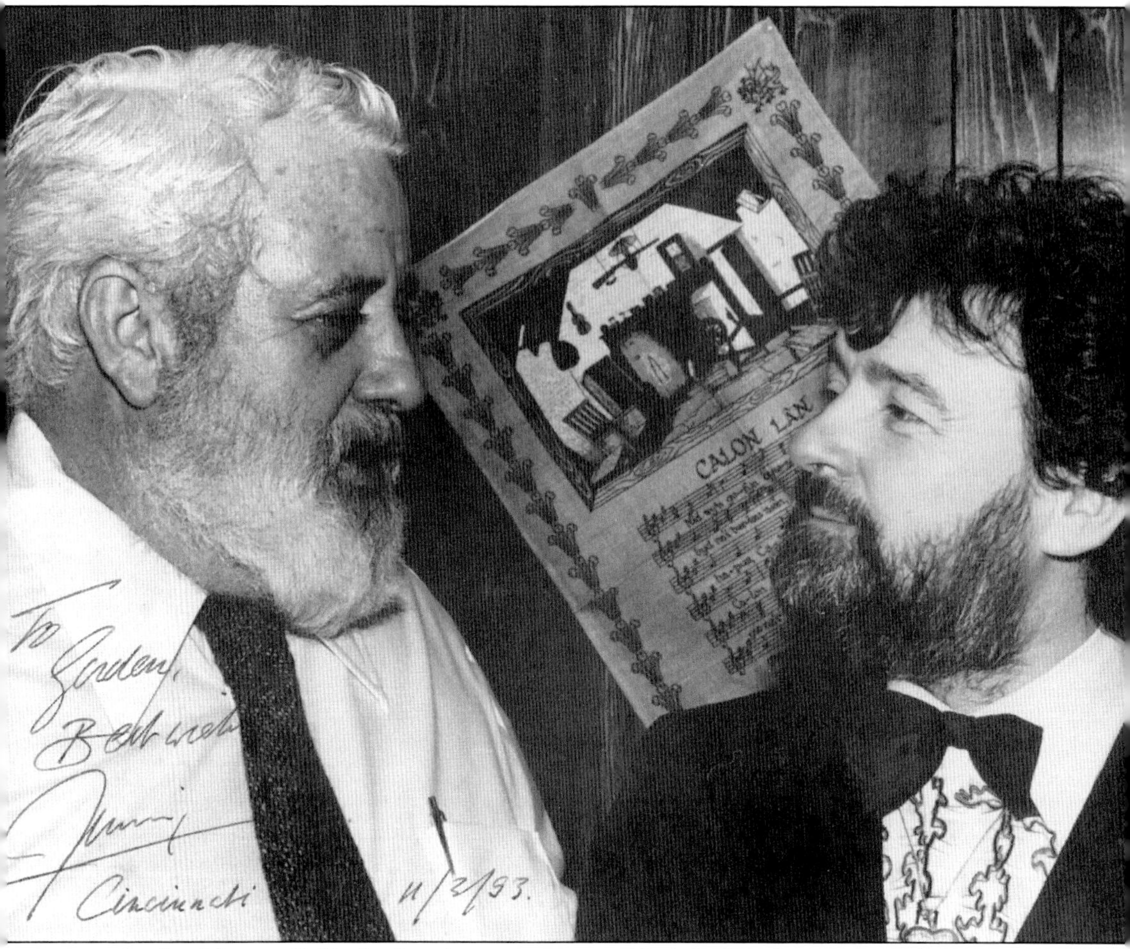

Gordon Thomas (left), the founding proprietor of Hap's Irish Pub in Hyde Park, was a man who embraced rugby, good *craic,* excellent beer, soccer, darts, and the neighborhood. Though he was not Irish himself, Thomas loved the pubs he visited on a trip to Ireland, so he opened Hap's in 1975. The pub soon became a home for the Irish in Cincinnati, either homegrown or visiting from home. Ever ethnically ecumenical, at one time Thomas served as president of the American-Irish Club, which listed over 200 members of multiple nationalities. Thomas also arranged rugby and soccer trips to Ireland for local teams and welcomed the Irish squads who came to Cincinnati. Occasionally, visiting musicians popped into the pub, including Irish flautist James Galway (right), straight from a performance at Cincinnati Music Hall. Thomas's love for all things Celtic is shown by the music pinned to the wall behind him: "Calon Lan," the beautiful Welsh hymn played before every national rugby team match in Wales. (Courtesy of Danny Thomas.)

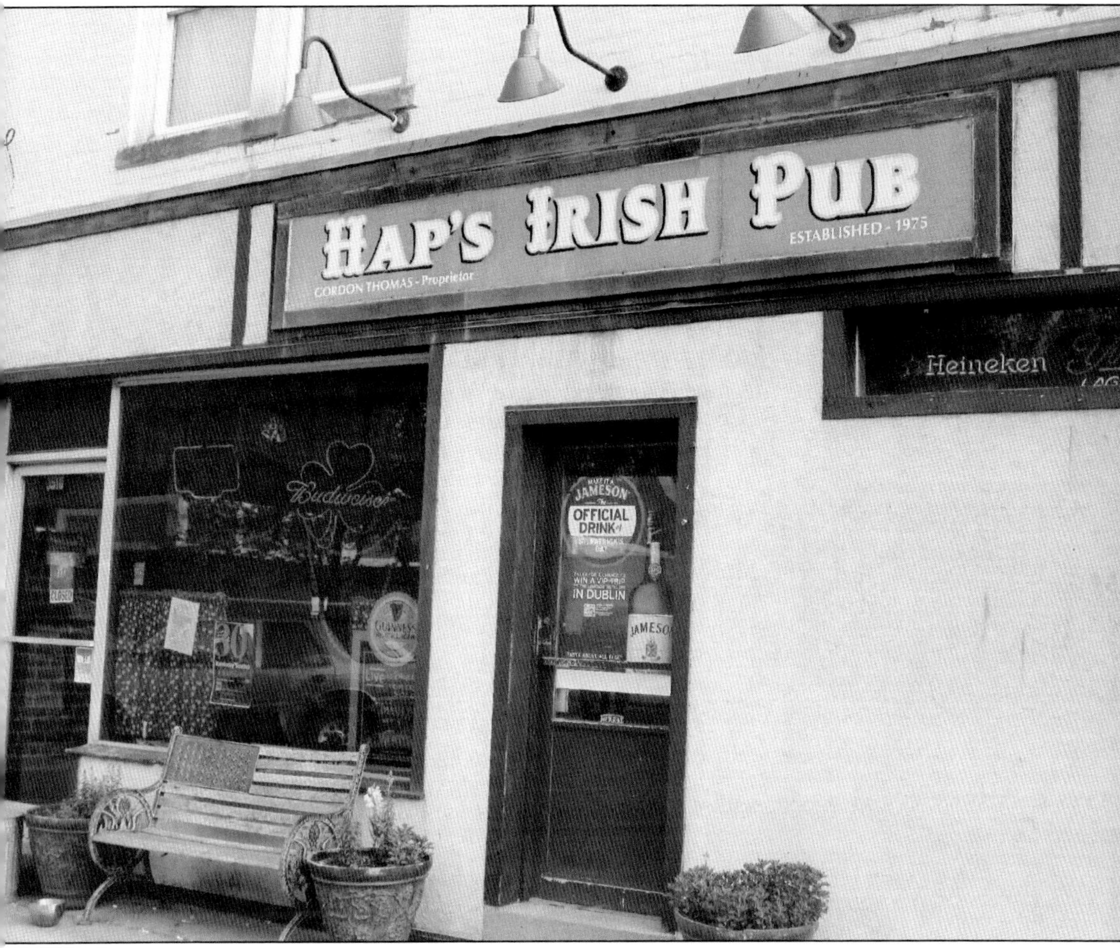

Now run by Gordon's son Danny Thomas, Hap's Pub still attracts a loyal clientele of Irish new to Cincinnati as well as the neighborhood regulars. Hap's was the first pub in Cincinnati to sell Guinness on tap. When Danny was in college, his father wanted to make a great event for the pub for a St. Patrick's Day celebration. The nearest distributor for Guinness at that time was four hours away in Cleveland, so young Thomas was instructed by his father to drive up there and bring back a couple of kegs. Eight hours and one flat tire later, Danny was back in the pub and the taps were pulled. But that was not the end of his day. Gordon instructed Danny to tend bar while he conversed with the pub patrons, so after the long drive, Danny put in another several hours behind the bar!

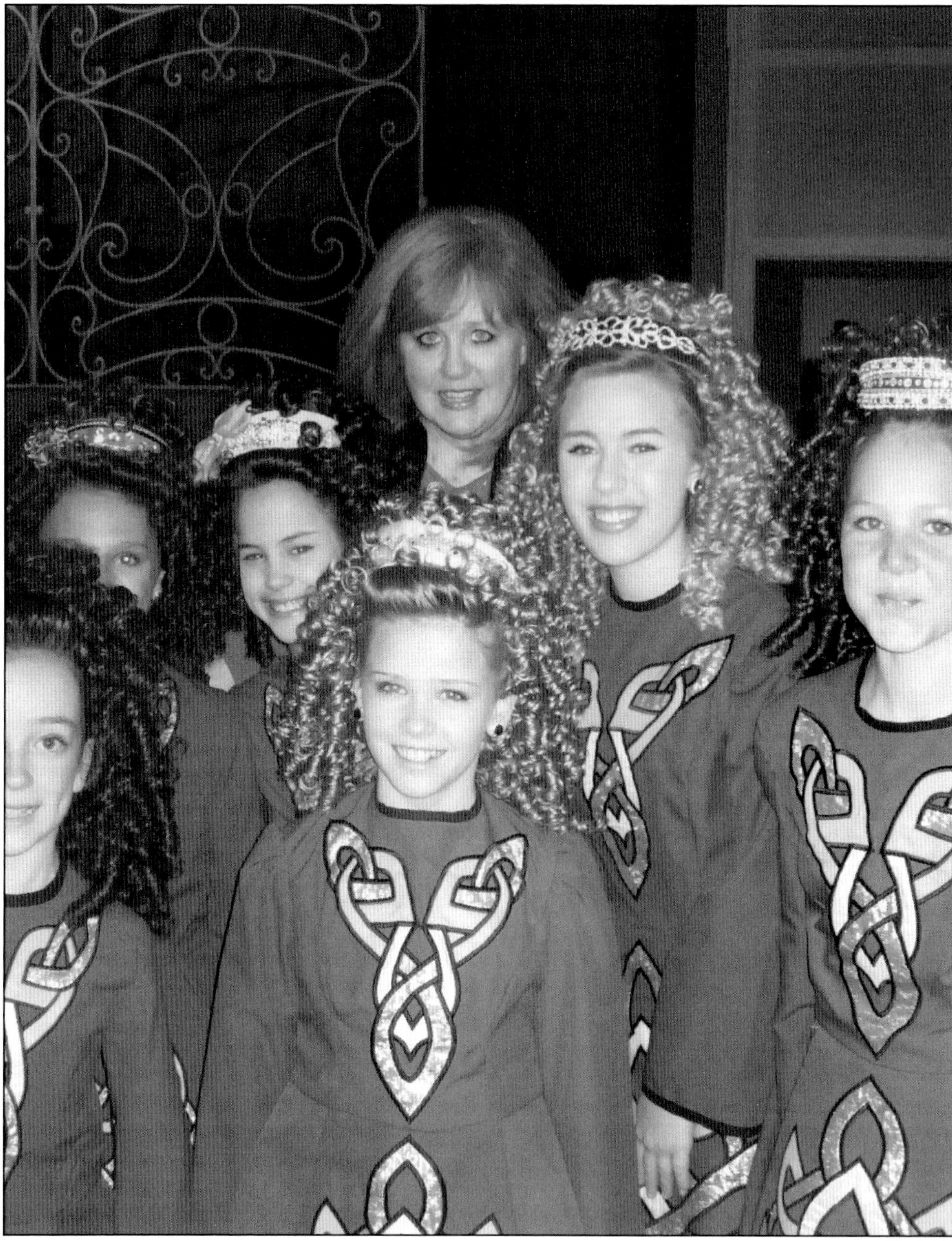

Mary McGing Duckworth is the founder and artistic director of Cincinnati's award-winning McGing Irish Dancers. McGing, whose parents emigrated from Ireland, began Irish dance herself at a Hibernian school at the age of seven and founded her troupe in 1981 while she was a student at the University of Cincinnati. In the decades since then, the dancers have won national and world accolades for their accomplished performances, and from a beginning enrollment of just a score of dancers, it has now grown to over 300. Pictured at top center with a group of students, McGing is also assisted by a teaching corps of Terry Gillian, Megan Collins, Shannon Henderson, Sarah McGing, Christine Carey Steele, Katie Behrle, Monica Bowen, Terry Sexsmith, Mary Kate Reilly, and Patti McGeever.

At the *ceili* presented by the McGing Irish Dancers and the Cincinnati Irish Cultural Society in February 2012, the ballroom at the music hall rang out with Caledonian pipes and drums as the dancers entered. From the smallest newcomers to adults, the dancing showcased a whirl of curly wigs and high stepping. In the photograph at right, some of the more experienced teen dancers perform one of their championship numbers, and in the photograph below, eight-year-old Erin Siler, after a year's instruction with the McGing school, takes a turn with her group.

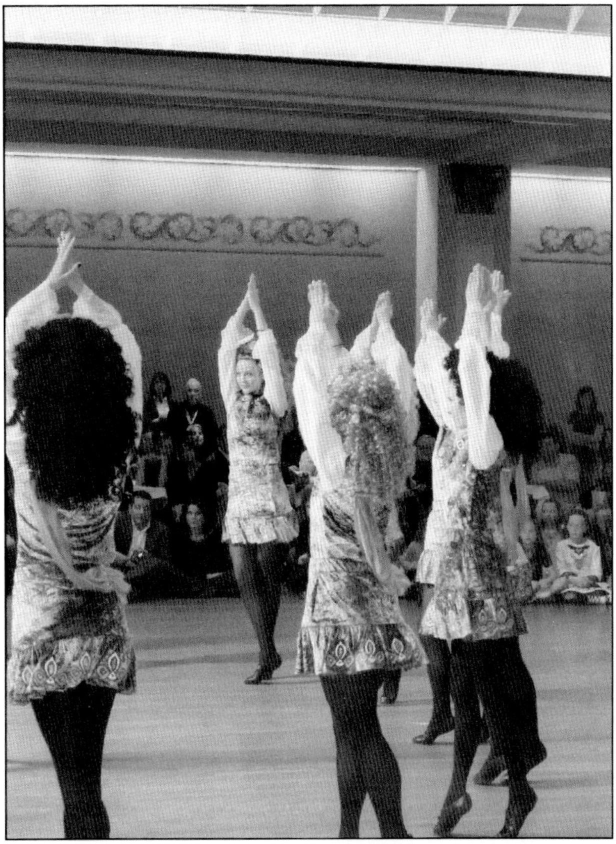

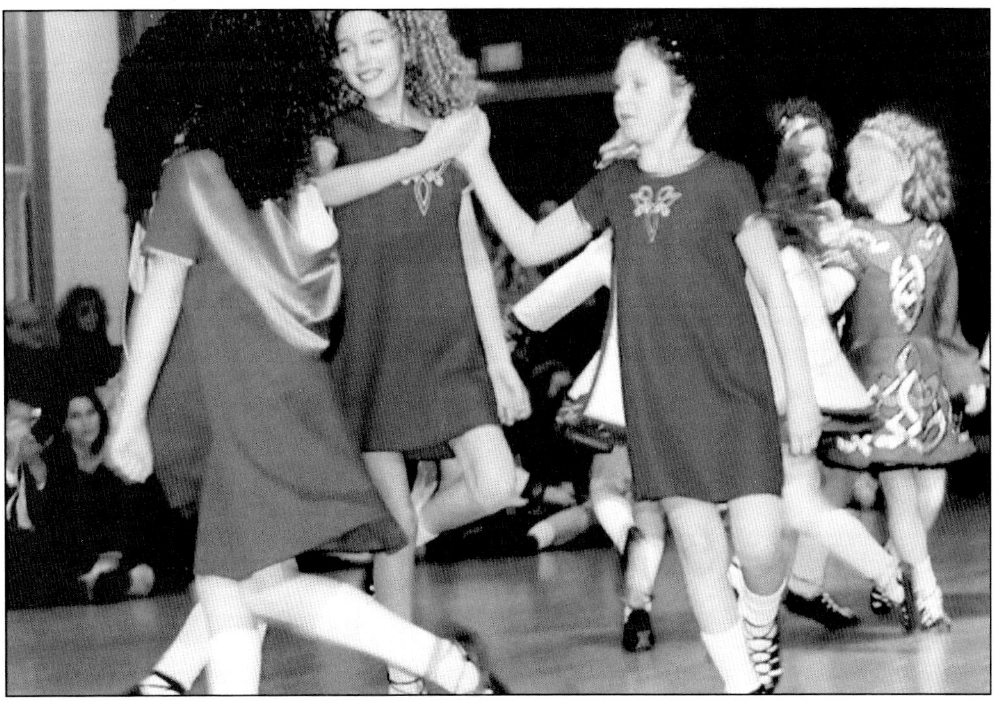

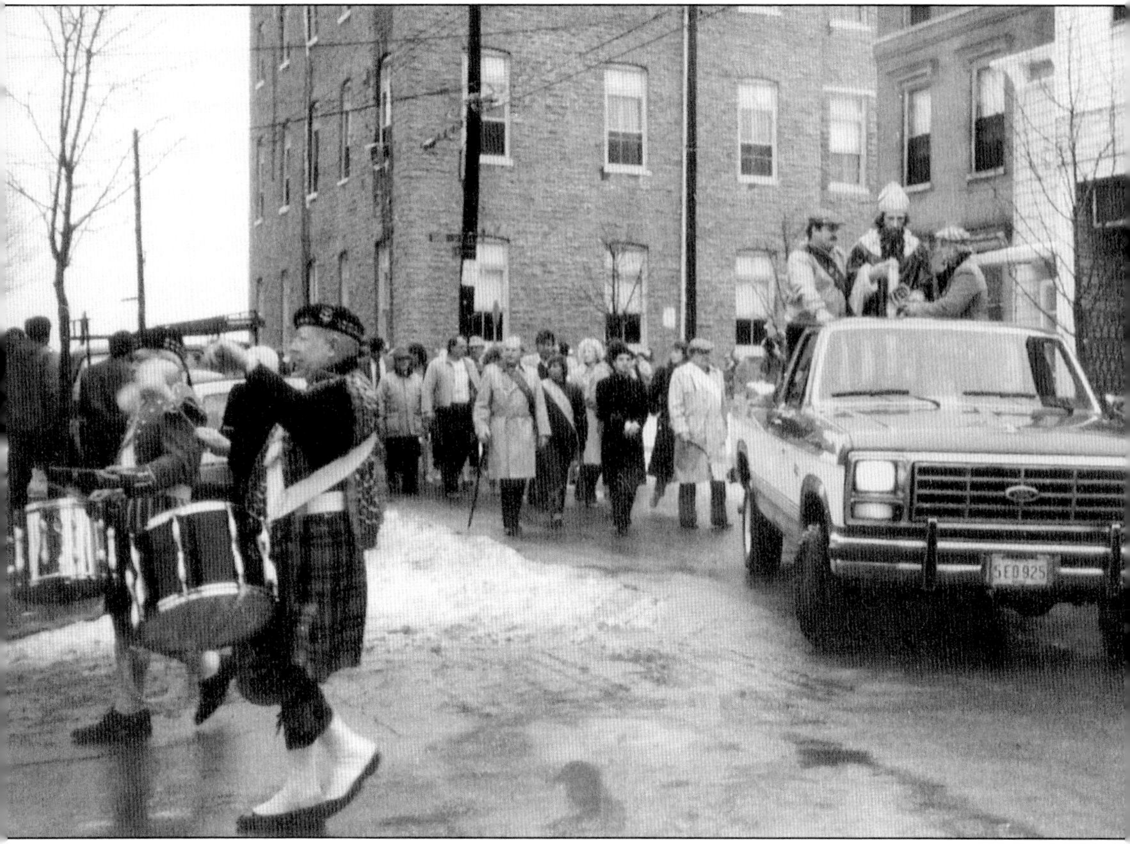

On a cold March morning, the Irish once again abscond with the statue of St. Patrick in Mount Adams. A tradition that had its beginning on March 15, 1970, the annual theft is now part of the festivities before the annual St. Patrick's Day Parade. Because of declining numbers of the congregations in the mid-1960s, the Irish Holy Cross Church was administratively consolidated with the German Immaculata Church. Holy Cross's parishioners were notified in 1970 when their church was finally closed. Jim Crowley asked Father Wilfrid Flanery if the St. Patrick statue could be moved to the German church to make the Irish more at home. The move could not be official, but the church door was conveniently left unlocked one night. Several Irish men in the parish took the statue and moved it to their "new" church. From that point, it became an annual event for the Ancient Order of Hibernians to steal the statue and hold it hostage until the parade. (Courtesy of Nancy Riesenbeck and Kevin Crowley.)

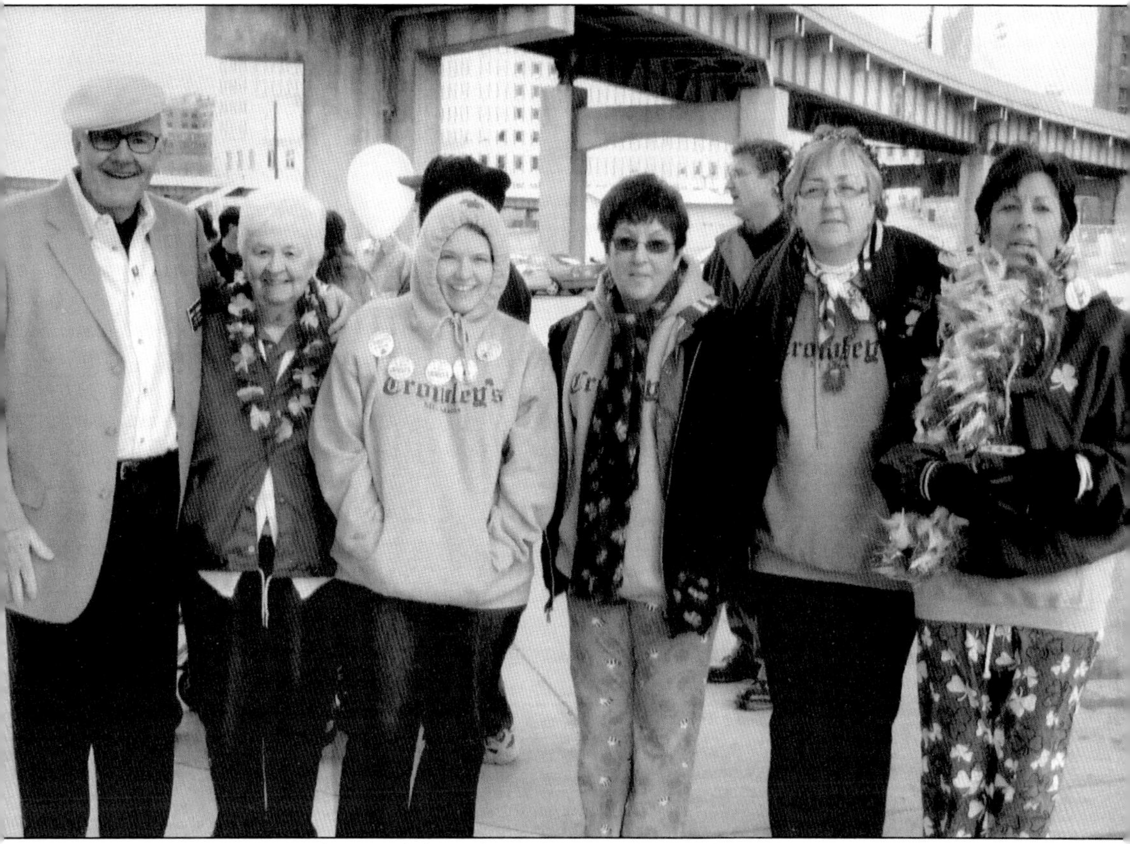

It seems, too, that the Crowley family has always been in the middle of the mischief, just as they have always been a stalwart part of the parade. A tale is told that one time, several drinkers over at Crowley's stole St. Patrick before the Hibernians could get there and left in its place a tiny St. Patrick statue. The statue was hidden away in a back room at the pub until the thieves released it to the Hibernians. Presumably, the Hibernians appreciated the joke, as the theft is always a time of good-humored celebration. For decades now, a contingent of Crowleys marches through the streets of downtown. In this photograph, dressed out in the holiday shamrock best, are (from left to right) David and Chick Crowley, Jill Kaffenberger, Nancy Riesenbeck, Jibber Stanley, and Colleen Munninghoff. (Courtesy of Nancy Riesenbeck and Kevin Crowley.)

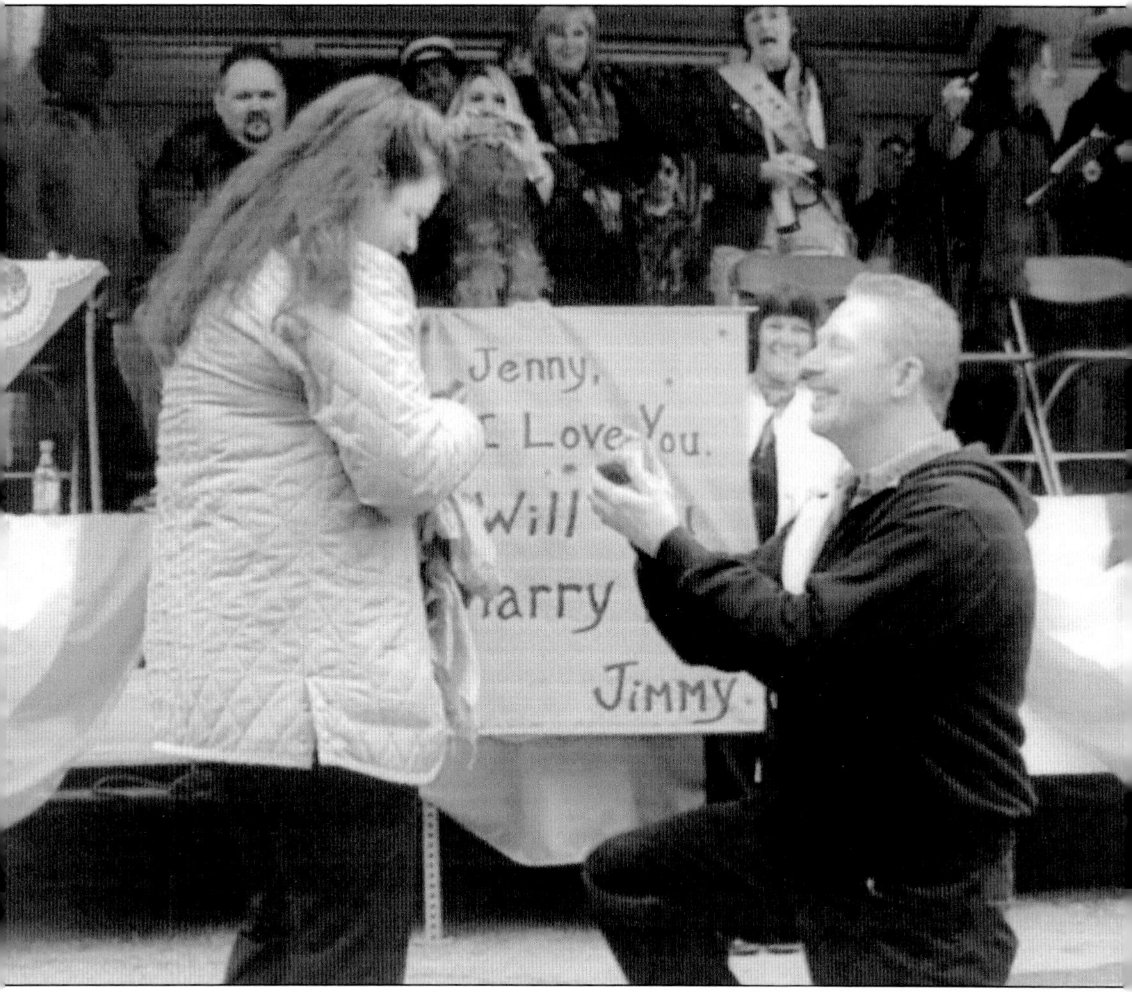

A new element of the St. Patrick's Day celebrations was Jim Williams's proposal to his girlfriend during the 2010 parade. As he marched in front of the reviewing stand, he dropped to his knee and popped the question to Jennifer Bell. As the crowd cheered him on, she said yes. In 2012, Williams served as the public address announcer for the parade.

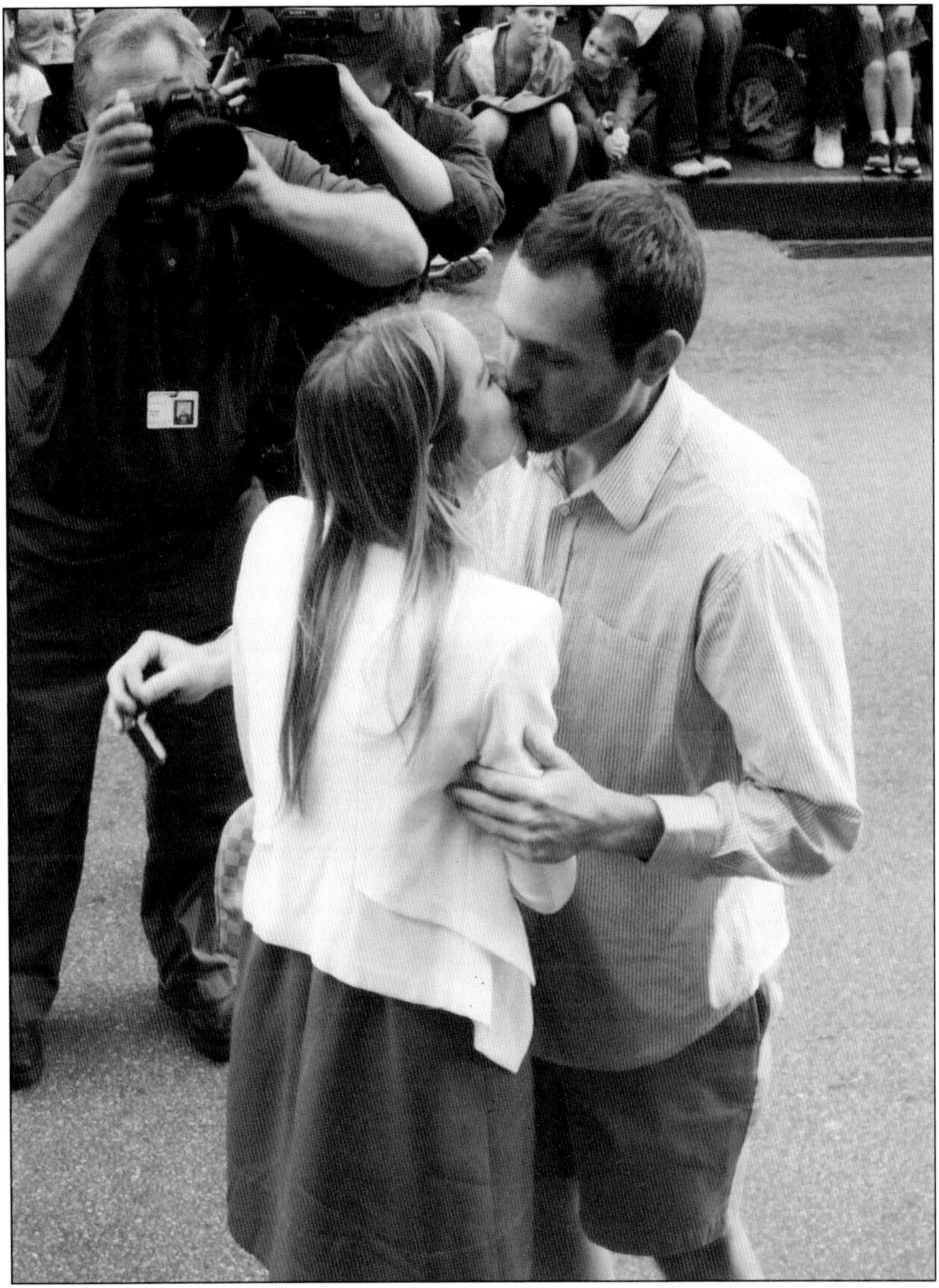

In 2012, parade-goers witnessed another marriage proposal. Grant Sharp, who had attended the parade for several years, thought it was the perfect spot to call out his girlfriend from the crowd. The marching bands stepped in place, the convertibles carrying officials idled, and the Shriners' mini-cars stopped in the middle of their figure eights as Sharp formally proposed in front of thousands of witnesses. He was backed by a banner that read, "Mary Patten, you are my pot of gold. Will you marry me?" Mary said yes.

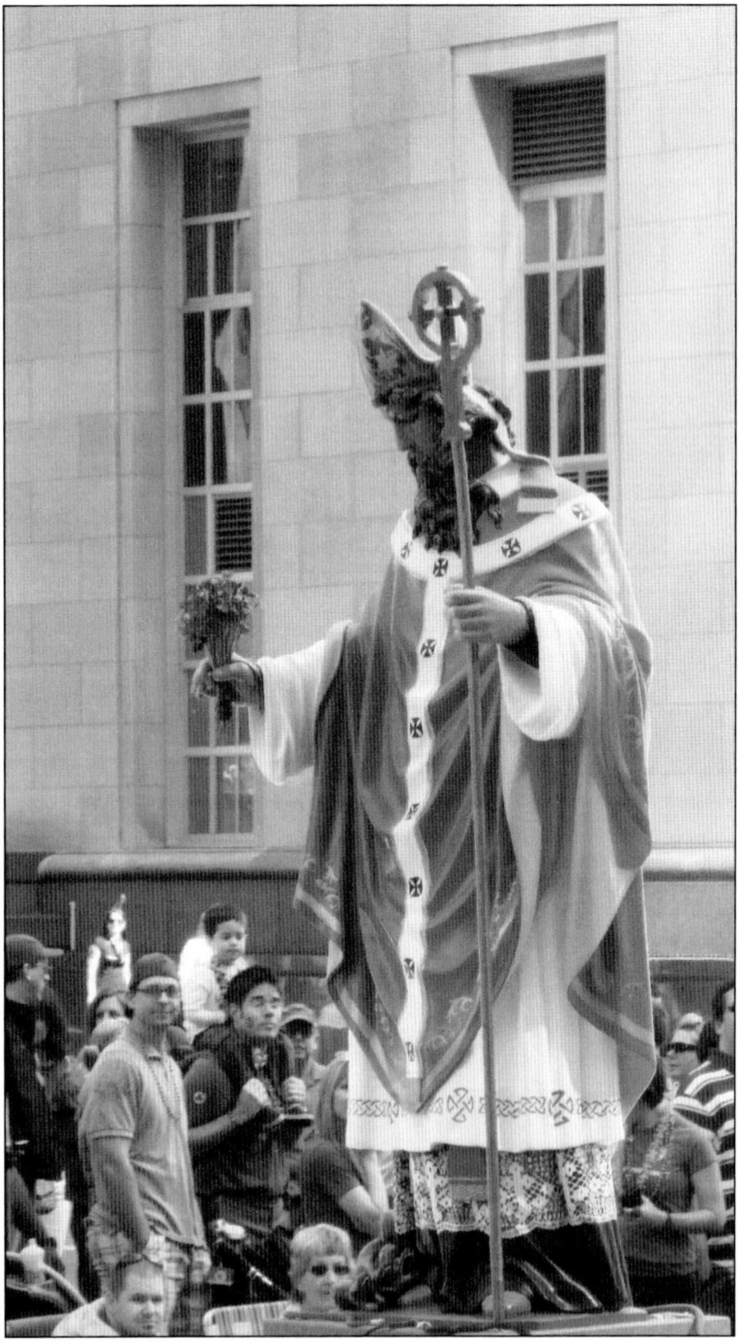

The stealing of the statue is now a highly anticipated part of the March celebration. As a pipe and drum corps marches down Pavilion Street in Mount Adams, a pickup truck full of Hibernians and one saint rolls along behind it through the narrow streets. The statue in Immaculata Church was donated to Holy Cross Church by James Healy in the 1920s, but it is no longer used in the parade downtown. Instead, the Ancient Order of Hibernians march with another one, a statue that once graced St. Patrick's Church. In 2012, this statue was repaired and repainted by artists Mike Hendley and Linda Mitchell, who kept it true to its original colors. (Courtesy of Bonnie Grace.)

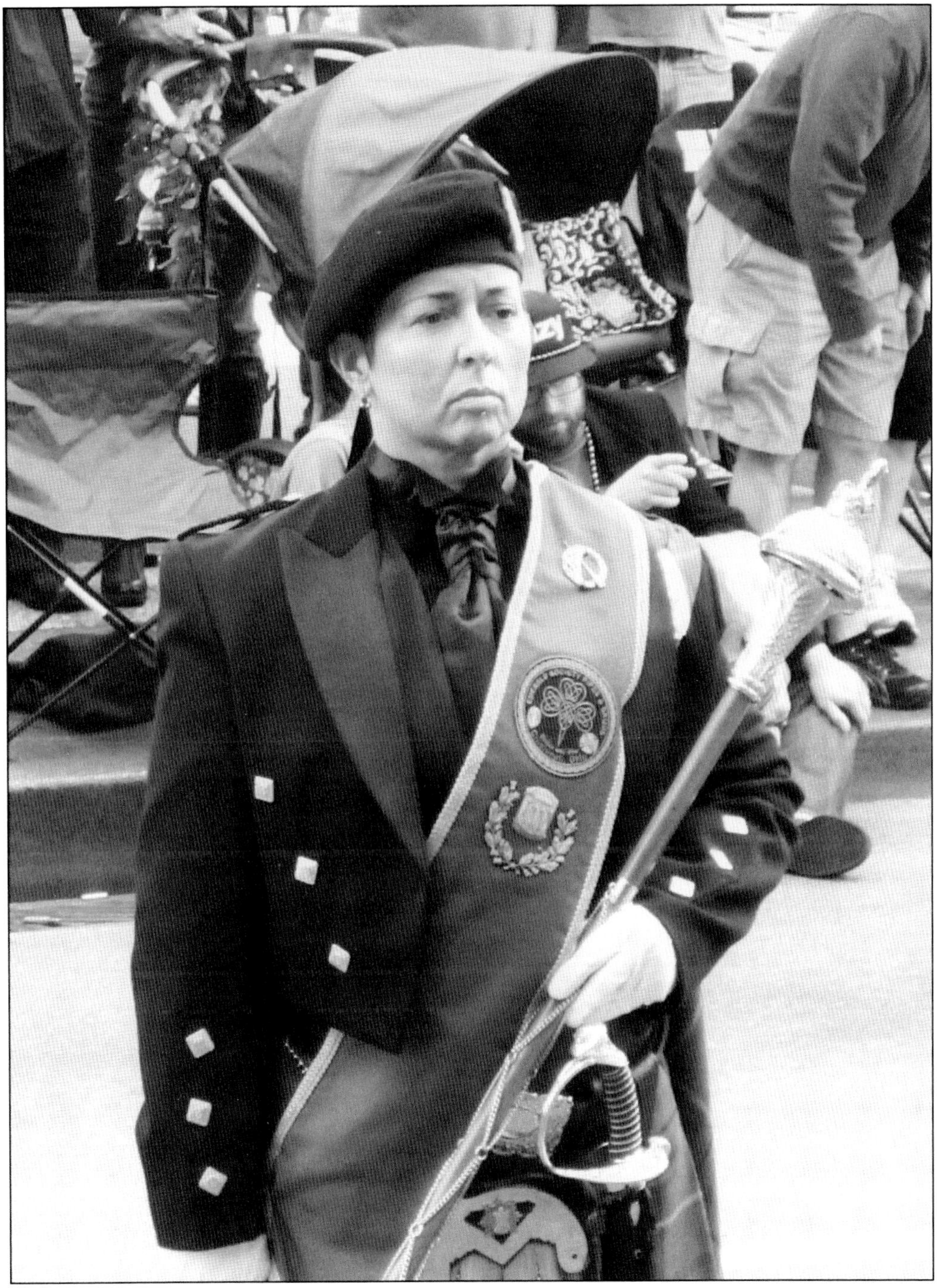

During the 2012 parade, drum major Robighn Woodbury for the Cincinnati Emerald Society Police and Fire Pipes and Drums Corps stops and stands at attention before the reviewing stand on Fifth Street. Formed in 2009, the corps is part of a larger, nationwide organization called the Emerald Society, which is made up of members who are of Irish or Scottish heritage. Cincinnati is one of several major cities in the United States that boasts a chapter of the Emerald pipes and drums.

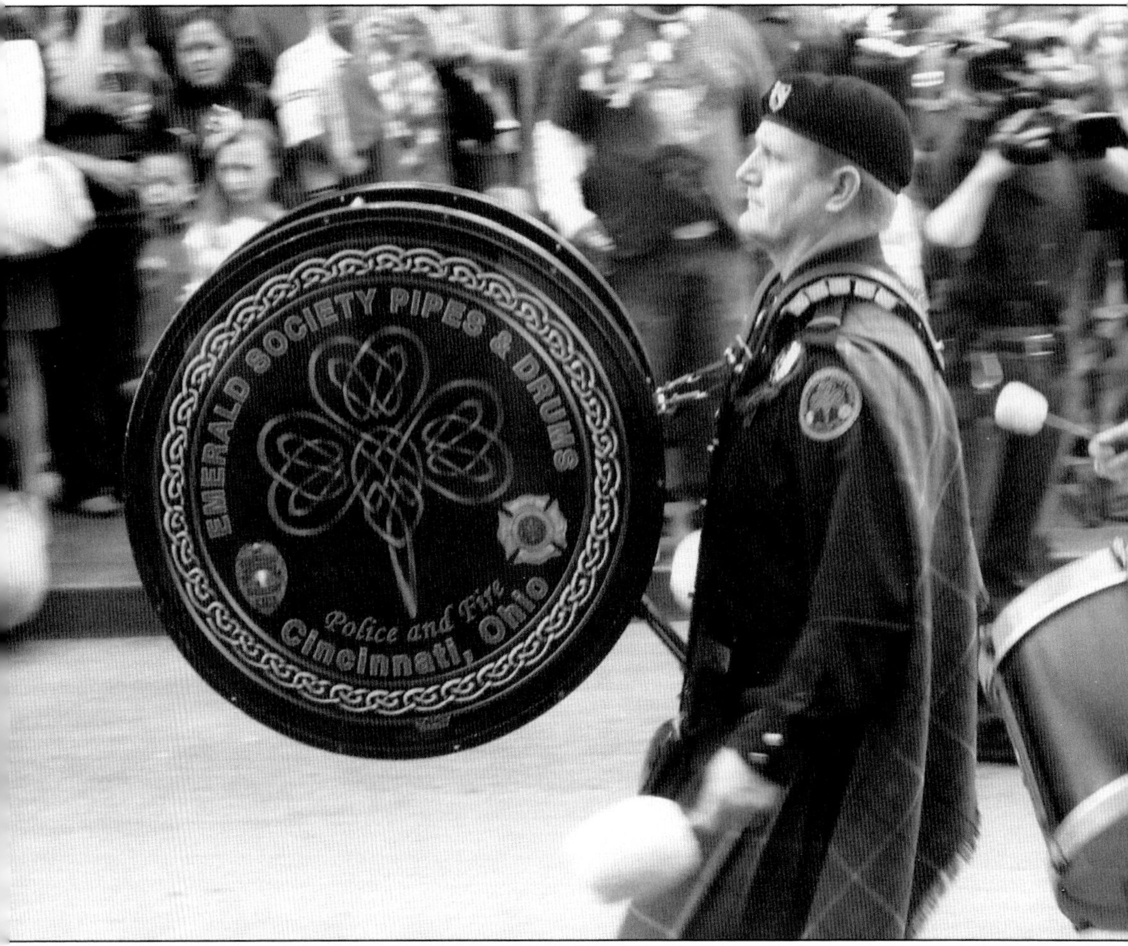

The corps's formal title is the National Conference of Law Enforcement Emerald Societies, and it has a number of society objectives, among them to build fraternalism among its members, to preserve Irish culture and promote the contributions of the Irish to American life, to work closely with civic and public safety organizations, and to recognize the accomplishments of Irish Americans in law enforcement and public safety organizations.

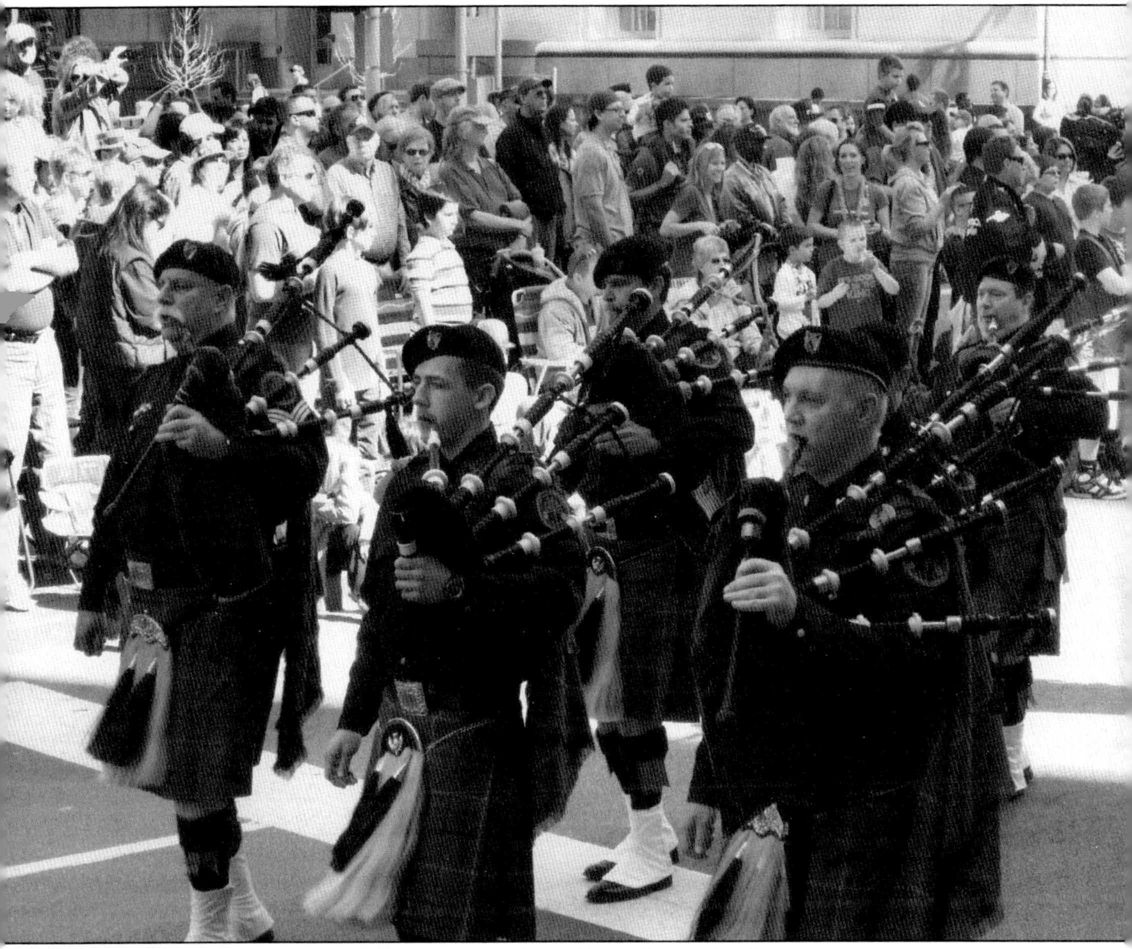

The Emerald Society pipers and drummers perform throughout the Cincinnati area, appearing at cultural events, parties, weddings, and other celebrations. The corps has also performed at funerals, a beautiful and somber appearance that first leads the cortege and then places a single piper in the distance to play the committal. The Cincinnati Emerald Society practices every Monday evening at Molly Malone's Pub, and it is fairly regimented: "pipes at seven, practice chanters at eight, and beer at nine."

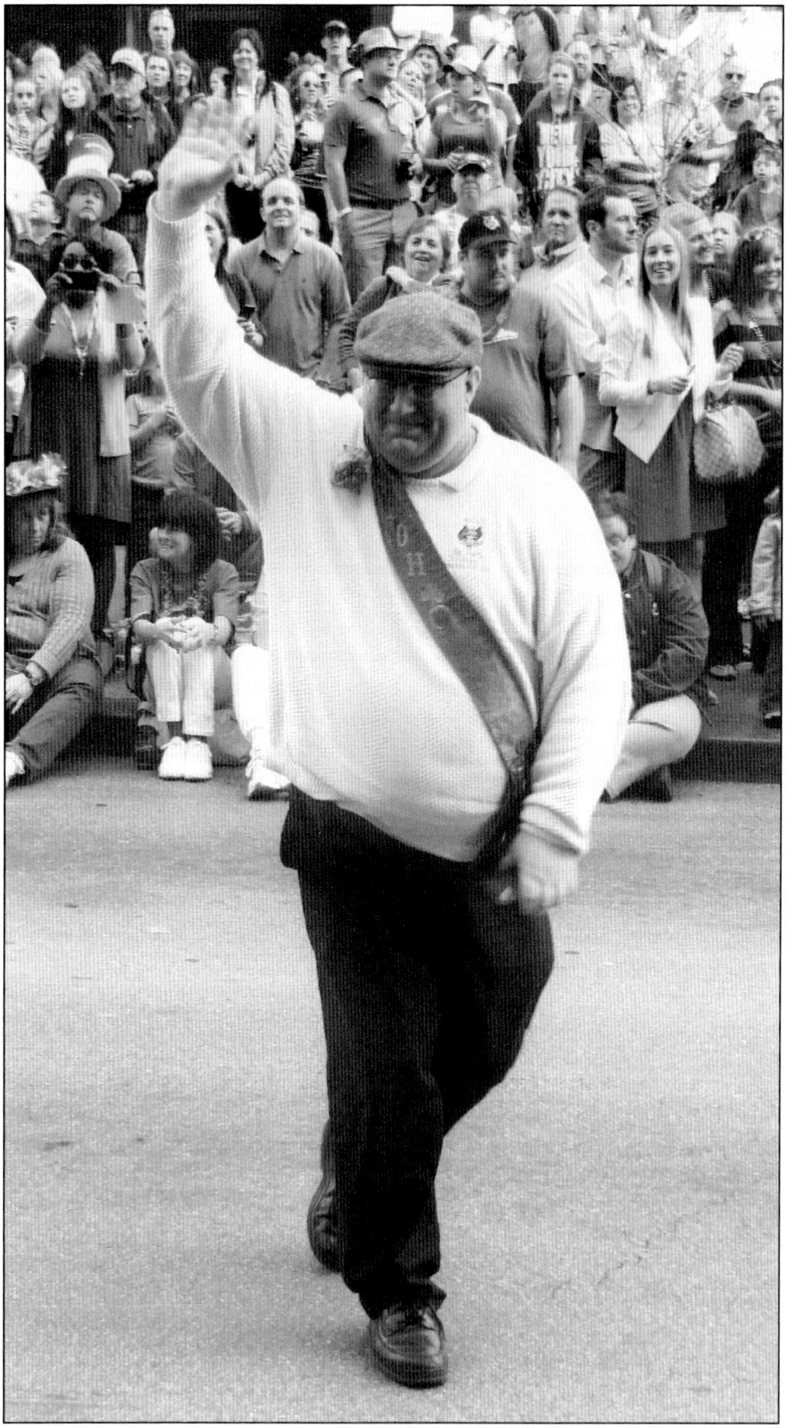

In 2012, Chris Schulte of the Ancient Order of Hibernians served as grand marshal of the St. Patrick's Day Parade. The first time Schulte marched in the parade, he was not even aware of it; his mother of loyal Irish heritage took part when she was several months pregnant with him. (Courtesy of Bonnie Grace.)

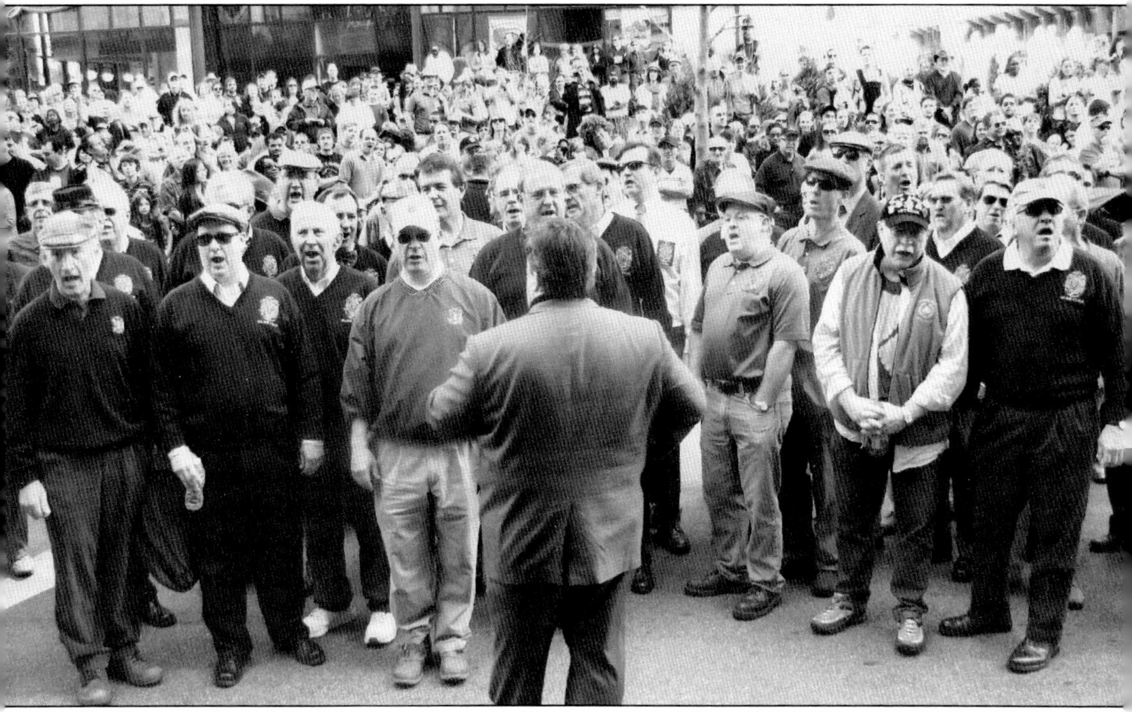

Pausing along the parade route during the 2012 St. Patrick's Day parade, the Friendly Sons of St. Patrick Glee Club entertains the crowds with a bit of song. The glee club began as a notion of Pres. Robert Manley in 1981 after he attended a concert of the New York Friendly Sons. Following an organizational effort in 1984 with Seamus Roche, Declan O'Sullivan, Bill Burke, and Richard Ormond, the glee club held its first practice with 16 initial singers in January 1985. Quickly joined by four additional members, the club gave its first Friendly Sons Banquet performance on St. Patrick's Day that March. Every year, the glee club performs regularly around Cincinnati. The club diligently rehearses every week at the Irish Heritage Center. (Courtesy of Bonnie Grace.)

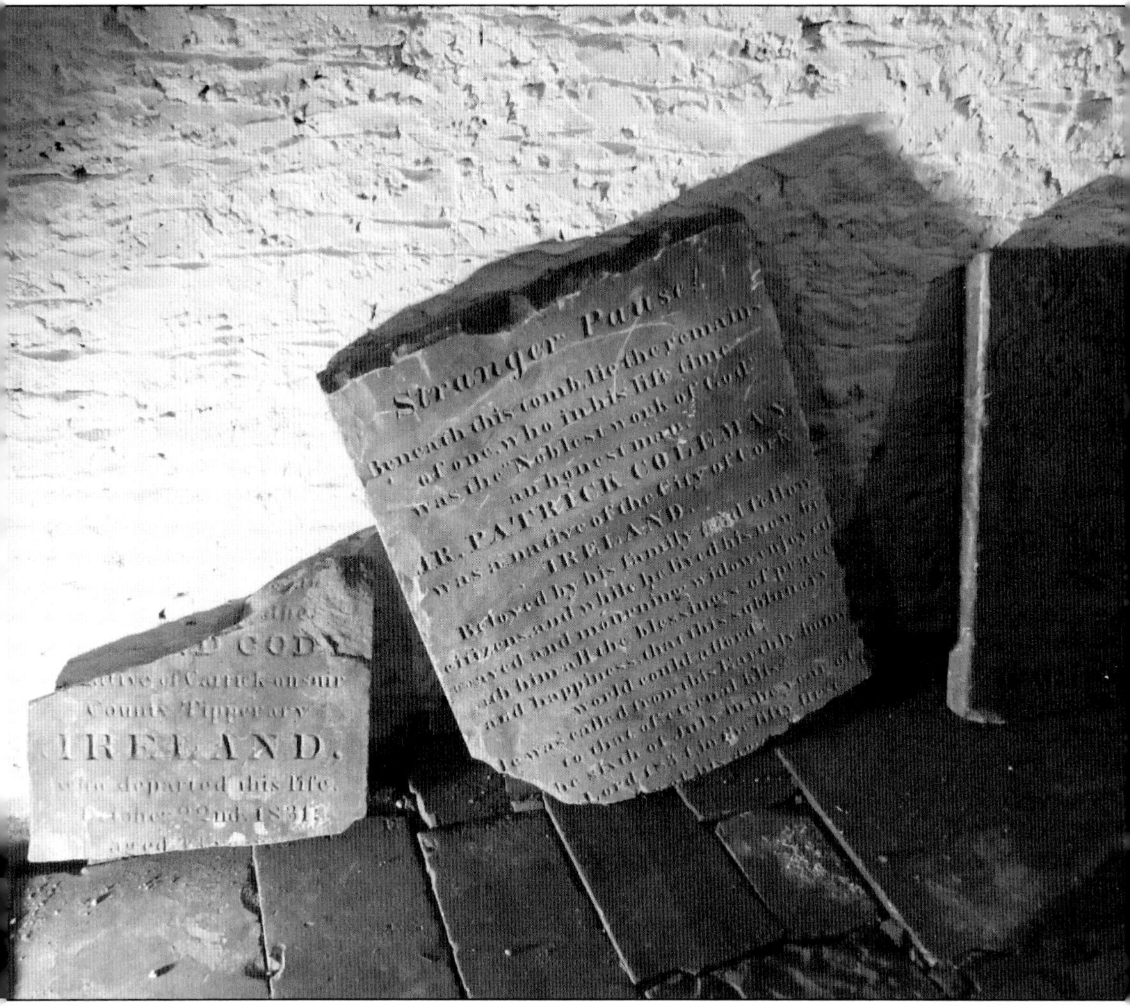

Deep underground beneath St. Francis Seraph Church in Over-the-Rhine, the floors are covered with accounts of the dead. Some of the original Irish congregants in Bishop Fenwick's Christ Church were buried in the churchyard that was located at Liberty and Vine Streets. Their tombstones tell the tales of the early immigrants, such as Patrick Coleman, a native of Cork City. Coleman "enjoyed all the blessings of peace and happiness the world could afford."

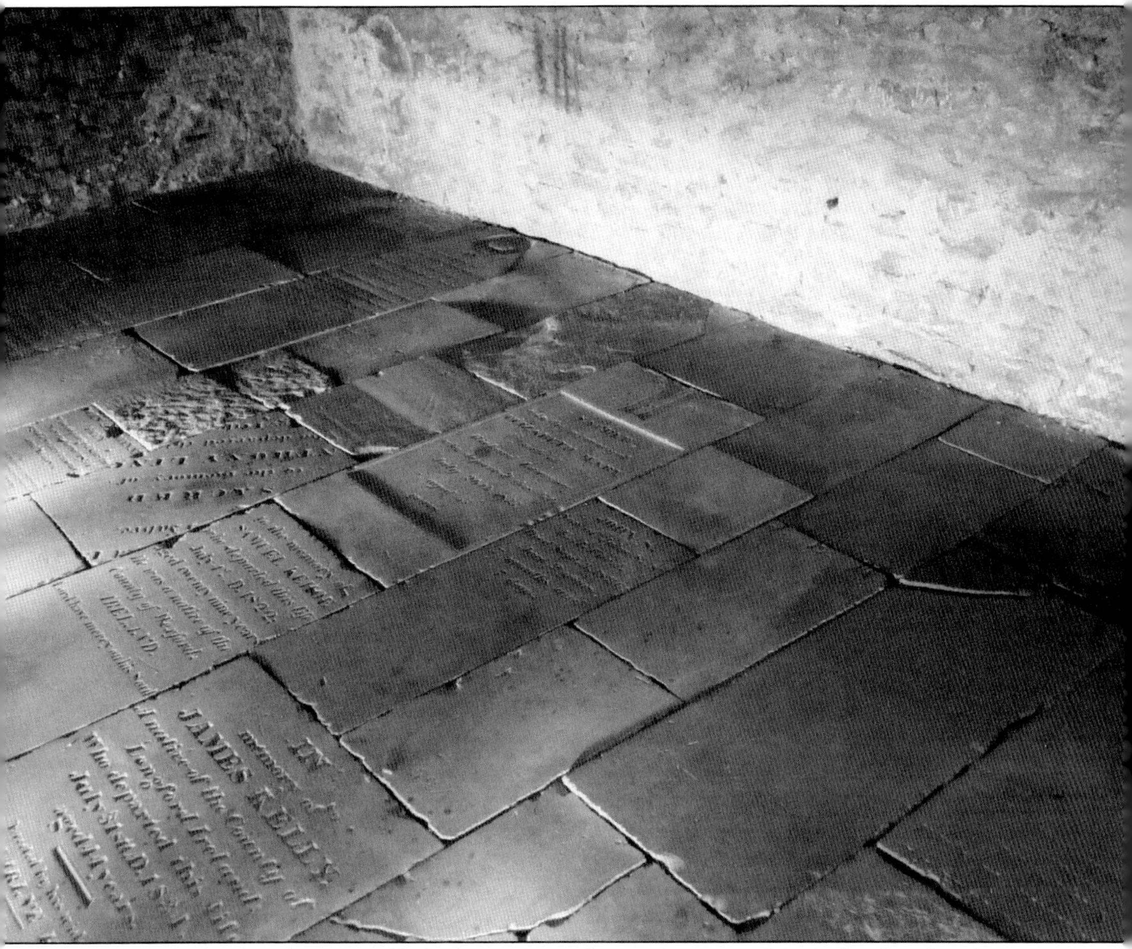

St. Francis Seraph Church was established in 1858, replacing the original Catholic church, Christ Church. Bishop Fenwick decided to move Christ Church closer to downtown after the ordinance was repealed that originally prohibited its establishment within the city limits. The new site was on Sycamore Street, where St. Xavier Church now stands. However, in moving the wooden structure along rollers, it fell apart. It was reconstructed and used until 1825. In 1844, German Franciscans were invited to Cincinnati by Bishop John Purcell to minister to the growing German Catholic population, and St. Francis Seraph was constructed for them. The descendants of the Irish who were buried in the original churchyard were invited to have the remains exhumed and moved, but in loyalty to the original Irish church, many decided to leave the graves as they were. The tombstones are now part of the floor in the subbasement.

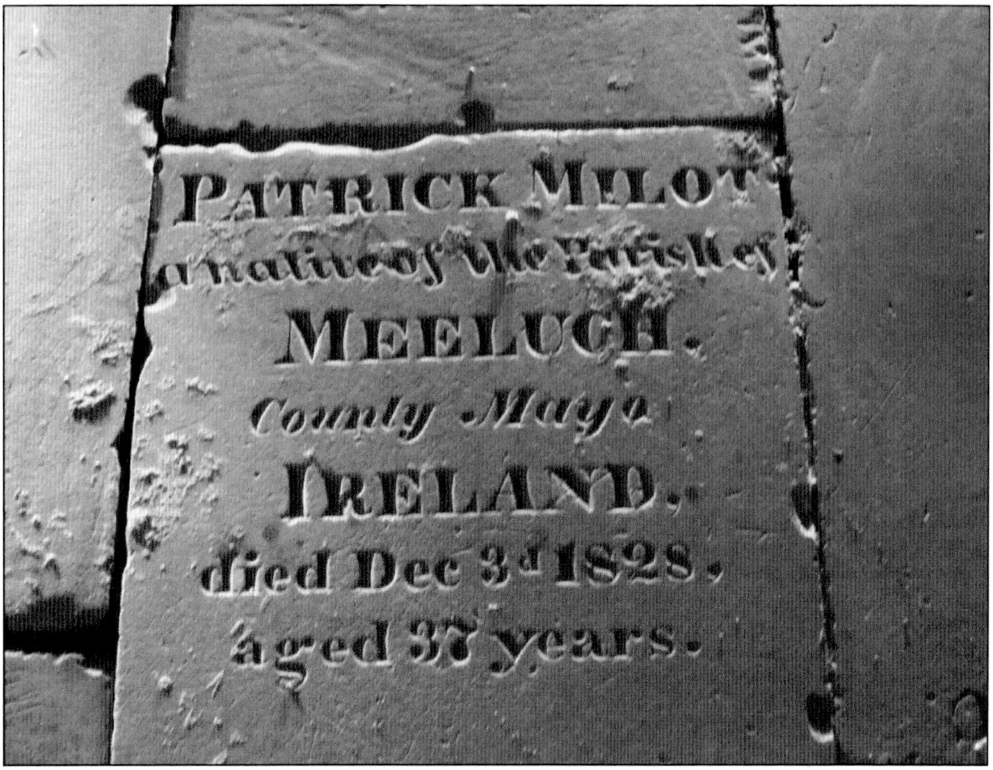

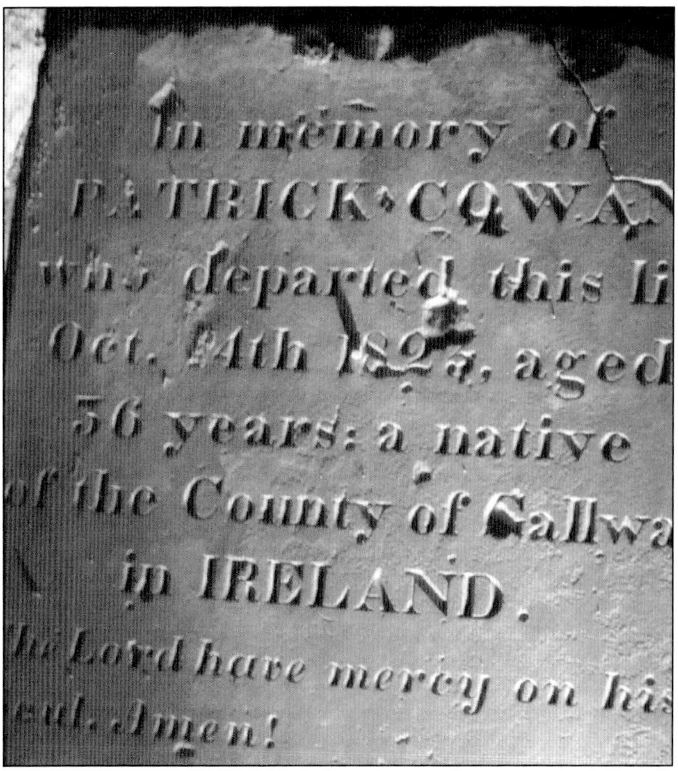

Under the direction of Brother Tim Sucher, the Irish graves at St. Francis have become an integral part of the church's legacy. The rooms where the tombstones are located and the stones themselves were carefully restored, thus preserving more of Cincinnati's Irish heritage. The St. Francis tombstones also became part of the Cincinnati underground tours, which provide an opportunity to view the city's past from the perspective of the beer lagering tunnels beneath the streets and buildings of Over-the-Rhine and the abandoned subway tunnels topped by Central Parkway.

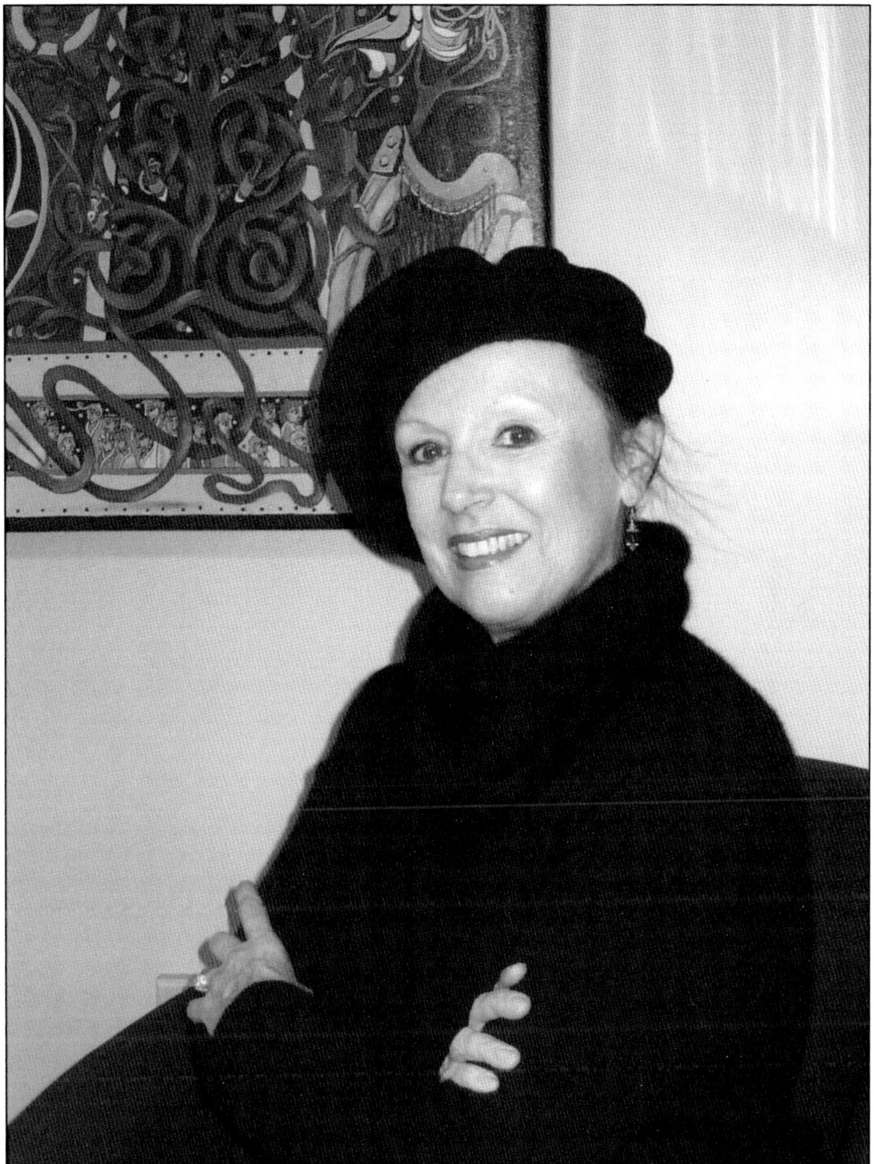

In November 2009, the celebration of Cincinnati's Irish heritage took a giant step forward with the purchase of an old McKinley Elementary School building on Eastern Avenue. Years in the planning, the Irish Heritage Center of Greater Cincinnati was the dream of Maureen Kennedy (pictured here) and her husband, Kent Covey. With a strong appreciation of her own Irish roots and a background in dance and theater, Kennedy formed the Irish American Theatre Company in Cincinnati, and she and Covey officially opened the center in 2010. Since then, with the help of dozens of volunteers, the building has been refurbished and is home to theatrical productions, a library, concerts, art classes, history lectures, exhibits, literary readings, dance instruction, and an Irish pub. In 2012, Irish sports were added to the variety of activities, and the center regularly hosts rehearsals for the Friendly Sons of St. Patrick Glee Club as well as the Cincinnati Chapter of Celtic Women International. Under the leadership of Kennedy and Covey, Cincinnati's Irish community comes together to actively live its ethnic legacy.

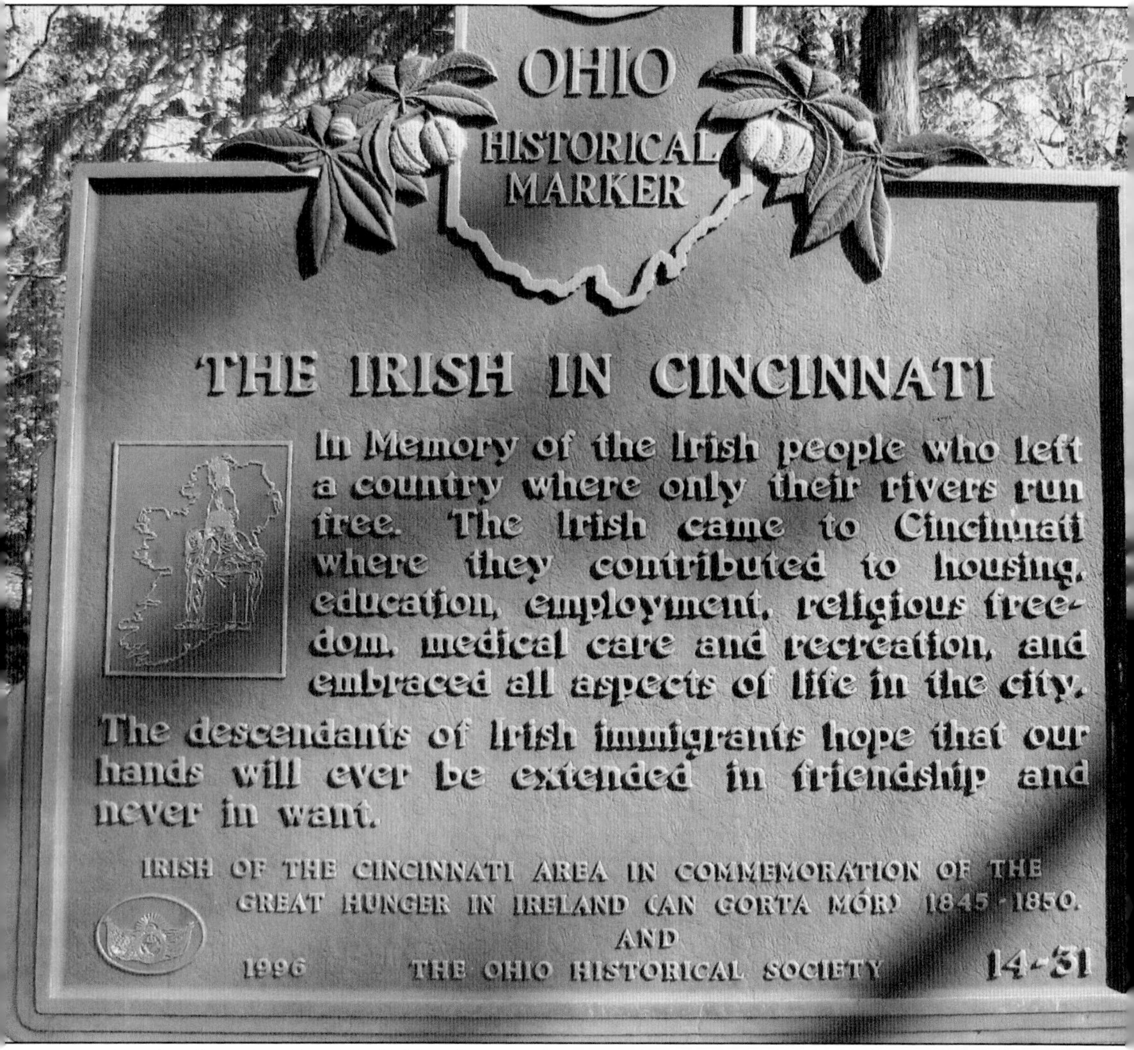

On Sunday, October 13, 1996, a historical marker indicating the contribution of the Irish to Cincinnati was unveiled along the path in Sawyer Point. The shady river path is the perfect location for the recognition, joining a number of other markers commemorating the contributions of other groups to the city's heritage as well. The Irish marker was part of the development of Bicentennial Commons, an effort to beautify the riverfront during the city's 200th birthday in 1988. Marshalling the support of 16 local Irish cultural organizations, an umbrella group called the Tri-State United Irish coordinated the funding and political backing to create the tribute. Much of the effort was led by Eileen McNeil, a second-generation Irish citizen, and Jane Davoran, who wished to commemorate her own heritage in this manner: "The descendants of Irish immigrants hope that our hands will ever be extended in friendship and never in want."

Suggestions for Further Reading

Barrett, James R. *The Irish Way: Becoming American in the Multiethnic City*. New York, NY: The Penguin Press, 2012.
Dezell, Maureen. *Irish America: Coming Into Clover*. New York, NY: Anchor Books, 2002.
Donnelly, James S. Jr. *The Great Irish Potato Famine*. Phoenix Mill, England: Sutton Publishing, 2001.
Flischel, Robert, et.al. *Messages of Glory: The Narrative Art of Roman Catholicism*. Cincinnati, OH: David-Flischel Enterprises, 2012.
Ford, Henry A. and Kate Ford. *History of Cincinnati, with Illustrations and Biographical Sketches*. Cleveland, OH: L.A. Williams & Co., 1881.
Fortin, Roger A. *Faith and Action: A History of the Archdiocese of Cincinnati, 1821–1996*. Columbus, OH: Ohio State University Press, 2002.
Greve, Charles T. *Centennial History of Cincinnati and Representative Citizens*. Chicago, IL: Biographical Publishing Co., 1904.
Hurley, Daniel. *Cincinnati: The Queen City*. Cincinnati, OH: Cincinnati Historical Society, 1988.
Kenny, Kevin, ed. *New Directions in Irish-American History*. Madison, WI: University of Wisconsin Press, 2003.
Lamott, Rev. John H. *History of the Archdiocese of Cincinnati, 1821–1921*. New York, NY: Frederick Pustet Co., 1921.
Meagher, Timothy J. *The Columbia Guide to Irish American History*. New York, NY: Columbia University Press, 2005.
Miller, Zane L. *Boss Cox's Cincinnati: Urban Politics in the Progressive Era*. New York, NY: Oxford University Press, 1968.
Rogers, Virgil A. *The Irish in Cincinnati, 1860–1870: A Typical Experience*. Unpublished master's thesis, Cincinnati, OH: University of Cincinnati, 1972.
Ross, Steven J. *Workers on the Edge: Work, Leisure, and Politics in Industrializing Cincinnati, 1788–1890*. New York, NY: Columbia University Press, 1985.
Writers Project of the Works Progress Administration, comp. *Cincinnati: A Guide to the Queen City and Its Neighbors*. Cincinnati, OH: Wiesen-Hart Press, 1943.